NATIONAL HEROES

MAINSTREAM | SPORT

NATIONAL HEROES

THE AINTREE LEGEND

REG GREEN

MAINSTREAM
PUBLISHING

EDINBURGH AND LONDON

First published in Great Britain in 1997 by
MAINSTREAM PUBLISHING COMPANY (EDINBURGH) LTD
7 Albany Street
Edinburgh EH1 3UG

This edition 1999

ISBN 1 84018 133 8

A catalogue record for this book is available from the British Library

Typeset in Adobe Garamond
Printed and bound in Finland by WSOY

FOREWORD

by

Richard Dunwoody

I feel privileged to have been asked to write the foreword to this latest book on what is widely regarded as the world's greatest steeplechase and which is written by the acknowledged authority on the race, Reg Green.

The Grand National holds many very special memories for me and I have experienced the tension of facing the starter every year since 1985.

Due to the very nature of this demanding event, many jockeys consider themselves lucky to even complete the course. I have been fortunate enough to ride the winner twice, with my old favourite West Tip in 1986 and on Miinnehoma eight years later.

The thrill of passing the post first in this race is indescribable – more so than in any other race. The atmosphere at Aintree is overwhelming, the reception the winning partnership receives dreamlike and one feels a sense of humility with the realisation that one is joining all those illustrious names of the past.

In this splendid book Reg Green has perfectly captured the anguish and joy which is inseparable from the race's colourful and unpredictable history.

I feel sure that you will derive as much pleasure from these pages as I have from riding in this unique event.

One

1839–1848

Queen Victoria was barely 20 years of age and in her second year as Britain's monarch when this country's oldest steeplechase drew a huge crowd of spectators to its inaugural running at Aintree, near Liverpool. Racing on the flat had taken place at Aintree since 1829 under the auspices of Liverpool hotelier William Lynn but after an experimental 'chase across country' in 1836, he finally laid plans for a major jumping event to rival that of Tom Coleman at St Albans.

Tuesday 26 February 1839 was the date chosen, and Lynn's diligent pre-race publicity for his project reaped rich rewards, with the hotels, inns and lodging houses of Liverpool benefiting enormously. Under somewhat mysterious circumstances and just three days before the race, William Lynn retired from his association with the racecourse and a syndicate was formed to administer Aintree's future, headed by a number of 'influential noblemen and patrons of the Turf'.

Of the 17 runners three made the journey across the Irish Sea to represent the leading Irish owner of jumpers, Tom Ferguson, who rode his chief fancy Daxon himself, leaving Barkston and Rust to the care of professional Byrne and amateur William McDonough. Long-time ante-post favourite The Nun lost favour with the public when she was seen to be rather too fat shortly before the race, and after a furious betting spree, Mr John Elmore's nine-year-old gelding Lottery wound up at the head of the market at 5/1. His superb jockey Jem Mason had won the Cheltenham Steeplechase but this newly devised event in which all the contestants would carry 12st was to prove the severest test of horse and rider ever encountered anywhere.

Because of errors in the weighing-out procedure and a number of false starts, the race finally began two hours late. Daxon made the early running out into the country with Captain Becher on Conrad close behind and the contest was trouble-free until the first dangerous obstacle on the course. This was a brook, eight feet wide, and approached across a ploughed field with strong, high palings bordering a jagged hedge on the take-off side of the water. Conrad hit the woodwork, throwing his rider over and into the brook beyond and although the gallant captain remounted when the rest of the field had passed, he fell again two fences later, exiting forever from the records of the race. The brook which gave him the soaking would thereafter and always be known as Becher's Brook.

The mare Charity came to grief at the treacherous wall in front of the stands, which was the halfway point and on the second circuit the Irish horse Rust was eliminated from the competition through an act of foul play on the part of a section of the crowd. Their money obviously laid elsewhere, they simply blocked him in a lane, refusing to allow his progress. Turning for home, with just two small flights of hurdles left to jump, Lottery had the race at his mercy and secured it with an incredible leap at the last, which was said to measure no less than 30 feet. Mr Elmore's favourite won convincingly by three lengths, from the Welsh horse Seventy Four, with Paulina a similar distance back in third place and just four other survivors plodding in at various intervals.

Lottery returned home to Uxenden, near Harrow, hailed as a hero and fêted as such, but his rest was brief, for he was soon back in training again with George Dockeray at Epsom for another tilt at the Liverpool steeplechase.

The Grand Liverpool Steeplechase of 1840 remains one of the events most clouded in mystery and uncertainty and there is confusion concerning who actually owned the eventual winner, Jerry. It was held on 5 March, contained the same conditions of entry as in the initial running and attracted 12 runners, but the ownership of at least three of the contestants went unrecorded. In the case of Jerry, there can be no question that certainly at one time he ran in the colours of Lottery's owner, John Elmore, a horse dealer. Lord Sheffield and Mr Villebois were both customers of Elmore's and although there remains the possibility that Jerry was owned jointly by these gentlemen, it is the latter who is associated officially with him on the day of the race.

The Nun was the best fancied at 3/1, with Lottery at 4s and Seventy Four on the 7s mark and Jerry among the outsiders at 12/1. Mr Power, who was partnering his horse Valentine in the race, had laid a hefty bet that they would be the first to reach the wall and, intent on winning his wager at least, set off right from the start at a cracking pace. At Becher's Brook he held a commanding lead, had increased it by the time he rounded the Canal Turn and then Valentine made as if to refuse the next brook. However, within strides of the obstacle, the horse had a change of heart and, with a spectacular corkscrew motion, cleared the jump. Thereafter this brook was ever to be known as Valentine's and as if to cap a memorable occasion, he carried his owner in the lead over the dreaded stone wall. Immediately behind the gleeful Mr Power, the wall wreaked havoc among some of the principal fancies, with Lottery, The Nun, Seventy Four and Columbine scattering stones in all directions as they crashed out of the race. Mr Power was still in front with Valentine over the second Becher's, where his nearest rival Arthur fell on landing but was quickly remounted by his brave amateur rider Alan McDonough. Jerry was brought with a determined run as they turned for home, staying on well to repulse the renewed efforts of both Arthur and Valentine and win by four lengths.

Jerry had only one race subsequently, finishing fourth behind Lottery in the Leamington Steeplechase.

Apart from his mishap in the 1840 Grand Liverpool, Lottery had gone from strength to strength, to such a degree that a new condition was added to the Aintree race for 1841. Mr Elmore's champion was handicapped with an extra 16lb for having won the Cheltenham Steeplechase, meaning that although his ten rivals all carried the usual 12st, Lottery was condemned to hump around an impossible and totally unfair 13st 4lb. Even so he started favourite again at 5/2 and it was perhaps a consolation to his many backers that the horrific wall had been replaced with a far less treacherous water jump.

For the first time the race started on time and on the first circuit there were but two casualties, Selim and Goblin, both at Becher's Brook, but the latter was immediately remounted by the previous year's winning rider Mr Bretherton. Jumping the newly instituted water jump in front of the stands the remaining nine runners were closely bunched, with Lottery well to the fore, but after clearing the second Becher's, jockey Jem Mason sensed the great horse starting to falter under his tremendous weight burden and wisely pulled him up. A terrific finish was in prospect as the two greys, Cigar and Peter Simple, raced stride for stride towards the final obstacles. Suddenly another appeared, running strongly and ridden in a very determined manner by Mr Powell. It was the mare Charity, and in a driving finish she got up to win by one length and half a length from Cigar and Peter Simple, with four others completing the course, including Seventy Four in sixth position and the remounted Goblin in seventh.

Lottery was again penalised in the 1842 race but the large betting public made him the 5/1 first choice in the betting on the 15-runner event.

Owner John Elmore had a second string to his bow in this race in the shape of the eight-year-old bay gelding Gay Lad, also well supported at 7/1 and ridden by one of the most colourful jockeys of that or any period, Tom Olliver. 'Black Tom', as he was affectionately known because of his swarthy complexion, was reputed to have spent almost as much time in various debtors' prisons as he had on the racecourse, but what is beyond doubt was his exceptional ability in the saddle.

From a good start Lord Waterford's Columbine took them along over the early fences, only to be outjumped at Becher's by Anonymous who then went on to the front for the remainder of the first circuit. Columbine regained the lead approaching Becher's for the second time, at which point Lottery seemed to be still well in the hunt. Jem Mason knew better though and again the weight had begun to take its toll and the favourite was pulled up after safely clearing the big brook. The grey Peter Simple pulled his way powerfully to the front after Valentine's and with both Seventy Four and Gay Lad moving up threateningly, the race lay between these three. Back on the racecourse Peter Simple was jostled so badly by some rowdies in the crowd that his rider was thrown from the saddle. With just one flight of hurdles left, Seventy Four and Gay Lad were both very tired horses and it was the mastery of Tom Olliver who conjured a late burst of speed from his mount which carried them to a four-length victory. After the unsporting interference of the crowd, Peter Simple was remounted to finish third, a long way in front of the only other two survivors, The Returned and Columbine.

Just six days after his historical Liverpool win, Gay Lad won a race in Oxford and was successful again later in the season at Nottingham and Chelmsford. He never competed in the big Aintree race again.

1843 brought two important changes to the race which were hardly seen as in any way significant at the time. The race was named 'The Liverpool and National Steeplechase' and became a handicap, attracting 16 runners with Lottery making his fifth and final appearance.

The stone wall was reintroduced and a welcome innovation was the distribution of race-cards showing the runners, riders, owners' colours and a map of the course.

Favourite on the day was Peter Simple at 3/1 and carrying 13st 1lb. He set off at a furious pace, fighting for his head every inch of the way and giving his jockey a most uncomfortable ride. It was not until they approached the second Canal Turn that the lead changed hands, with Peter Simple losing his place through tiredness and Dragsman striking the front in the very able hands of his amateur rider Crickmere. The pair seemed certain winners at the last fence before the straight, but the horse swerved for no apparent reason, jumped a gate and bolted down a lane, leaving the race between Vanguard and Nimrod. Tom Olliver got a great jump out of Vanguard at the final flight, who then ran on strongly to secure a three-length success and provide Olliver with his second win in the race within 12 months. Nimrod was second, with Dragsman performing a minor miracle to not only get back in the race but finish a close-up third of the nine which finished.

In seventh place came the horse whose name became a legend in just a few short years – Lottery. For a short time he became the hack of his trainer, George Dockeray, but sadly ended his days pulling a cart around the back streets of Neasden.

Tom Olliver apparently had a higher regard for Vanguard, for when that horse died, the jockey had a sofa made from his hide.

At last the Aintree executive decided to do away with the dreadful wall but on the day of the 1844 National the weather seemed to disapprove of the alteration to the course; the rain poured down all day long.

There was only one previous winner in the line-up of 15, the popular mare Charity. Of the joint favourites, Discount and Marengo, it was the former who had the most interesting, if unusual, background, for the six-year-old was not only an entire but was actually registered in the General Stud Book. Formerly named Magnum Bonum, the chestnut proved completely useless as a flat racehorse, resulting in countless attempts to sell him, but time after time he remained unwanted. Eventually a horse dealer, Mr Quartermaine of Piccadilly, became the owner after a prolonged negotiation during which he kept offering less and less than the asking price. As a result the son of Sir Hercules was renamed Discount.

At the reinstituted water jump Charity came down, leaving Marengo, Lather, The Returned and Discount to chase Tom Tug back out on to the second circuit. As they emerged from the mist towards the final obstacles it could be seen that five horses were closely grouped, then Mr Crickmere, who had done so well to secure third place the previous year, produced a brilliant run from Discount to strike the front at the last flight and come home a very easy winner by 20 lengths.

In due course Discount won a further two races, before being sold for 1,100 guineas at Tattersalls and he was then heard of no more.

Sixteen riders weighed out for the 1845 race but only 15 horses lined up at the start because the favourite The Knight Templar injured himself shortly before the off. One of the newcomers was a brown gelding described at the time as a 'rather coarse-looking individual'. His name was Cure-All, somewhat appropriate under the circumstances, for his sire was the stallion Physician, and he was bred in Yorkshire and bought for just £60 by William Loft at Horncastle Fair. After laming himself badly while jumping some rails, the gelding was put in the care of Mr Loft's groom, a remarkable female named Kitty Crisp. She not only nursed the horse back to fitness, but walked with him every inch of the way from Grimsby to Liverpool to enable him to take part in the big race. Cure-All ran in the colours of Mr W. Sterling Crawford who had purchased a share in him, and co-owner William Loft, despite his inexperience of race-riding, took the mount.

It was so cold at Aintree on the day that the Liverpool and Leeds Canal was frozen over and so treacherous was the state of the going that a number of owners objected to the event being held. After taking a vote of all the owners, the decision to go ahead was made and Vanguard went into a clear lead the moment the starter's flag fell. The favourite's attempt to repeat a double victory was short-lived, for on the approach to Becher's Brook for the second time Vanguard became exhausted and was pulled up. As they rounded the Canal Turn The Exquisite was at the head of affairs making the best of his way home on the energy-sapping ground and it was at this point that William Loft discovered a lengthy strip of better land on which to continue his efforts with Cure-All. Galloping on much less taxing a surface, Cure-All was able to issue a challenge as they came to the final obstacle, sweeping into the lead as they landed on the flat and holding on for a two-length win from Peter Simple and The Exquisite.

Kitty Crisp made the return journey back to the east coast with Cure-All, again on foot all the way, arriving to the chiming of Healing's church bells which were rung in their honour.

There could be no complaints about the weather, or the state of the going for the 1846 Liverpool and National Steeplechase. The sun shone, visibility was clear and the ground perfect. Jem Mason was on the favourite Veluti, backed down to 11/2, and there was good money also for Eagle, Firefly, Lancet and Mameluke, but 1845's first and second, Cure-All and Peter Simple, were among the outsiders. There was one horse who received the unkind description from a paddock observer of being 'a rough-looking fellow, very poor in condition'.

The 'fellow' in question was the six-year-old Pioneer, owned by a Mr Adams and ridden by the unknown jockey W. Taylor. Few riders could have received more of a blow to any confidence they may have held than did Taylor when, just a few days before the race, Mr Adams announced publicly that there was no way he would risk a penny of his backing Pioneer.

Peter Simple was very prominent in the early stages, and was still in front nearing the halfway stage, but he fell soon after beginning the second circuit. Culverthorpe led over Becher's from Switcher, Firefly and Veluti, with Pioneer for the first time coming into the picture as he made ground rapidly through the field. A surge of premature cheering broke from the packed stands as the favourite Veluti came back onto the racecourse looking all over a winner, but at the second last he broke down and finished his day being walked back by the dismounted Jem Mason. This left Culverthorpe with the race at his mercy, but from seemingly nowhere after jumping the last, Pioneer came with a powerful run to capture the prize by three lengths from Culverthorpe, Switcher, Firefly and the only other to complete the distance, Eagle.

For the second year running, the result was a complete surprise to everybody, with Pioneer being totally unquoted in the betting. The horse subsequently proved his victory was no fluke by later in the year succeeding in the valuable Leamington Grand Annual Chase.

It was in 1847 that for the first time the great steeplechase was named the Grand National and even more horses turned out for the event than the year before. The one most talked about as the likely winner was the brilliant, if elderly, Irish mare Brunette who had carried all before her in her native land and would benefit from the assistance of the most brilliant of all amateurs, Alan McDonough.

There was, however, another challenger from across the Irish Sea who on the day became not only the Aintree punters' choice, but the hope of all in Ireland who could spare a few coppers to back him. The brown gelding was called Matthew and although many criticised the conformation of his 'stilty' legs, he carried his head proudly and possessed a bold glint in his eyes. He was owned by a Mr Courtenay, ridden by his fellow countryman Dennis Wynne, and was at 4/1 until just moments before the start, when inexplicably he drifted out in the betting to share favouritism with Culverthorpe at 10/1.

From a good start Cumberland Lassie dictated the pace, until losing her way near the end of the first circuit, when she swerved away from the racecourse to fall in a lane at the side of the canal. This left Jerry in front and he strode out well as if aware that he had conquered this place before. Still showing the way over the second Becher's, Jerry by now had but a handful of rivals following him, the nearest of them being Culverthorpe, Pioneer and St Leger, the latter partnered by Tom Olliver. At the last flight of hurdles, the crowd were on their feet, cheering the prospect of another close finish as Jerry held a half-length lead over the fast-finishing St Leger. All attention was focused on the desperate struggle as St Leger gained on the leader stride by stride, when suddenly and almost unnoticed another horse appeared with a storming challenge up the straight. Matthew was simply flying at the end of the race, getting up in the very last strides to snatch victory by a hard-fought length from St Leger, with Jerry the same distance away in third place.

Matthew and Dennis Wynne immediately became the toast of the Emerald Isle, and rightly so, for their success, the very first in the race by an Irish horse, restored some faith and hope to a people sorely in need.

Despite the ever-increasing popularity of steeplechasing, the keeping of accurate records of the sport had still not become an important aspect to the organisers, principally because there was no governing body.

This deficiency was most graphically demonstrated in the 1848 National when, among the 29 runners, there appeared two of the same name – Pioneer. One can but imagine the confusion this caused both the betting public and the bookmakers.

Tom Olliver took the mount on the 6/1 favourite, The Curate, with Ireland's hero Matthew second in the market at 8/1 and a 12-year-old gelding Chandler at 12s. It was Chandler whose early history endorsed the fairytale quality already becoming such an endearing feature of the great 'chase.

Chandler was bred by Sir Edward Scott of Great Bar, who unkindly referred to the animal as a 'fiddle-headed brute', and like others before him this gentleman was to be made to eat his words. In time the horse was sold to a chandler named Wilkinson, who used him between the shafts of his cart in the furtherance of his trade around the streets of Sutton Coldfield. As a result of this initial occupation came the name Chandler. Eventually becoming the property of Captain 'Josey' Little, a former officer in the King's Dragoon Guards, the humble cart-puller won 'chases in the hands of this man at Worcester and Windsor. By the time they came to Aintree, Chandler was jointly owned by Captain Little and his friend and brother officer Captain Peel.

Ashberry Lass made the early running, jumping well in the poor conditions, but a groan of anguish came from the crowd when Matthew was brought down by a horse falling directly in front of him. At the second Becher's Brook there were now only a few left in the race with any chance at all and racing back for the final time it was British Yeoman who was in front. Joined by The Curate at the last flight of hurdles, it was obvious there was to be another close struggle to the line and with the favourite going so well the spectators gave frantic vent to their feelings. With barely 400 yards to run it was The Curate going away, but yet again that final dash to the winning post was to prove decisive. Captain Little produced Chandler at precisely the right moment with a blistering run to win by just half a length from The Curate, with British Yeoman one and a half lengths back in third place.

This tenth Grand National had like all before produced the tension, excitement and thrills which were to become synonymous with the race and which had brought a new meaning to the words courage, tenacity and perseverance.

Two

1849–1858

As if to confuse the thousands flocking to the race in 1849, among the 24 competitors was a horse named Peter Simple, who to many had already given a meritorious account of himself during his six attempts in the race. As too often in the past, however, the latest Peter Simple to bid for Aintree glory had nothing whatsoever to do with the earlier version.

Unlike the grey 'Peter', who many claimed the newcomer was named after, this Peter Simple was a bay gelding by the stallion Patron and although a very good jumper, was a painfully slow performer on the racecourse. This fact was well known among the betting fraternity, which allowed him to start an unconsidered outsider at 20/1. The most heavily backed at 5/1 was Tom Olliver's mount Prince George, with The Curate, The Knight of Gwynne and Proceed the best supported of the remainder.

From the outset the proceedings matched the prevailing weather conditions, as the starter desperately tried in vain to recall the runners after what was blatantly a false start. Urged on by the freezing crowd, the jockeys ignored Lord Sefton's pleas to return for another try and galloped away, with Peter Simple well to the fore. Peter Simple was the only one completely at home in the treacherous conditions, striding out well in the lead and jumping fluently throughout. He jumped brilliantly all the way and came over the last with his race well won. It was at this point that his jockey, Cunningham, heard the first shout of temptation from his nearest rival, Captain D'Arcy, astride The Knight of Gwynne. In the most flagrant display of bribery, D'Arcy called upon the rider ahead of him to 'take a pull' for a financial inducement which ranged from £1,000 to begin with and reached £4,000 as they drew nearer to the winning post. To his eternal credit Cunningham ignored all offers, riding out Peter Simple to a comfortable three-length victory. A long way back in third place came the favourite Prince George, with just three others surviving the rigours of a very gruelling contest.

Proud of the fact that steeplechasing owed its origins to their homeland, the

Irish had from the very beginning recognised the Liverpool 'chase as an event worthy of their attention and their fervour for the event had been increased through the success of Matthew in 1847.

Twenty years before that popular victory set Irish eyes a-smiling, Henry Osborne of Dardistown Castle, County Meath, was returning home by coach and ferry from London. His educated eye fell on one of the team pulling the coach, a bold-looking mare, which he discovered before the journey ended was for sale at an asking price of 40 guineas. Without hesitation, Osborne puchased her, took her back to Ireland and, after naming her English Lass, won many races with the mare, including the Bachelor's Plate at Bellewstown.

When put to stud, English Lass delivered nine foals, all of which, except the eighth, proved most disappointing as racehorses. That single exception was a tiny colt foaled in 1842 and given the name Abd-El-Kader. He demonstrated very quickly that he possessed more than just a measure of his mother's jumping ability. The pony-sized 'chaser soon became affectionately known as 'Little Ab' among the Irish racing fraternity, winning races the length and breadth of the Emerald Isle, while displaying in the process a tenacity remarkable from such a diminutive frame.

By the time the 1850 Grand National came round 'Little Ab' was running in the colours of Henry Osborne's son Joe, an individual no less interesting than the horse representing him at Aintree. Besides training the horse, Joe Osborne was an acclaimed journalist. A regular contributor to *Bell's Life*, he was the compiler of *The Horsebreeder's Handbook* and one of the first men to take the trouble to keep accurate records of steeplechasing. As a pilot for his horse he chose the professional jockey Chris Green, the son of a Norfolk farmer and a widely admired horseman over fences. Both Green and Abd-El-Kader were making their first appearance in the National.

Thirty-two runners lined up for the 1850 Grand National, with last year's winner Peter Simple leading the betting at 5/1. Despite his impressive record in his native land, Abd-El-Kader was completely unquoted in the betting, more than likely because of his very small size.

There was no problem with the start on this occasion, the whole field getting away to an even break, with Sir John, Half-and-Half, Hope and Peter Simple leading them on into the country. Returning to the racecourse a great cheer went up when The Knight of Gwynne and Peter Simple were seen to be sharing the lead. Until this stage of the race Chris Green had guided Abd-El-Kader patiently in mid-division, steering his mount carefully through a path strewn with fallen horses and those without their riders. On the run back to Becher's though, he made his move, taking Abd-El-Kader to the head of the field with an amazing turn of foot. Jumping the Brook like a stag, the little gelding outran his opponents from there on, increasing his advantage with every splendid leap on the way to the final fence. The Knight of Gwynne put in a determined effort as they rose at the last obstacle but Abd-El-Kader stoutly refused to relinquish the lead, holding on to win by a length. Sir John was three lengths back in third place, with only four others completing the course.

The brilliance of 'Little Ab's' victory was reflected when it was announced that he had broken the time record for the race, reducing it to under ten minutes for the first time since its inauguration.

In 1851 the Great Exhibition was staged at the Crystal Palace in London, attracting countless thousands from far and near. For racegoers the excitement began early in the year, with the usual throngs converging on Aintree for the latest episode in the Grand National story.

With 21 runners, ranging in the handicap from 11st 12lb down to 9st 4lb, the emphasis this time seemed to be on quality rather than quantity. Rat-Trap was the principal choice of the punters, favourite at 6/1, with Lord Waterford's Sir John sharing second place in the market with his fellow countryman Abd-El-Kader, at 7s. Fickle as the betting public usually are, they chose to ignore completely last year's favourite, the former winner Peter Simple, who was deemed not even worthy of a quote in the market.

There was a conspicuous jockey change for this race, involving none other than Abd-El-Kader. Possibly through injury, Chris Green was unable to ride, being replaced by the little known T. Abbot, the rider who safely guided Farnham into fifth place in 1850.

From a perfect start the field thundered away at a cracking pace, headed by Sir John, Peter Simple, Maria Day, Tipperary Boy and Half-and-Half, with Abd-El-Kader well to the rear. At the halfway stage Tipperary Boy led narrowly over the water jump from Peter Simple, with Sir John in hot pursuit followed by Volatile and the improving Abd-El-Kader. Abbot was enjoying a dream of a ride on 'Little Ab', who was jumping like a stag and appeared able to go to the front whenever he chose. At the last ditch before returning to the racecourse, four of them jumped in line abreast, Sir John, Tipperary Boy, Abd-El-Kader and Maria Day, and as they touched down together the cheers from the distant stands rose in anticipation of a great finish. At the final obstacle Abd-El-Kader struck the front, striding away at full pelt towards the winning post but the race was far from over. Maria Day, found hidden reserves of energy and the two battled on up that cruellest of all run-ins, horses and riders somehow conjuring up the brand of courage which is the essence of greatness. They flashed past the post together, still locked in combat, yet thankfully at last relieved from competition and content that they had given their all, a fact so obvious to all who witnessed that glorious display of bravery and total commitment.

Abd-El-Kader had held on by the narrowest of margins, the judges' difficult decision being that he had won by half-a-neck. He was the first horse to record a dual victory in the great race.

Then as now record-breakers guaranteed increased attendances wherever they appeared and with the possibility of an unprecedented third victory for Abd-El-Kader, the public flocked to Aintree in March 1852.

For the third year running 'Little Ab' found himself with a new partner in the form of Dennis Wynne, the jockey who tasted the sweetness of success five years earlier aboard Matthew. The pair started second favourite at 9/1 behind the 6/1 shot La Gazza Ladra, considered by many a blot on the handicap with just 9st 12lb.

Although the race attracted 24 runners, only eight received quotations in the betting, with Royal Blue, the mount of 19-year-old George Stevens, earning his place in National history as the first competitor ever offered at the extreme odds of 100/1.

Among the majority considered unworthy of a starting price was a bay mare, who in her early years must have been the most maligned animal ever to carry a saddle. Miss Mowbray by the stallion Lancastrian out of Norma and bred by Mr Boulton at Pitmore in Bedfordshire, soon became the very bane of her breeder's life. Time after humiliating time she was sent to Newmarket, examined by countless trainers and returned to Boulton as being utterly worthless. Even when at last a buyer from Manchester was found for the sum of 100 guineas, hardly a week had elapsed before Miss Mowbray was back at Pitmore and the frustrated Mr Boulton had to refund the purchase price. In desperation he finally put the mare to hunting, a sphere in which she displayed enough promise to catch the eye of no less a personage than Mr T.F. Mason. Having once ridden the unwanted mare, Mason bought her cheaply from the relieved breeder with a view to testing her mettle 'between the flags'. She duly rewarded his judgement by developing into a fine 'chaser endowed with abundant stamina and followed up a victory in the Warwickshire Hunt Cup with a fine win in the Leamington Open Steeplechase the year before making her début in the Grand National. Sharing her introduction to Aintree was her rider, 30-year-old Alec Goodman, a native of Peterborough who, although acknowledged as a fine horseman, was considered too old and somewhat out of his class in this company.

For the third time in as many years, the going was good, the weather fine and the starter did his duty to perfection in getting them all away well and evenly. Abd-El-Kader thrilled the crowds with a succession of brilliant leaps at each of the obstacles on the gallop to Becher's Brook, where again the little fellow was foot perfect but at which juncture there was a frightful pile-up. Two fences later, at the Canal Turn, Abd-El-Kader was overtaken by the free-running Chieftain and these two continued making the pace, leaving behind them another jumble of casualties which included Maley, Peter Simple and Bedford. Agis refused to go any further at this point. Passing the stands at the end of the first circuit Chieftain had increased his lead to six lengths over Abd-El-Kader, Sir John, Maurice Daley and the remounted La Gazza Ladra, with Miss Mowbray being beautifully coasted along by Alec Goodman. Before reaching the second Becher's the furious gallop proved too much for 'Little Ab', jockey Wynne showing sympathy for his plight by pulling him up. Approaching the final half mile Chieftain was still in front but now strongly pressed by Maurice Daley, Sir Peter Laurie and the fresh-looking mare Miss Mowbray. Striking the front over the final flight Miss Mowbray ran on with remarkable ease, withstanding the final courageous challenge of Maurice Daley by a length, with Sir Peter Laurie five lengths back in third place. Chieftain was fourth, in front of La Gazza Ladra, Warner and Sir John.

Mr Mason made plans for a return to Aintree with his heroine and Alec Goodman proudly returned to his farm at Willow Hall, Thorney, near Peterborough. It was to be 14 years before he would find a horse good enough to justify his talents in the National again.

A prolonged winter followed by a late thaw not only brought disruption to the training schedules of contenders for the 1853 Grand National but brought once more dreadful conditions for the running of the race. Slush and mud made it a certainty that the event would develop into a gruelling slogging test in which only the bravest and luckiest could survive.

Making his fifth successive appearance in the race was the former winner Peter Simple, a 9/1 shot possibly through a combination of sentiment and the fact that he would have in his saddle that veteran of so many Nationals, Tom Olliver. Already with two victories to his credit in the race, the jockey was said to know Aintree 'like the inside of his pocket'. Peter Simple, having failed to get round since his triumph four years earlier, had changed hands frequently over the years and again this year he was carrying a new set of colours. It can truly be said that the life of Captain John Lockart Little had been as chequered as that of his new representative, Peter Simple.

Born in 1821 at Chipstead, near Redhill, Surrey, 'Josey' Little, as he affectionately became known, was commissioned in the King's Dragoon Guards until 1848. At that time his finances suffered the severest of blows when the bank holding his money collapsed and he was forced to transfer to a less high profile and expensive regiment, the 81st Regiment of Foot. Like many cavalry officers of his era, 'Josey' Little benefited from the excellent coaching of none other than Tom Olliver, developing into not only a superb horseman but attaining a standard of jockeyship which was the equal of most professional flat-race jockeys. The irony of this relationship was perfectly displayed in the 1848 National when Captain Little proved the stronger in a very close finish to defeat his mentor aboard Chandler.

Sent on their way at 4.25, the field splashed through the heavy going led by Maurice Daley, with Bourton and Peter Simple in close attendance. Poll, The Dwarf, and Betsy Prig all came down at the third, while at the head of the field Peter Simple had taken up the running. Going into Becher's a loose horse cannoned into the leader, causing Olliver to take evasive action by swerving his mount to the left. The manoeuvre, however, placed the pair in serious danger of jumping the wrong side of a flag, until through an incredible stroke of luck, Sir Peter Laurie came through on Peter Simple's inside and knocked him back on a straight course. Undeterred by the incident, both took the Brook in stylish fashion, sharing the lead until the Canal Turn, where Sir Peter Laurie dropped back, to be replaced by the challenging Abd-El-Kader. The dual winner pressed on at a good gallop, taking up the running after Valentine's with such zest that by the time they stretched out over the water jump his advantage had increased to fully 100 yards. The order remained unchanged back over Becher's and beyond, but after clearing Valentine's both Miss Mowbray and Peter Simple began making ground towards the leaders. Approaching the second last Abd-El-Kader began feeling the strain, fading rapidly as he was overtaken by Oscar who at once found himself challenged by his stable companion Miss Mowbray. Timing his run to perfection, Tom Olliver brought Peter Simple to pass them both over the final flight of hurdles. Striding away in the conditions he so relished, Peter Simple came home a comfortable three lengths to the good from Miss Mowbray, with Oscar five lengths back in third place. Of the only other four to finish, Sir Peter Laurie was fourth, just in front of the gallant Abd-El-Kader.

It was a truly outstanding performance by Peter Simple, only the second horse to twice succeed in the Grand National and to this day the oldest at 15 years of age to win the race. Captain Little's fortunes were finally restored and a third riding victory in the race for Tom Olliver placed him firmly at the forefront of the all-time greats.

Treachery was the forerunner of the 1854 Grand National and as if that were insufficient to blight a fine occasion, a double tragedy was to be its sequel.

For many weeks before the race, Miss Mowbray had been all the rage among the betting public, many thousands of pounds being placed on her to improve on her splendid attempt in second place the previous year. Certain bookmakers were in fact in danger of being totally wiped out if she won and there can be little doubt that it was this situation which led to an act of infamy. Shortly before the 21 runners were due to assemble in the paddock, Miss Mowbray was found to have been blistered on her near foreleg, rendering the limb useless and causing her to be withdrawn from the race. Those responsible were never apprehended, bringing a fresh outcry for the formation of a governing body to supervise the sport.

Rapidly forming a new market, the bookies brought in the bay gelding Bourton as a 4/1 favourite, one point ahead of Tom Olliver's mount Maurice Daley. Owned by William Mosley and ridden by the almost unknown jockey J. Tasker, Bourton had failed to get round the National course in the previous two years and prior to that had raced under the name Upton. In view of his short starting price this time, it appeared that someone somewhere knew more than his form indicated.

When the starter lowered his flag at 3.46, the 20 runners charged towards the first fence *en masse*, with Dennis Wynne holding a fractional advantage aboard the lightly weighted Crabbs. At Valentine's Burnt Sienna, another from the bottom of the handicap, went to the front from Crabbs and Lady Arthur, the trio staying in this order back to the racecourse and on over the water. One by one those chasing the leaders dropped from the race and clearing Becher's for the second time, less than half the original starters were still in the contest. Tasker had brought Bourton smoothly through and as Burnt Sienna began to tire down the canal side, they were in a challenging position. Moving past Crabbs as they ran to the last, Bourton romped away, increasing his lead with every stride to pass the post in little more than a canter.

Delighted with his National success, Mr Mosley decided that Bourton had earned his retirement and incredibly passed on his champion to a gentleman from Leamington for the sum of £50. The assurance given by the purchaser that the horse would never race again was sadly dishonoured when Bourton appeared in a steeplechase at Warwick the following season, fell at the water and was so badly injured that he had to be put down. In the cruellest of ironies, his partner in Aintree glory, jockey Tasker, had been killed at almost the same spot on that racecourse just six weeks earlier.

For Britain's military leaders the year 1855 was causing great concern due to the situation in the Crimea, with epidemics of typhus and cholera among the troops costing more lives than those of battle wounds. Not even the news from Africa that David Livingstone had become the first white man to cast his eyes on the majestic beauty of the Victoria Falls was enough to ease the public anxiety for their soldiers' misery in the war against the Russians.

According to the sports writers of the day, things had also reached an all-time low in the affairs of the Grand National. Commenting on the quality of the field for that year's event, *Bell's Life* made the observation that it was 'the worst field which ever started for the race'.

Of the 20 runners Miss Mowbray looked to be the only animal of any class and thankfully this time avoided the attentions of villains. She went to the post 4/1 second favourite behind Mr Mosley's Trout.

A bay entire, owned by Mr Dennis and ridden by J. Hanlon, Wanderer received the scathing description of being a 'rough, undersized, common-looking brute' from a member of the journalistic profession.

Trout and Garland led the field over Becher's, only to be passed approaching the Canal Turn by Bastion and Wanderer, the latter taking up the running shortly after negotiating Valentine's. At the water jump Trout moved up again, joining the two leaders as the three leapt the final obstacle on the first circuit. Back out in the country the greatly reduced field struggled on the heavy going, with Bastion holding a marginal advantage from Wanderer and the improving Freetrader. Tom Olliver appeared to be fully in command on Bastion as they led into Becher's Brook but his mount slipped in the mud within strides of the fence and both crashed to the ground. This mishap now left Wanderer in front, with Freetrader pressing hard as they jumped the Canal Turn almost together. As they re-entered the racecourse, Wanderer was passed by Freetrader, at this point going so well that he appeared unbeatable. Hanlon aboard Wanderer, however, felt differently, remaining unflurried to the extent that he took a pull to give the horse a breather. The only danger to Freetrader looked to be the fast-finishing Maurice Daley as the two charged at the final hurdle, which they both knocked down. As they began the long run to the winning post, Wanderer came with an unstoppable sprint on the stands side to grasp victory by two lengths from Freetrader, with Maurice Daley a game third four lengths further back.

It was a surprised and somewhat disgruntled Mr Dennis who led in his winner Wanderer, for he had not fancied his representative in the slightest and had, in fact, wagered a substantial sum of money on the stable's other runner Boundaway.

It was with genuine feelings of relief that Britain celebrated victory in the costly war against Russia in 1856. Serious shortcomings within the army's ability to care for its sick and wounded had been exposed in a manner which thankfully was to lead to improvements all round for the troops. The only other good thing to emerge from the Crimean War was the institution of the nation's highest award for gallantry on the battlefield, the Victoria Cross.

At Aintree, Mr Edward William Topham took control of the racecourse, having been a diligent official at the venue since before Lottery's victory. One of the finest handicappers of thoroughbreds in the history of the sport, Topham began his managerial duties confidently by extending the Grand National meeting to two days, with the big 'chase held on the second day. Although there could be no way of knowing it in 1856, the Topham family were to be associated with Aintree for the next 117 years.

The top weight was awarded to Sir Peter Laurie at 10st 12lb, and also to one of two challengers from France, Franc Picard. It was the first time the French had launched an assault on the National, an indication that the race had aroused international interest and it was quite significant that one of the pair, Jean du Quesne, headed the betting at 9/2. Another man making a dual attempt that year was retired army Captain W. Barnett, with Sir Peter Laurie and the seven-year-old Freetrader, who had been so close to victory 12 months before. Unimpressed by that performance, the public neglected Freetrader to such an extent that he started at 25/1.

A bay entire, he was by the stallion The Sea which, owned and ridden by the Marquis of Waterford, had finished fourth in the 1840 National. Having shown some promise on the flat, Freetrader went on to win over hurdles before graduating to 'chasing and the keen-eyed Captain Barnett managed to buy him for just 90 guineas. As his jockey, the owner chose an up-and-coming young rider named George Stevens, another protégé of Tom Olliver and like Captain Barnett, a son of Cheltenham.

From the off The Forest Queen dashed to the front, with the favourite Jean du Quesne and Emigrant attempting to keep pace with her. There was no let-up in the strong pace set by The Forest Queen, the mare seeming intent on making every post a winning one and once again she jumped Becher's Brook in splendid style. Through no fault of hers, her race came to an end at the very next fence. Foot-perfect at the obstacle, a foolish bystander chose the moment she landed to run across the course, causing her to swerve off the track. This left Jean du Quesne with the advantage and the French horse brought them back onto the racecourse seemingly with the race at his mercy. Tiring quickly, however, he was passed on the run to the penultimate flight of hurdles by Freetrader, Minerva and the fresh looking Minos, this trio entering into an exciting tussle at the end of their gruelling journey. All the way up that punishingly long straight the three outsiders produced the kind of finish more reminiscent of an Epsom Derby. Producing one of the coolest displays of jockeyship yet seen in a National finish, George Stevens snatched victory on Freetrader by half a length from Minerva with Minos staying on to secure third place. The only others to finish were Hopeless Star, Little Charley and the luckless Emigrant.

For the bookies it was a benefit day, as none of those which finished were in the top seven of the market.

If Freetrader's triumph proved a field day for the bookmakers, the National of 1857 was to prove extremely profitable for two members of that fraternity, as well as placing them in the record books.

Messrs Hodgman and Green were well-known and much-respected members of the gambling profession who became owners of a racehorse, appropriately enough, through the turn of a card. Trainer and former jockey, Ben Land, had set his heart on winning the big Aintree steeplechase, firmly believing when he came into the possession of Emigrant that at long last he had the means of realising his ambition.

Unfortunately for Land, when attending Shrewsbury races in 1855 he found himself in dire straits through a run of atrocious luck in a card school. One of the onlookers at the game, George Hodgman, came to his aid by offering to buy Emigrant from him for £590. A quick return for Hodgman's investment came the following day when the gelding romped home in a 'chase at Shrewsbury. Delighted with his good fortune, Hodgman gladly paid Ben Land a further £100 as agreed when concluding the purchase and in due course sold a half share in the animal to his friend and colleague, Mr Green. Their first tilt at the Grand National proved promising with Emigrant bravely finishing sixth in 1856 despite encountering trouble early in the race.

It was another foul day at Aintree as the 28 runners made their way to the start, the rain lashing down incessantly and the ploughed expanses of the course reduced to squelchy mud.

After seven false starts the drenched runners were finally sent on their way. Garry Owen and Emigrant led across the first two fields, from which point Emigrant gained the upper hand, to quickly open up a good lead. Maintaining a steady gallop, jockey Charlie Boyce kept Emigrant in front over Becher's while realising that the glue-like ground would be a strain on the stamina of the greatest horse. Swinging sharp left at the Canal Turn, the observant rider noticed a good strip of more solid land on the wide outside, on the very bank of the Liverpool and Leeds Canal. On the long run back to the racecourse, Emigrant raced alone far to the right of his rivals, going the longest way round but benefiting from the better underfoot conditions. Striding out freely now, he raced back towards Becher's and with his pursuers struggling in the mud Emigrant cleared the Brook fully 50 yards ahead of them. Moving over again to the firmer ground on the approach to Valentine's, Boyce again took a pull on his mount, preserving what energy he could for the final haul to the finish. At the anchor point, with just two jumps left, Weathercock moved up threateningly, the only horse near enough to offer any danger to the leader. Despite a spirited effort on the part of his jockey, Chris Green, Weathercock was unable to match the pace of Emigrant over the last half mile and Emigrant stayed on strongly to win somewhat easily by three lengths. Treachery finished third just ahead of Westminster and four weary stragglers.

Gleeful owners, Hodgman and Green, netted a small fortune from their bets, while commiserating with Ben Land, second with Weathercock behind his former property Emigrant.

It was only after the race that Charlie Boyce's ride to victory received the acclaim it deserved, when it was discovered that he had ridden with an injured arm strapped to his side.

The 1858 race saw the reappearance of Abd-El-Kader, now 16 years old but still affectionately remembered as the first dual winner, who so many times had given cause to believe that his heart was surely bigger than his tiny frame. Reunited with his first National jockey, Chris Green, 'Little Ab's' presence brought the only glimmer of pleasure to an otherwise severely bleak afternoon. That year saw the first-ever parade for the race – and it was held in a blizzard!

Making his fourth attempt in the National was ten-year-old Little Charley, considered no better than a 100/6 chance by the bookies, though staunchly supported by the gambling inhabitants of Cheltenham. It was from this Gloucestershire town that the owner, Christopher Capel, trainer William Holman and jockey William Archer all derived.

Away to a first-time start, Harry Lorrequer set the early pace but to everyone's dismay Abd-El-Kader made an early exit when misjudging his take-off at the second fence. Conrad headed Harry Lorrequer at Becher's, this pair disputing the lead to and beyond Valentine's, while Escape, Little Tom and Moire Antique came to grief just behind them. With a clear lead approaching the stands, Conrad took the water jump in fine style, followed by the improving Little Charley, Weathercock, Xanthus and Harry Lorrequer. Up front, however, a tremendous tussle was in progress, with Conrad, Weathercock and Little Charley battling against each other, the stinging snow and savage wind. From the Canal Turn back towards the finish, these three had the race to themselves, only a handful of stragglers remaining a long way behind and when Conrad fell three from home it looked odds on that Weathercock would take the race. Like the fine jockey he was though, William Archer was merely biding his time, saving his mount for a final dash once the last hurdle was crossed. Gauging his effort to the second, he pounced the moment they touched down on the flat, Little Charley responding instantly to race away for a four-length victory over Weathercock. Fifty yards back came Xanthus in third place, with only Morgan Rattler and the remounted Conrad surviving a most unpleasant contest.

It had been one of the slowest and most exhaustive Nationals up to that time and many pundits of the day considered the brightest thing to emerge from the race was the superb jockeyship of William Archer. At the time of his success, his son Frederick was a little over 12 months old. Before his tragic death by his own hand, 28 years later, Fred Archer became the most successful flat-race jockey of his and many other generations. William Archer outlived his more famous son by three very unhappy years.

Three

1859–1868

An unwanted prelude to the 1859 Grand National was the widespread rumour that the fences had been seriously tampered with, to such a degree that the event would be reduced to little more than a long-distance hurdle race. In his capacity as Senior Steward, Lord Sefton rode out and examined every obstacle, discovering to his horror that the claims were indeed well-founded. He then personally supervised the restoration of every fence to its correct dimensions, insisting that they should be carefully watched until after the big race.

The mount of Chris Green, Abd-El-Kader's former jockey, Half Caste, was a six-year-old brown horse owned by Mr Willoughby, with but 9st 7lb in the handicap. In his only previous steeplechase, Half Caste had fallen, so it was a surprise to many that he figured so prominently in the betting.

Little Charley, now owned by Mr W. Barnett, was trying for a repeat victory and his former owner, Christopher Capel, had his colours carried by Anatis. With three French challengers in the field, the race had an interesting flavour about it, but still a number of sporting scribes described its content as 'mediocre'.

The favourite The Brewer led the way over the early fences, followed by Xanthus, Gipsy King and Flatcatcher. An untidy jump at Becher's relegated The Brewer, who was passed by Xanthus, Flatcatcher, Anatis and Ace of Hearts and in this order they continued round the Canal Turn and over Valentine's. Passing the stands they jumped the water with Flatcatcher now in front but closely followed by Xanthus, Anatis, Jean du Quesne, Half Caste and Ace of Hearts and well to the rear The Brewer, who fell bodily into the water. With the positions the same jumping Becher's for the second time, Huntsman and Midge moved into contention and with the fall of Xanthus at the Canal Turn the race was wide open. Half Caste, now left in front, proceeded to make the best of his way home but there were at least four well in touch and at this stage nothing was travelling better than the French horse Jean du Quesne, ridden by Yorkshire-born Harry Lamplugh. Anatis also produced a good turn of foot as they faced up to the final hurdle, racing alongside the two leaders. In a furious race to the winning post, Half Caste just held on to win by the narrowest of margins, a short neck, from Jean du Quesne, with the game Huntsman a length away in third place.

While those connected with the winner celebrated in time-honoured fashion, there was sympathy for the runner-up and also once more for Ben Land. His Huntsman had run a tremendous race in the hands of the owner's son, Ben Land junior, but still his ambition to win the National remained unfulfilled.

With both the Crimean War and the Indian Mutiny fading into painful memories, British Army officers were once more able to pursue the pastimes peacetime service afforded them and steeplechase racing was to the majority the chief choice.

Curiously, as most of these gentlemen were the products of semi-aristocratic families, there remained large sections of this strata of society which vehemently objected to everything associated with 'racing across country'. The result of this situation was the practice of many amateur riders to conduct their affairs in the saddle under the guise of assumed names.

Among the most prominent and certainly most talented obliged to resort to such methods were Mr Thomas, whose real name was Thomas Pickernell; Mr Edwards, preferring to compete under that title rather than his actual identity, which was George Ede, and a certain parson named Drake.

In the case of Drake, he simply reversed the letters of his name to partner Bridegroom in the 1860 National as plain Mr Ekard. It is not recorded if this subterfuge was intended to mislead his parishioners or to avoid the anger of his bishop.

Of the 19 runners assembled on a cold and windy National day, the hot favourite at 7/2 was Christopher Capel's ten-year-old mare Anatis, a very creditable fifth on her introduction to Aintree the year before. She was trained by William Holman and ridden by Tommy Pickernell, better known to racegoers as Mr Thomas. The belief among the betting public that Anatis had been laid out for this race originated from the fact that the mare had not taken part in one single race since the 1859 Grand National, but the fact of the matter was that the mare had very dicky forelegs and her trainer did not risk her over even a practice jump.

Ben Land had sold Huntsman and he was now owned by Captain G.W. Hunt and ridden by Captain Townley, who appeared a good bet at the generous odds of 33/1.

There was little delay at the start, from which Goldsmith attempted to cut out the running, securing a five-length lead over the second fence at which Miss Harkaway and Congreve both refused. Still in front clearing Becher's, Goldsmith failed to withstand the strong run of Xanthus going into Valentine's and quickly losing ground was also passed by Telegram, Anatis and Huntsman as they returned to the racecourse. In line abreast, Xanthus, Telegram and Anatis jumped the water, with Huntsman three lengths back, ahead of the well-strung-out remainder. At the second Becher's it was still Xanthus showing the way from Anatis, whom Mr Thomas was still gently nursing round, as Telegram and Tease fell by the wayside. A mistake by Huntsman at the Brook resulted in his rider losing both stirrup irons and as Captain Townley struggled to regain them, the two leaders drew further away from him. Coming to the penultimate flight of hurdles Xanthus gave way to Anatis at the precise moment that Huntsman began a devastating run from the rear. Over the last there was absolutely nothing between Anatis and Huntsman, both giving their all in full flight and their riders going with them every inch of the way. It was only in the final yards of the race that Tommy Pickernell took his whip to the courageous Anatis for the first time, driving her past the winning post half a length in front of the brave Huntsman. Six lengths behind came the evergreen Xanthus, followed in by four others, including Bridegroom with the galloping parson aboard.

For the second time in three years Mr Capel enjoyed the thrill of leading in a Grand National winner and the crowds went home content not just at the favourite's success, but that they had witnessed a finish never to be forgotten.

The outbreak of the American Civil War in 1861 was to have a severe effect on the cotton mills of Lancashire and Yorkshire. At Aintree Edward Topham had shown that he was a more than worthy presenter of the great steeplechase and this time round his efforts attracted a record 89 entries for the race, with a tempting £985 on offer to the winner. Reduced to just 24 runners by National day, the crowds were far from deterred, most of them being convinced that Anatis was certain to repeat her success.

Mr Capel's mare was again favourite at 4/1, with another of her sex, Jealousy, one point behind on 5s. A seven-year-old, owned by Mr Bennett, Jealousy had run unplaced in the race two years before, but upon publication of the weights was chosen this time by no less a person than George Stevens as his mount at Liverpool. Stevens was offered 13 other horses to ride in the National, yet turned them all down in preference to Jealousy. Sadly, and to Stevens' eternal regret, George was claimed by one of his retained owners for the big 'chase, forcing Mr Bennett to engage J. Kendall as the rider of Jealousy. Ironically, on the eve of the race, George Stevens was left without a ride when his horse was withdrawn through injury.

Xanthus was again prominent from the start, quickly opening up a good lead across the early fences, but at the first Becher's lost his advantage when Redwing sprinted past him. Over Valentine's, Redwing was well clear of Xanthus, Cockatoo, Old Ben Roe, Brunette and The Freshman, but the latter joined the rising list of casualties when losing his footing after clearing the obstacle well. Turning towards the halfway point, Xanthus moved up to join Redwing on the run to the water, which they jumped together some way ahead of the rest. Having been patiently ridden up to this juncture, Jealousy was now moved into contention with a well-judged run which took her to the heels of the leaders. The long-time front-runner, Redwing, cleared Valentine's three lengths to the good, only to collide with a casualty from the first circuit still prostrate on the turf. Over the second last the order remained the same and continued so until Kendall set his mare alight at the final flight of hurdles, Jealousy romping clear for a two-length victory from the fast-finishing The Dane, who appeared on the scene late and seemingly from nowhere. Old Ben Roe was third, in front of the only other two to finish, Bridegroom and Xanthus.

The year came to an end in deepest mourning when, 11 days before Christmas, Prince Albert died at the age of 42 from typhoid.

Only 13 horses took part in the 1862 race and the favourite was a horse which had already come close to success in the race twice before. Huntsman, a nine-year-old entire, first ran in the National of 1859 when ridden by Ben Land junior, the son of the owner. Finishing third, he represented Captain Hunt the following year when second, just half a length down in that tremendous finish with Anatis. Changing hands immediately after the 1860 event, Huntsman was bought by Harry Lamplugh on behalf of his patron, the French nobleman Viscount de Namur, who apparently was as determined to win Aintree's great 'chase as Huntsman's original owner Ben Land senior was. Trained by his jockey, Lamplugh, the horse had a season free of Aintree exertions but was now a roaring 3/1 first choice of the punters who remembered his past gameness.

It had been 15 years since Dennis Wynne steered Matthew to a famous Irish victory and the now-retired jockey was delighted to watch his young son James attempt to emulate his success on the outsider O'Connell. On the morning of the race, father and son received the dreadful news that the sister of James had died at home in Ireland. Upon being informed, the owner of O'Connell, Lord de Freyne, considerately offered to excuse the young jockey from his commitment to ride but in true professional manner, James Wynne insisted on fulfilling his obligation. It was to be a fateful decision.

After a delay of almost half an hour, the runners at last began their journey with that popular front-runner Xanthus once more making the running, but there was a groan from the crowds at the first fence when the second favourite

Thomastown made a premature exit. At Becher's Xanthus held a narrow lead from Willoughby and Bridegroom, the trio setting a very searching pace and at the next fence The Tattler collided with Bucephalus, costing the latter some valuable ground but those looking for Anatis were out of luck for she had already been pulled up. With the pacemakers taking the gorse fence before the water in precise style, Playman surged forward just to their rear and, completely missing his stride, plunged through the barrier, tumbling in an untidy heap. Already in mid-flight, both Willoughby and O'Connell were unable to avoid slamming into the sprawling animal in front. In the ensuing pile-up James Wynne was crushed beneath the rolling Playman, his inert body left forlornly injured as the race continued. Without any delay the young man was rushed to hospital, from where just a few hours later came the distressing news that James had died from his severe internal injuries. With the stands occupants more concerned with the disaster in front of them, the leaders were making their way back to Becher's Brook, headed briefly by George Stevens on Harry, whose prominence was curtailed when stumbling out of the race two fences before the Brook. From there on it became a three-horse race, Bridegroom holding a fractional advantage over Huntsman and Romeo, and when the latter had to retrace his steps after going the wrong side of a flag, the prize lay between just two. Allowing Bridegroom to precede him all the way back along the canal, Harry Lamplugh coasted Huntsman along, keeping something in reserve for the final run to the line. His strategy worked a treat for, after clearing the last, Huntsman raced away from his rival to win comfortably by four lengths. A long way behind came the only other survivors, Romeo, Xanthus and Bucephalus.

As a winning favourite, Huntsman, the first French-owned horse to succeed in the race, received a distinctly muted reception returning to the winner's enclosure. The death of James Wynne had cast the darkest of shadows, bringing an awareness that steeplechase jockeys risked their all on a daily basis.

Changes were made to the Grand National in preparation for the 1863 renewal, with the distance being increased by about a quarter of a mile, to a total just short of four and a half miles and alterations were made to a number of fences. Posts and rails were erected at both Becher's and Valentine's, adding to the severity of both obstacles and the fence which cost James Wynne his life became an open ditch. It can only be assumed that the reasoning behind changing the latter was the hope that a ditch on the take-off side would bring caution to competing riders.

Making a concentrated attempt to lift the prize was one of the most respected patrons of the turf, George William Coventry, ninth Earl of Coventry, with a seven-year-old chestnut mare named Emblem. Sired by the 1851 Derby winner, Teddington, from a mare called Miss Batty, Emblem won seven races on the flat before being bought by Lord Coventry who sent her to be trained at his family estate, Croome Court, Kinnersley, in Worcestershire, by Tom Golby.

The Welsh-bred mare provided some initial problems at the beginning of her training, but it soon became evident to Tom Golby that Emblem was a natural jumper after a day's hunting with the North Cotswold Hounds at Northwick Park. She was ridden in the National by George Stevens, a close friend of Lord Coventry's. Emblem was the 4/1 second favourite.

The customary cheers as the starter sent them on their way turned to guffaws of laughter at the antics of The Orphan, whose amateur rider Mr Bevill became an embarrassed passenger as his mount buck-jumped in reverse for anxious moments before being persuaded to proceed in the right direction. Accompanied by the riderless Inkerman, The Freshman landed first over the Brook, from Jealousy, Yaller Gal and Medora and still in this order they cleared Valentine's. Returning to the racecourse, it was Jealousy and the loose Inkerman leading the field, from Master Bagot, Yaller Gal and Medora. At the new open ditch before the water jump The Orphan came down and at the water itself Jealousy had secured a six-length lead over the blundering Medora. For the first time, Emblem appeared among the leaders, moving into a handy position on the run back into the country. Losing her place nearing Becher's, Jealousy was led over the Brook by Yaller Gal and Arbury, with George Stevens riding a waiting race tucked in just behind. The two leaders engaged in a ding-dong tussle all the way back from Valentine's, entering the racecourse some three lengths ahead of the coasting Emblem. Between the last two flights of hurdles, Emblem raced to the front, rapidly opening up an unassailable advantage over the other two, which inspired tremendous cheers from the packed stands. A last-minute blunder at the final hurdle almost put Emblem out of the race when she slid on landing, but a brilliant piece of horsemanship by George Stevens saved the day and they raced home, winning by 20 lengths. Arbury got the better of a tense struggle to finish second, two lengths ahead of Yaller Gal, and last of the three others to complete was the 1861 winner Jealousy.

All who witnessed the winning jockey's stupendous recovery at the most crucial stage of the race agreed that his reflex action deserved the highest praise and none was more appreciative of George Stevens than the grateful owner, Lord Coventry.

In America the Civil War dragged on and in March 1864 President Lincoln promoted General Ulysses S. Grant to command all the Union armies. Less than three months later, though, the general suffered a humiliating defeat by the Confederate General Robert E. Lee at Cold Springs Harbor.

Increased prize money in excess of £1,000 attracted 25 runners to Liverpool for that year's Grand National, with 'Mr Edwards' teaming up with the 9/2 favourite Jerusalem.

With Emblem unable to run through injury, Lord Coventry was represented by a most appropriate substitute, his National winner's full sister Emblematic. Two years younger than her famous sister, she had also raced on the flat and was also chestnut in colour.

There, however, the similarity ended. Emblematic had long weedy legs and hardly any quarters to speak of. Whatever her appearance, though, the public plunged on the mare sufficiently for the bookies to install her in third position in the market at 10/1. Of course, the fact that she would be ridden by George Stevens was enough to make anyone part with their money when it came to the National.

In the brightest sunshine, they got off to a fine start, Wee Nell and Ireley taking them over the first and on to the next, a ditch and bank. The usual groan when the favourite is involved in disaster came from the crowds when Jerusalem went sprawling to the ground from a clumsy jump and was joined at once by Stanella. With the favourite's jockey struggling to remount, 'Mr Edwards' was knocked sideways and back again by passing horses before eventually regaining the saddle, to continue some 200 yards behind the rest. With Ireley now in front over the third, he left behind him even more grief than before, with several of the runners falling and a number refusing. Up front though, Ireley was setting a merry old gallop, taking Becher's Brook ten lengths clear of Bell's Life, Thomastown and Portland. In mid-division round the Canal Turn, Arbury and Emblematic were close together, jumping well but constantly hampered by a posse of loose horses.

Portland came down just after Valentine's and with Ireley racing clear onto the racecourse, Real Jam came with a flourish to join him on the run to the water. A length up on Arbury leaping this obstacle, Real Jam looked full of running as he made the turn back to the country, while behind him the water jump had claimed some victims. Romeo, Martha and Harry came down with a splash and it was only the perfect balance of George Stevens which kept Emblematic in the contest as she slipped badly on landing. There was a cheer from the crowd when Jerusalem passed them, carrying on in hopeless pursuit after a second fall and now more than a quarter of a mile behind the others. Giving the mare time to recover, Stevens began getting Emblematic into a useful position approaching Becher's, which she jumped in fourth place behind Arbury, Ireley and Chester. After clearing Valentine's side by side, Arbury and Emblematic were left with the race to themselves as the remainder dropped away or were pulled up and another close finish appeared on the cards as the pair galloped neck and neck to the final obstacle. Once on the flat though, Emblematic sprinted away from her rival to win easing up by three lengths. A very long way back came the only three others to survive a most eventful contest, Chester, Thomastown and Ocean Witch.

For the second year in succession George Stevens was acclaimed as the perfect jockey for Aintree, his recovery at the halfway point displaying his abilities to the full and his calmness at the finish a joy to behold.

Both Emblem and Emblematic were eventually despatched to stud, where they each produced useful offspring for flat racing.

In 1865 the American Civil War mercifully came to an end, with Lee's surrender to General Grant at Appomattox Courthouse, signalling a peace which had cost 618,000 lives. Sadly, America's pain was not over, for five days after the surrender President Abraham Lincoln was assassinated at Ford's Theatre in Washington.

In the UK it was a welcome change to have some gentlemen of the press actually praising the efforts being made to put steeplechasing in general and the Grand National in particular on a more organised footing. Predominant among those striving to establish a governing body for the sport were the Old Etonian Mr B.J. Angell and Mr W.G. Craven who had dedicated themselves to making jump racing 'respectable'.

A staunch supporter of 'chasing, Mr Angell had on two occasions come close to winning the National with Bridegroom and his Ireley had run well for a long way the previous year, until being knocked over in the closing stages. His representative in 1865 raised many eyebrows among the more knowledgeable of racing's hierarchy. It wasn't just that Alcibiade was only a five-year-old, nor that the animal was French-bred. The very real concern revolved around the fact that the horse had never before competed in a steeplechase and for the owner to choose the Grand National as Alcibiade's début over fences was viewed not merely as the height of folly but dangerous in the extreme. Despite his deplorable lack of any experience whatsoever, Alcibiade was surprisingly handicapped to carry 11st 4lb and to make matters appear worse, his rider was also facing Aintree for the first time and was considered by most as nothing more than 'a swell from the Guards'.

Captain Henry Coventry was perhaps something of a swell and he most certainly was an officer in the Grenadier Guards, but he was also a most accomplished horseman and a cousin of the man who owned the past two winners, Lord Coventry.

Both Emblem and Emblematic were among the 23 runners, the latter carrying the bulk of money wagered at 5/1 and the dubious Alcibiade receiving some attention in the market on 100/7.

The starter, Mr McGeorge, at last sent them on their journey with Meanwood going on at a cracking pace. Over Becher's Meanwood maintained a clear lead from Hall Court, Alcibiade, Tony Lumbkin and Arbury, with the field so well strung out that a quarter of a mile separated the first and last horses.

Coming back to his field as they reached the racecourse, Meanwood was caught and passed by Arbury, who led over the water followed by Joe Maley, Merrimac, Emblem and Flyfisher. Riding a waiting race, Captain Coventry concentrated on steering a safe path with Alcibiade and it was probably this which saved the day, for at the second Becher's there was an unholy crash. Young Ben Land now found himself well clear of the remainder on Merrimac and kicking on for home, jumped Valentine's 25 lengths in front of Hall Court, The Czar, Flyfisher and the smoothly moving Alcibiade. Toiling in the rear were the only others with a remote interest in the outcome, Emblematic, Mistake, Philosopher and Lightheart. With just two obstacles left to jump, Hall Court had easily overtaken the tiring Merrimac, looking all set to record a shock victory at 50/1, but Captain Coventry was poised with Alcibiade just behind. Touching down over the last with a half-length advantage, Captain Tempest on Hall Court raced for the winning post with a flourish of energy which brought great cheers from the crowds and an immediate response from his brother officer, Captain Coventry. Gaining stride by stride up the long run-in, Alcibiade drew level with Hall Court with less than 200 yards to go and with both riders pushing their mounts for all they were worth, the brave pair battled on, neck and neck to the line. It was only in the very last strides that Alcibiade forced his nose in front to win by a head from a most courageous Hall Court, in a finish which would be talked about for many years to come. Persevering with Emblematic, George Stevens secured third place on the favourite, some 50 yards to the rear of the epic struggle.

The triumph was a fitting reward for owner Mr 'Cherry' Angell, who had worked long and vigorously to create an authoritative organisation to control steeplechasing. As the first five-year-old to succeed, Alcibiade had run the race of his life, the more so for it being his initial outing over fences. Although he was to appear at Aintree again, catching the judge's eye on more than one occasion, he never won another race.

Messrs Angell, Craven and their associates gained the maximum satisfaction in 1866 with the formation of the Grand National Hunt Committee, the long-awaited body which would henceforth administer everything to do with steeplechasing.

Among the distinguished field of 30, the largest to face the starter since 1850, were two very outstanding French-bred horses, L'Africaine and Laura. The public showed their preference for Laura, by making her the 7/1 favourite. Then at 8s came a newcomer, Cortolvin, 1865's hero Alcibiade at 9/1 and, at the long and seemingly generous odds of 30/1, Hall Court.

At even longer odds was another newcomer, Salamander, who from the day of his birth in 1859, had faced derision from first one quarter and then another. Bred by Mr Bourchier in County Limerick, even this man despised the foal the moment he set eyes on him, for the unfortunate animal was born with a crooked foreleg. Time and again Bourchier tried to sell the horse, meeting always mocking laughter instead of offers to purchase. Eventually Mr Hartigan of Limerick bought Salamander for half the asking price of £70, then turned him out in his paddocks to mature. Some months later, a wealthy retired indigo planter by the name of Studd, who often bought horses from Hartigan, purchased 'the crooked-legged bay' in a package with two other hunters for £450 the lot. Mr Studd trained his own horses in Rutland and after intensive work with Salamander, discovered that the leg deformity in no way impeded his ability to jump. Mr Studd and his family were convinced their horse stood an excellent chance at Aintree with only 10st 7lb to shoulder. So confident remained the owner that he backed Salamander to win £40,000 to £1,000 on the day of the race. The man chosen to ride the horse was the 45-year-old amateur Alec Goodman, one of the best horsemen in an age of superior riders and, of course, one who knew his way round Liverpool. Fourteen years earlier he had partnered Miss Mowbray to victory when she had been at even longer odds than Salamander.

A huge crowd in excess of 30,000 willingly suffered the chill of a snowstorm shortly before the start, fully appreciating the quality of the contest they were about to witness. After two false starts, the race began, except for Sir William who dug his toes in and refused to budge. It could well have been an indication of the drama so soon to unfold. Ace of Hearts was quickly into his stride, taking the first fence some three lengths ahead of the rest and looking intent on setting a scorching pace. At the very next obstacle though, the front runner whipped round at the last moment, falling into the ditch from where he ran to and fro along the face of the fence. In one fell swoop Ace of Hearts put 20 runners out of the race, causing a scene of sheer bedlam as jockeys rolled and tumbled amid the falling, scrambling horses. Of the lucky handful which avoided the chaos, Creole showed the way, on and over the third where another three came to grief. Creole was still going well as he led back onto the racecourse, but his jockey, George Waddington, was having a fearful time trying to fend off the attentions of two loose horses directly alongside him. Early on the second circuit Laura fell and Alcibiade went out at Becher's Brook. At the Canal Turn Thomastown moved up smoothly within a couple of lengths of Creole, only to fall at the next, Valentine's. With just the riderless Hall Court ahead of him, Creole appeared to have the race in his pocket on re-entering the racecourse, but suddenly and at great speed a challenger came on the scene. Alec Goodman had simply hunted round the whole way, avoiding the falls and mayhem to bring Salamander with a well-judged effort at just the right moment. Streaming away, Salamander ran out a very convincing winner by ten lengths from Cortolvin, who relegated

Creole to third place close home. Lightheart and Merrimac were the only others to survive a most disastrous race.

It was a highly jubilant Mr Studd who welcomed back the heavily bewhiskered Alec Goodman to the winner's circle and although the rider's exertions had left an uncharacteristic frown on his face, Goodman also had every reason to rejoice.

One week after his celebrated Grand National victory, Salamander romped home in the important Warwick Grand Annual 'Chase, dispelling any thoughts that his Aintree victory had been a fluke. Tragically Salamander was never allowed the opportunity to prove himself at Liverpool again for, in April 1866, he broke his back at an innocuous fence in a very minor event at Crewkerne.

If the world of racing had witnessed a bargain purchase in the form of the 1866 Grand National winner, there occurred an even greater snip the following year in the sphere of international commerce. William Seward, United States Secretary of the Interior, finally achieved what he had campaigned for over many years, the purchase from Russia of Alaska. That vast expanse of near wilderness in the Far North would for some time to come be laughingly referred to as 'Seward's Folly', yet the cost to the American government of just over $7,000,000 represented a mere two cents per acre.

Aintree's recognition as the Mecca of steeplechasing received overall acceptance that year with the Grand Military Meeting being added to its spring fixture, so making the Grand National meeting a three-day affair.

The big race drew 23 hopefuls, the most fancied being King Arthur, Shakspeare and Fan, and although sadly without last year's winner Salamander, that owner's colours were carried by the promising young Shangarry.

Third in the handicap, and penalised an extra half stone for his good performance behind Salamander, came Cortolvin, considered by many to be unreliable in a test of stamina. Bred by Michael Dunne at Ballymanus in Ireland, Cortolvin caught the eye of a man with a penchant for horses from across the Irish Sea, that loyal friend of 'chasing, Lord Poulett. Perhaps it was the suspicion that his horse did not truly stay which persuaded his lordship to accept an offer from the Duke of Hamilton to buy, and it was in the duke's colours that Cortolvin made a second attempt at the National. It was by all accounts to be a final spin of the dice for the Duke of Hamilton, who had recently encountered financial difficulties and plunged heavily on Cortolvin in a last desperate attempt to restore his fortunes. Ridden by one of the most stylish jockeys of his generation, the Warwickshire-born Jesse Page, Cortolvin went off at 16/1.

On a bright, clear Wednesday afternoon in early March 1867, the starter got them away cleanly and at a cracking pace Thomastown, Cortolvin, King

Arthur, Plinlimmon and Sea King attempted to out-run each other to the first fence. It was the favourite, King Arthur, who landed first on the other side, but when he'd set the crowds on their toes he refused at the very next obstacle. Cortolvin now took them along, maintaining a strong gallop down to and over Becher's and it was only as they approached the Canal Turn that his jockey decided to hold him in check. Adopting this strategy just at that time prevented Cortolvin getting caught up in the catastrophe which almost immediately developed. As those jostling for the lead rounded that extremely sharp corner, Havelock crashed to the ground, directly in the path of Little Frank and Astrolabe, who were both brought down. Their exit in turn interfered with Fan and Marengo, the former losing many lengths in the process. To the surprise and amusement of the spectators, the pony-sized Globule now took up the running. His smallness only added to the amazement of the crowds as he jumped the fences and ditches with a fluent precision, leaping the water jump like a stag, clear of Sea King, Revolver, Genievre and the remounted King Arthur. Levelling up for the Canal Turn, Cortolvin came on the scene, striding out well as he overtook the leader and proceeded to make his run for home. From a long way back, the mare Fan suddenly appeared with a threatening run towards the leader, only to find that Cortolvin still had something in reserve as the gelding increased his tempo to skip over the final hurdles and pass the post five lengths to the good. Mr Studd's Shangarry was a further four lengths behind Fan in third place, just a neck in front of the unfortunate little Globule. Another six horses completed the course a very long way behind the winner Cortolvin, who answered the questions concerning his genuineness in a most emphatic manner.

As may well be expected, winning owner the Duke of Hamilton was beside himself with joy, heaping praises galore on both his horse and the astute jockeyship of Jesse Page. In a sporting style typical of the man, Lord Poulett, who had sold Cortolvin to the Duke, congratulated the winning owner and jockey after first performing his customary practice, that of checking that his own runner and jockey were safe and well. Poulett's horse Genievre finished tenth and last.

Having carried the biggest weight to victory in the race since it became a handicap in 1843, as well as straightening out his owner's financial problems, Cortolvin never ran in another race.

There was a continental flavour about the 1868 Grand National, with the French mare Astrolabe and the Hungarian gelding Buszke among the 21 runners. They shared top weight of 12st with the favourite, Lord Coventry's representative, Chimney Sweep.

Undaunted by having parted with the previous year's winner Cortolvin before its day of glory, Lord Poulett staked his hopes this time on a diminutive grey entire called The Lamb. Bred in County Limerick, he was sired by the stallion Zouave, the property of Mr Courtenay who had owned the first Irish-trained National winner Matthew in 1847. The link with past Aintree worthies did not end there for The Lamb's grand-sire on the female side was none other than Arthur, runner-up to Jerry in the 1840 contest. Barely 15½ hands high, The Lamb was very delicate as a youngster, to such an extent that the idea of putting him to racing was never considered. Offered for sale to the English owner Edward Studd, of Salamander fame, the grey was contemptuously dismissed as being 'not fit to carry a man's boots'. As The Lamb thickened and matured, though, he attracted the attention of Dublin veterinary surgeon Joseph Doyle, who bought him and for whom the tiny grey won the valuable Kildare Hunt Plate at Punchestown when only five years old. At the end of 1867 The Lamb was leased to Lord Poulett for the remainder of his racing life and his preparation for a tilt at the forthcoming National began. A founder member of the recently instituted National Hunt Committee, Lord Poulett acquired his love of steeplechasing when stationed in Ireland as a captain in the 22nd Regiment. When his military duties permitted, he rode in numerous cross-country races, quickly developing a strong affection for Irish-bred horses. An excellent judge of riders as well as horseflesh, Lord Poulett chose well in engaging the very talented all-round sportsman George Ede to partner The Lamb at Liverpool. Better known to the racing public as 'Mr Edwards', Ede was a brilliant cricketer who, in conjunction with Lord Poulett, founded Hampshire Cricket Club, scoring 1,200 runs for them in 1863. In his very first Grand National ten years earlier, 'Mr Edwards' finished second on Weathercock behind Little Charley.

Racegoers at Liverpool in 1868 really took the little grey son of Zouave to their hearts, amazed and delighted at the gentleness of The Lamb, a trait which in fact had given him his name. Encouraged by the escape of a small lamb seen fleeing from a cattle truck on a nearby railway siding, the public considered it an omen and backed him into third slot in the market at 9/1.

From a good start, the 21 runners sped away on the run to the first fence when, with just a little over 200 yards covered, tragedy struck. Chimney Sweep, the favourite, brushed against one of the large boulders marking the route across the road, shattering the pastern of his near foreleg. To save the creature further suffering there was no alternative but to put him down at once. Captain Crosstree led the remainder over the first fence, continuing in front of Daisy and The Lamb. Fan, who had done so well as runner-up the previous year, proved a very stubborn character at the second obstacle, refusing to jump every time his jockey desperately tried to get her over. At Becher's

Brook Garus also refused and within seconds Mentmore, Kingswood and Thalassius crashed out of the race, while Captain Crosstree went on in front, closely followed by Daisy and The Lamb. Back on the racecourse Captain Crosstree gave way to the sweetly moving Pearl Diver who, 24 hours before, had proven his usefulness by winning a hurdle race at Aintree. Leading over the water jump, Pearl Diver took them back into the country, with The Lamb, Captain Crosstree and Alcibiade hard on his heels, but upon reaching a severe stretch of plough, several runners found the going too heavy and called it a day. A terrific struggle evolved coming into Becher's, with Alcibiade striking the front when producing a mighty leap over the Brook, while Captain Crosstree renewed his challenge all the way to the Canal Turn. The latter forged to the front as Alcibiade began to tire coming back to the racecourse, but at the penultimate hurdle Captain Crosstree ruined his chance by whipping round when just about to take off. In an instant The Lamb and Pearl Diver swept past, matching strides over the last and engaging in a ding-dong tussle all the way up the straight. Sticking dourly to his task, The Lamb gradually gained the ascendancy in the final 60 yards to win by two lengths from Pearl Diver, with Alcibiade ten lengths back in third place.

A highly jubilant crowd cheered the little grey long and loud as he was led to the winner's enclosure by a very proud Lord Poulett, whose faith in his horse and rider had been so well justified.

Four

1869–1878

Across the Atlantic in 1869 Americans celebrated as only they know how with the completion of a railroad linking the nation from coast to coast. As the final spike was hammered at Promontory Point in Utah, so the journey time between New York and San Francisco was reduced from three months to just eight days. This triumph of engineering skill was accomplished two months after the inauguration of the former general, Ulysses S. Grant, as the 18th President of the United States.

At home, there was little cause for rejoicing among the connections of The Lamb who, since his exertions in winning the National, had suffered from a wasting disease. In the grey's absence Fortunatus was a short-priced favourite in the 22-runner line-up, with Fan and Despatch also at cramped odds. Of the old brigade, Hall Court, Alcibiade and Globule were trying again, but of the newcomers there was a brilliant six-year-old hurdler deservedly commanding much respect.

Although only once having run in a steeplechase, which he won, The Colonel had proved near unbeatable under big weights over the minor obstacles. Bred by John Weyman in Shropshire, the graceful near-black entire was prepared for racing by a farmer named Roberts at Bishop's Castle and served Mr Weyman well by carrying his colours to victory five times from nine outings before taking a tilt at the National. Fourth in the betting at 100/7 was an indication more of the confidence punters had in the jockey, George Stevens, rather than for The Colonel, about whom there remained a serious doubt concerning his lack of 'chasing experience.

For some unaccountable reason Fan again showed her dislike of the second fence, stubbornly refusing and bringing about the fall of Bishopton, Orne and Knave of Trumps. Guy of Warwick and Dick Turpin went out at the next, but up front Globule, Despatch and Gardener were jumping well, leading over Becher's in that order. At this stage of the race, The Colonel was well to the rear,

George Stevens riding the young entire the way he preferred to avoid possible interference. Shortly before returning to the racecourse, Globule gave way to Gardener, only to regain the advantage as they leapt the water jump and it was as they turned back into the country that The Colonel began moving through the field. Stevens produced a prodigious leap from his mount at Becher's Brook, placing The Colonel right in the firing-line among the leaders and he was galloping far more easily than his opponents. Still held in check from the Canal Turn, The Colonel lay third behind Fortunatus and Gardener over Valentine's, where suddenly from the rear came those two great old rivals, Hall Court and Alcibiade. With the favourite Fortunatus still in the lead three from home, the crowds began cheering him home, only to see their hopes dashed when he was pulled up before entering the racecourse. The Colonel drew level with Gardener two out, racing easily in the magical hands of George Stevens, and after leading over the last, The Colonel strode away to withhold the late challenge of Hall Court. At the post the winning margin was three lengths, Hall Court finishing second one length ahead of Gardener, with the gallant Alcibiade the same distance back in fourth place.

It was apparent to most that The Colonel had won with something in hand, inspiring the belief that with such a young horse the possibility of future success existed. With that thought in mind they looked forward to the prospect of perhaps The Lamb and The Colonel pitting their skills against each other in 12 months' time.

Europe felt the thunder and tragedy of war again in 1870, with the outbreak of the Franco-Prussian War, a conflict which was to see Paris besieged and France crushed. At the age of 58, the novelist and social reformer Charles Dickens died, leaving his latest work, *Edwin Drood*, unfinished.

An air of sadness also prevailed in Liverpool upon the death of William Lynn, the man whose dreams of a steeplechase to stir the imagination of people everywhere had come to fruition in a way not even he could have hoped for.

With The Lamb still afflicted with illness, the hoped-for 'match' between the little grey and The Colonel would have to remain in abeyance for some time yet. So far as The Colonel was concerned, the public looked upon him as virtually unbeatable, so comfortably had he triumphed in the race last time. Not even an additional 19lb imposed by the handicapper could deter the punters, who made him 7/2 favourite. This time running in the colours of a Mr Evans, though still officially the property of Mr Weyman, The Colonel was again partnered by the incomparable George Stevens.

With hardly any delay, the field got away to a capital start at the first time of asking, with Gardener and Primrose cutting out the early work ahead of a well-bunched pack. Traveller was the only casualty at the first, but true to form, Fan refused at the second fence for the third year running. The Elk, ridden by Ben Land the younger, cleared Becher's in impressive style four lengths ahead of the rest, a lead he increased to 12 lengths by the time they were over Valentine's. Briefly accompanied by Guy of Warwick as they ran to the water, The Elk was soon back with a commanding advantage when the former fell. Two fences before the second Becher's, The Elk was pulled up as he came to the end of his tether, his place being taken by Karslake, who jumped the Brook just ahead of Surney, Cristal and Primrose. This quartet dominated the proceedings until after jumping Valentine's, where Pearl Diver and The Colonel joined the struggle for supremacy, raising dust clouds as their hooves beat a rapid tattoo over the last field of plough. Galloping on the wide outside, The Colonel was tucked in just behind the leading pair, Surney and Primrose, as they came back on the racecourse for the final time and with Cristal and Pearl Diver dropping away through exhaustion, the outcome seemed to rest between the three. With just one flight of hurdles left, The Doctor came with a blistering run from way off the pace at the exact moment that The Colonel struck the front. Primrose was also about to make her effort when her opportunity was destroyed, being barged off her stride by Surney, leaving The Colonel with but one horse to beat. Every yard of that cruelly long run-in was fought for with a tenacity, determination and bravery, which is truly the hallmark of greatness. Neck and neck, The Colonel and The Doctor brought the crowds to their feet in a crescendo of cheering as they dug deep into their final reserves of energy to gain those precious, glory-winning inches. It was only with his very last stride that The Colonel prevailed, by the agonising distance of a mere neck from the resolute The Doctor. Five lengths behind in third place came the luckless Primrose, followed by Surney and four others, the last of which was that most reliable performer Alcibiade.

For everyone, except the bookmakers, it was a very popular result, with the first three home featuring in the exact same order in the betting. Winning jockey George Stevens had written his own special chapter into the annals of Grand National history, riding his fifth winner of the race.

Tragically, the following day, another outstanding rider bade his farewell to Aintree in the saddest way possible.

George Ede, who as 'Mr Edwards' had partnered The Lamb to victory just two years before, died from injuries he received when falling in the Sefton Steeplechase over one circuit of the National course. He was 35 years of age at the time of his death, which was an enormous loss to horseracing.

Grand National day in March 1871 had a joyful, carnival air about it, which even the weather apparently recognised, for the crowds of over 40,000 basked in sunshine more in keeping with mid-July.

For those at Aintree that day there occurred an extra reason to rejoice, the return of the little grey horse who had captivated racegoers when triumphant in the National three years earlier. Now trained by Chris Green, successful in the race as a jockey aboard Abd-El-Kader and Half Caste, The Lamb had at last been restored to fitness by his new handler and although this was to be his first race in more than two years, the public rushed to back him. A new jockey had of course to be found for the grey. The sad and untimely demise of 'Mr Edwards' created a problem regarding who should be entrusted with The Lamb after such a long lay-off. Incredibly, Lord Poulett, the owner, woke up one morning with what he believed was the perfect answer. During the night his lordship had had a dream, which he swore was as clear as daylight, in which The Lamb was ridden to victory in the Grand National by Tommy Pickernell, alias 'Mr Thomas'. Wasting no time, Poulett wrote to the rider concerned, informing Tommy of his vision and requesting an immediate answer as to his availability for Liverpool. What 'Mr Thomas' really thought of Lord Poulett's dream is unknown, but remembering how The Lamb had made light of Aintree's demanding obstacles in 1868, he didn't hesitate in accepting the mount. The pair started second in the betting at 11/2, despite The Lamb's absence from racing for so long and the fact that his handicap mark of 11st 5lb was asking a lot from such a small horse.

Most heavily backed of the 25 runners was the hardy-annual Pearl Diver at 4/1, with The Colonel at 8s and Despatch, Cecil and The Doctor also well supported. Uppermost in the thoughts of all as the horses paraded before the start, however, lay the question concerning the prospect of The Colonel winning an unprecedented third Grand National. His journey to Liverpool was considerably longer this time, for he was now owned by Baron Oppenheim of Germany and he travelled from Berlin to compete.

From the first-time start Rufus was the first to show, bowling along to the first fence and scattering a party of picnickers who had foolishly settled themselves in the lee of the obstacle. St Valentine came down at the second, where The Doctor, after at first refusing, was persuaded to jump it at the second attempt and The Colonel was as usual bringing up the rear. Still in command over Becher's, Rufus was setting a merry gallop, with Souvenance vainly trying to match strides with him and the remainder already well strung out. It was noticeable that The Lamb was having difficulty crossing the ploughed stretches of the track, the dust from the soil hindering his vision as it rose from the galloping hooves, but 'Mr Thomas' persevered, keeping well in touch with the leaders. Rufus and Souvenance rose together at the water, clearing it well and set off back into the country followed by a cluster of runners, with The Colonel still being waited with at the rear. On the run back to Becher's The Lamb lost more ground again on the plough, yet the plucky little grey made it up when meeting the turf and cleared the Brook brilliantly, right on the heels of the pacemakers. As he began his challenge at the Canal Turn, two horses fell directly in front of The Lamb and displaying exceptional agility, the grey put in another leap to clear them both as well as the fence. With The Colonel now making a forward move, the race was opening up. Rufus touched down over Valentine's a fraction before Despatch, with Souvenance tiring as Pearl Diver, Scarrington and The Lamb swept past and George Stevens seemed set to pounce with The Colonel. The cheers from the stands began as the principals raced to the penultimate flight of hurdles and as The Lamb outjumped Despatch at the last the noise was deafening. Sprinting to the post the tiny grey was never in danger of being caught, his winning margin over Despatch being a comfortable two lengths, with Scarrington four lengths further back in third place. The Colonel bravely stayed on to finish sixth of the eight which completed the course.

Surrounded by a near hysterical mass of excited people, Lord Poulett led in The Lamb to a hero's welcome, losing in the process his pocket-watch to a swift-fingered pickpocket, whilst his gallant winner had half his tail snatched away by frenzied souvenir hunters.

Barely three months later the dreadful news that George Stevens had been killed left an unfillable gap in the world of jump racing. After so many years of surviving the hazards of steeplechasing, the Cheltenham-born maestro lost his life in a quiet country lane near his home on Cleeve Hill, Cheltenham. While enjoying a leisurely hack far from the hurly-burly of the racecourse he knew so well, his mount shied and threw him from the saddle. The greatest jockey yet seen round Aintree died without regaining consciousness after smashing his head against a stone wall. George Stevens was 38 years old at the time of his death, his record of five winning rides in the toughest race on earth stands to this day and is likely to stand forever.

It seemed fitting with George Stevens no more to be seen demonstrating his brilliance over Liverpool's unique fences, that his partner in two memorable victories, The Colonel, should also bid farewell to Aintree. Returning to Germany, The Colonel took up stud duties at the German government's horse-breeding establishment in Beberbeck. As a stallion he proved most successful and such was his fame and splendid appearance, on several occasions he was Kaiser Wilhelm's charger for ceremonial events.

Apparently smitten by the appeal of the Grand National, Baron Oppenheim sought a replacement for The Colonel to represent him in the 1872 race. Thus, for the sum of £1,200 The Lamb moved from the ownership of an English nobleman to that of a German one. Again to be ridden by 'Mr Thomas', The Lamb was dealt harshly by the handicapper, topping the weights with the massive burden for such a tiny horse of 12st 7lb. Even his army of admirers considered it an impossible task and the grey was easy to back at 100/8.

After failing to complete the course in the last two years, Casse Tête was trying for a third time in the company of jockey Jesse Page, the man who had steered Cortolvin to victory five years earlier. Bred by the Duke of Newcastle, Casse Tête was a seven-year-old chestnut mare by Trumpeter out of Constance, whose early displays on the flat were modest to say the least. After being bought by Mr Brayley she was put to jumping, at which she showed much improved form and, despite her unimpressive attempts at Liverpool in the last two Grand Nationals, this time the mare found support from some quarters to start at a rather cramped 20/1. Mr Brayley had made a small fortune in the theatrical world after starting his working life as a Punch and Judy man and being completely enamoured with steeplechasing, like many before him, set his heart on winning Aintree's famous event. He came close to achieving that aim when his Pearl Diver got within two lengths of The Lamb in 1868.

With the going very hard indeed, but with a bright, clear sky, the crowds waited anxiously as the starter, Mr McGeorge, brought the runners into line before despatching them at the first try. Royal Irish Fusilier led them over the first, proceeding to take them along at a good pace, so good in fact that by the time he landed over Becher's Brook his pursuers were spreadeagled with the tail-enders fully 300 yards to the rear. Rufus and Primrose joined issue at the Canal Turn, to such effect that the pair led the rest of the way back to the racecourse and were first over the water jump. As Rufus and Royal Irish Fusilier faded, Scots Grey moved up to dictate the proceedings over Becher's, while Ryshworth failed to survive the Brook. The Lamb, Scarrington and Casse Tête came with a flurry at the Canal Turn, carefully giving a wide berth to the falling Cinderella and the colliding Franc Luron and Acton. At full gallop they raced back to the racecourse, with Mr Arthur Yates suddenly bringing Harvester into the fray, and as Scots Grey dropped back The Lamb, Casse Tête, Scarrington, Despatch and Harvester raced towards the second last with the prize between them. The applause which heralded the little grey's momentary spell in front shortly before the final flight fell away as quickly as The Lamb's effort, as the weight took its toll and he tired. This left Harvester with the race at his mercy, but he too became the victim of fate. His overreach at the last obstacle caused immediate lameness, leaving owner-rider Arthur Yates with no option but to pull the horse up. Casse Tête cleared the last well, quickly putting the result beyond issue as she raced on to the post, leaving the struggling Scarrington toiling in her wake. At the line six lengths separated the first two, Scarrington being hampered by a twisted shoe which seriously impeded his progress. Six lengths further back came Despatch, just depriving The Lamb of third place. Five others managed to complete the course at varying intervals.

As a result of the outrageous misfortune which beset at least three horses in the closing stages of the race, Casse Tête was considered a very lucky winner, a view obviously not shared by her connections. Page had ridden a perfect race and the mare had made not a semblance of a mistake throughout the trip and most importantly of all, Casse Tête was exactly where she needed to be to succeed. During the next three seasons Casse Tête ran in a total of seven races without ever winning.

The Lamb returned to Germany after giving such a brave display in the National to finish fourth and sadly he was never to appear at Aintree again. Whilst in the lead close to home in a steeplechase at Baden-Baden in September 1872, The Lamb ran into a patch of boggy ground barely 100 yards from the winning post, breaking his leg so badly that he had to be destroyed. It was a most tragic end to a very courageous horse.

The Grand National of 1873 came around with bright skies and good ground and although the crowds grieved the passing of The Lamb and the retirement of The Colonel, a field of 28 for the big race drew many thousands to Aintree.

Top weight with 11st 11lb was the six-year-old entire Disturbance, owned by a remarkable and often fiery character by the name of Captain James Machell. Born at Beverley in Yorkshire in 1838, Machell resigned his commission in a line regiment in 1862 to set up a training establishment at Newmarket. An excellent judge of a horse, he was a very heavy gambler who made great sums of money for himself and his associates by preparing horses for specific events and getting his money on when the price was right. After watching Mr Barber's Disturbance win a hurdle race at Aintree the day after Casse Tête won the 1872 Grand National, Machell purchased the bay, with the object of getting him ready for a tilt at the 1873 National. It was a most ambitious plan for a horse as yet with no experience of 'chasing. Disturbance in fact had his introduction to the larger obstacles at Aintree in November 1872, when he fell while contesting the Grand Sefton 'Chase. Obviously a very quick learner, Disturbance came out the very next day to romp home an easy winner of the Craven Steeplechase over one circuit of the National course. Needing to know the answer to one final question, whether or not his horse could stay the distance, Machell brought him out barely three weeks later in the four-mile Great Metropolitan 'Chase at Croydon. Without putting a foot wrong at any time, Disturbance beat his 14 opponents, hard held by a length. Completely satisfied with the ability so far displayed by his horse, the owner put him away for the winter and the big Liverpool test four months hence. An essential element in the Machell success at this time was the man who both trained and rode for him, John Maunsell Richardson. A fine all-round sportsman, Richardson was born at Limber Magna in Lincolnshire in 1846, was educated at

Harrow and Cambridge and rode his first winner when an undergraduate at the latter seat of learning. He excelled at most sports, particularly running, fencing and cricket, being a member of the Varsity team against Oxford in 1866, 1867 and 1868. A natural and polished horseman, Richardson became champion amateur rider in 1872 after riding 56 winners.

Favourite on the day was Mr Moreton's Footman, but it was the second in the betting which attracted most attention in the paddock, the seven-year-old Ryshworth. This individual certainly brought a touch of class to the race, having been good enough on the flat to take part in the 1869 Epsom Derby. Casse Tête was at 10/1, as was Cecil, but despite having proved he could jump the course, Disturbance was allowed to start at the generous odds of 20/1. With the benefit of hindsight, it may well have been a ploy of Captain Machell's to give the horse such a long lay-off, for most people felt by the time the National came round that Disturbance would be in need of a race. Among some interesting newcomers was a five-year-old chestnut horse owned by Lord Aylesford by the name of Reugny, who had competed against Disturbance over hurdles and of whom more would be heard before long.

It took the starter three tries to get the field away, it being Ryshworth who was first to show on the gallop to the first fence. As the product of classic blood-lines, Ryshworth behaved in a most disorderly manner, while still preceding the others, constantly swerving from side to side as his jockey frantically struggled to control him. This behaviour led to trouble at Becher's, when Ryshworth put in an untidy jump, knocked the nearby Cecil to the ground and created such disruption that Ismael refused and carried Huntsman off the course. Lord Stamford's New York now took up the running, thankfully in a far more sedate fashion and was only overtaken by Solicitor as they neared the water jump. The favourite Footman crumpled out of the race at the second fence back in the country, taking with him New York, Lingerer and True Blue, who all fell over him. The mare Columbine moved up prominently hereabouts and after the grey Broadlea fell and brought down Solicitor and Red Nob at the fence after Becher's, was left in the lead. Soon three lengths clear, Columbine took the Canal Turn and Valentine's well and began making the best of the way home. Chased by Ryshworth, Alice Lee and Disturbance, Columbine came to the second last gamely holding on to her rapidly diminishing advantage, but she had given her all and rising to the obstacle was passed easily by Ryshworth. The crowds began cheering home the second favourite as he came to the final hurdle full of running, but their joy was premature. Richardson, aboard Disturbance, knew the horse in front of him particularly well, having both trained and ridden Ryshworth in his younger days. He was fully aware that Mr Chaplin's horse thoroughly disliked close company when jumping, to such an extent that

Ryshworth usually declined to continue his effort when challenged. As both rose for the final jump, Richardson's assessment of his rival proved correct and Disturbance forged ahead to win well by six lengths. Columbine was ten lengths behind the runner-up, with just three others coming home after her.

The huge grin on Captain Machell's face in the winner's enclosure spoke volumes. He collected a huge amount of money from the bookies, heaped praise on his rider and immediately began to plan for the next Grand National. John Maunsell Richardson, it was widely agreed, had given a superlative exhibition of jockeyship and his meagre £10 bet on Disturbance brought him a richly deserved £1,000.

Ryshworth was brought out within 24 hours to contest Aintree's Sefton Steeplechase, which he won in a common canter, thus paying the highest compliment to his conqueror in the National, Disturbance.

Watching the Sefton 'Chase was the astute Captain Machell, whose interest was aroused not by the winner but by the horse which finished second. A French-bred five-year-old called Reugny, it soon became the property of Machell, to be added to his plans for a future Grand National.

Of the 93 subscribers named as the entries for the 1874 Aintree renewal of its most important event, just 22 stood their ground as actual competitors.

Launching a three-pronged assault on the race, Captain Machell ran Disturbance, Defence and the now six-year-old Reugny and it was the early installation as favourite of Reugny which led to an unseemly and very bitter dispute.

All three were prepared by Mr Richardson at Limber Magna, Lincolnshire, and the trainer made no secret of his preference for the youngest of the trio, Reugny. His many friends in the area at once began investing heavily on the French-bred horse, while the owner for once delayed placing his bets. By the time Captain Machell got his money down, the best available price was 5/1, causing an explosion of anger directed at John Maunsell Richardson. Confronting his trainer-rider, Machell declared that he didn't keep horses just for Lincolnshire farmers to bet on and even went so far as to threatening to withdraw Reugny from the race. Equally angry, Richardson responded that if the threat was carried out, he would accept the ride on Mr Bruce's Furley in the National and win with it. The last straw for the rider was Machell's suggestion that Richardson should deliberately mislead the public as to which horse he would partner at Liverpool. Subterfuge in any form was totally abhorrent to the sportsman and he was emphatic in stating that the only Machell runner he would ride was Reugny and that, furthermore, after the Grand National he would never compete in another race. The previous year's winner, Disturbance, was this time ridden by Joe Cannon, but shouldering the impossible burden of 12st 9lb, was at longer odds than last time at 25/1.

With the acrimony existing between the connections of the favourite, the atmosphere in the paddock was tense, to say the least, and John Maunsell Richardson must have been relieved when the signal to start the parade was given. After one false start the race began with the usual dash to the first fence, headed by Daybreak, Eurotas, Ouragan II and Bretby. Ouragan II was first over Becher's from Bretby, Daybreak and Merlin, closely followed by Machell's trio, Defence, Disturbance and Reugny. With little change in the order they proceeded without incident to Valentine's, where Columbine moved smoothly into third place and Furley joined the tightly bunched pack on the heels of the leaders. For the observers in the densely packed stands the scene at the water jump was a thrilling one, with a host of horses in contention slightly to the rear of Columbine, who went back into the country ahead of Daybreak, Ouragan II, Merlin, Eurotas and Chimney Sweep. All the way up to Becher's Brook and then on to the Canal Turn, first one then the other showed briefly in front and at Valentine's Reugny was still some distance off the pace. At the Anchor Bridge Crossing, with only two obstacles left to jump, Chimney Sweep and Columbine were racing stride for stride with each other, having opened up a gap of several lengths between the rest. With the mare Columbine tiring as they straightened up for the penultimate flight, Chimney Sweep drew clear by five lengths, appearing to have the race in his pocket. Bringing Reugny with a perfectly timed run, Richardson judged his challenge to a nicety, but it was only when he saw Chimney Sweep fail to respond to some slaps from his jockey's whip that he knew the race was his. In spite of making a slight mistake at the last, Reugny rallied well to his rider's urging, gaining the upper hand within strides and racing clear to a six-length victory from the exhausted Chimney Sweep. Merlin stayed on to secure third place from Defence, who was followed home by the weary survivors, Master Mowbray, Disturbance, Columbine and Ouragan II.

John Maunsell Richardson quietly unsaddled Reugny in the winner's enclosure, the second time in 12 months he had enjoyed the experience, while Captain Machell revelled in the congratulations on having his three runners finish in the first six.

The vast crowd celebrated as only they who have backed a Grand National winning favourite know how and the jockeys weighed out for the next race, while the man who only moments before had won his second National unobtrusively left the racecourse. True to his word, as always, John Maunsell Richardson never rode in another race again.

So far as worldwide matters were concerned, 1875 was as eventful as any other year. In the United States, residents of Clay County, Missouri, described the bombing by the Pinkerton Detective Agency of the home of the outlaws Frank and Jesse James as 'the crime of the century'. With the notorious brothers absent from the premises at the time, the Pinkertons understandably lost quite a lot of credibility. In Boston much greater expertise was demonstrated by Alexander Graham Bell when he pioneered the telephone. The recently completed Suez Canal, providing a shorter shipping route to the Far East, came under the jurisdiction of Britain. French composer Georges Bizet died at the age of 36, just a few months after the first production of possibly his greatest work, *Carmen*.

Steeplechasing in general, and the Grand National in particular, received a welcome boost when a notable journalist described the sport as 'providing such a wonderful spectacle as almost sufficient to menace the position of flat racing'. This, of course, was a tremendous tribute to the energy and initiative of the National Hunt Committee, which was not yet ten years old.

With this Grand National being worth just under £2,000, it was rather disappointing that no previous winner was among the 19 starters. Congress, Furley and Clonave were at the head of the handicap, but it was the French-bred five-year-old mare, La Veine, which attracted most money as 6/1 favourite. Captain Machell attempted a third victory in the race, this time with the professionally ridden Laburnum, yet without the assistance of the highly regarded Richardson the punters looked elsewhere.

Taking part in his 15th National, 'Mr Thomas' took the leg up on Pathfinder, a somewhat lightly raced eight-year-old bay gelding who had previously raced under the name of The Knight. Having been bred by John Cowley near Rugby, the horse changed hands on a number of occasions, once being claimed for 100 guineas after winning a selling 'chase at Daventry. Eventually passing into the joint ownership of Lord Huntly and Herbert Bird, and now running as Pathfinder, he carried the colours of the latter at Liverpool, having been trained for the race by Mr W. Reeves at Epsom.

On very heavy going, the runners raced away at the first attempt, with rank outsider Sailor heading the charge, much against the wishes of his rider's struggles to restrain him. On the testing ground most of the runners were finding difficulty with their jumping and in well-strung-out order they took Becher's with Congress, Sparrow, La Veine and Miss Hungerford making the pace. Remaining in this order over Valentine's, Jackal and Victoire joined them returning to the racecourse and as they straightened up for the water, Pathfinder began making ground. Congress was in front going back into the country, where at the second obstacle Miss Hungerford came to grief, as did Sailor. 'Mr Thomas' felt concern for his mount as they pursued the leaders across a stretch of plough, Pathfinder showing a distinct dislike of the heavy ground there and losing a considerable amount of ground. Over Becher's Congress touched down in front, only to be passed by Victoire, while, many lengths behind, 'Mr Thomas' seriously considered pulling up Pathfinder. Finally deciding the joint owners deserved a run for their money, he persevered, clearing the Brook in fine style. The mare Dainty moved steadily into second place behind Victoire after jumping Valentine's, with Congress starting to feel the pace and La Veine staying on well, and Pathfinder seeming much happier during the final mile of the race. As those around her faded, Dainty hit the front over the second last, full of running and with her amateur rider, Mr Hathaway, sitting confidently as he kicked for home. Coming from a very long way back, Pathfinder surprised her rider more than anyone else by suddenly finding his second wind to close on the leader at the last hurdle. A tremendous race developed as they landed together on the flat, the mare and the gelding galloping flat out all the way to the winning post, with Pathfinder just prevailing by half a length from Dainty. Three lengths behind came another mare, the French-bred La Veine in third, just ousting Jackal at the line.

As congratulations were heaped on the owners, Lord Huntly and Herbert Bird, the story broke that at the start Tommy Pickernell had found it necessary to ask a fellow jockey to point him in the right direction. His practice of taking a nip of something strong before the big race as a fortifier had apparently exceeded the usual dosage this time, leaving him a little confused. Certainly nobody would have guessed this from the manner in which he demonstrated his mastery in such a close finish, to notch his third Grand National victory.

The west was at its wildest in America in 1876: Wild Bill Hickock was shot in the back while playing poker in a saloon at Deadwood, Dakota, while further south the Indian chief Geronimo began a ten-year war against the white man. General George Armstrong Custer's Seventh Cavalry, consisting of 264 men, was massacred by the Sioux at the Battle of the Little Big Horn. At home, the British Parliament passed the Royal Titles Act, making Queen Victoria Empress of India.

Racegoers at Aintree felt extremely privileged this year, being able to declare that they had seen in the flesh what everybody accepted as the finest example of a steeplechaser to step on a racecourse in many years. The animal in question was a beautiful-looking chestnut entire called Chandos, owned by none other than Captain James Machell. From the moment the weights were published, Chandos was spoken of as a virtual certainty for the Grand National, with such conviction that he was at the head of the betting from the time the first book was formed.

The previous year's winner, Pathfinder, was trying for that elusive double, now partnered by the professional W. Reeves, as 'Mr Thomas' was this time aboard Defence. Others among the 19 runners with past experience of the race included Jackal, Chimney Sweep and Congress, but to most observers each of these were way past their best.

With Chandos a rampant 3/1 favourite on the day, Captain Machell was alleged to be more than satisfied with the extended odds he had received, while declining to divulge the fact that he had secured a healthy 'saver' on his other runner, Regal.

This five-year-old black gelding was by Saunterer out of the mare Regalia who, in 1865, had won the fillies classic, the Oaks, at Epsom. Also in Regal's favour was the fact that he, unlike his stablemate, Chandos, had won over fences, his most creditable performance to date being a sparkling victory three months before the National in the Great Sandown Steeplechase over four miles. Twenty-seven-year-old Joe Cannon had recently become Captain Machell's private trainer and with James Jewitt booked for Chandos, Joe accepted the double duty of partnering Regal, believing his mount would cope better with Liverpool than the favourite. Still, to the majority of gamblers, the thought which preserved their faith in Chandos was the knowledge that he had finished fourth in racing's premier classic, the Derby.

From a first-rate start, Chimney Sweep dashed into the lead, with the whole field leaving the first fence behind without any upset. Still in front over Becher's, Chimney Sweep brought a roar from the crowd with a big leap, closely followed by The Liberator, Master Mowbray and Rye, and in this order they rounded the Canal Turn and down that long run back to the racecourse. Most of those which started were still in the race as they ran towards the water jump, with The Liberator now holding a narrow lead from the improving Shifnal, who in fact landed first over the last obstacle on the first circuit. Directly on the heels of the leading group over the water, Chandos caused all in the stands to gasp with anxiety as he landed on his head in such an alarming way that it looked a certainty he would part company with his jockey. Clinging to his mount like a leech though, James Jewitt performed a minor miracle of horsemanship, making an incredible recovery which brought cheers from the excited spectators.

Back in the country again The Liberator resumed command, striding out well ahead of Shifnal, Jackal, Master Mowbray and, moving up quickly from the rear, Zero. The whole complexion of the race changed dramatically at the fence before Becher's with The Liberator coming to grief and Thyra refusing. Defence was pulled up and Gamebird fell at the Brook, leaving Phryne in front and all at once Captain Machell's pair moved into forward positions. Chandos and Regal were well within striking distance of the leader as they took the Canal Turn, as also were Jackal, Congress, Rye and Shifnal, but all eyes were on the favourite Chandos as he took Valentine's well in his stride. At the very next fence, however, Chandos fell, followed one obstacle later by the departure of Zero, whose rider was badly injured. Three horses rose at the final flight together, Shifnal, Congress and Regal and, landing as one, began that make-or-break struggle to the line. Halfway up the straight Shifnal cracked, leaving Regal and Congress fighting out an epic climax over the remaining couple of hundred yards. It was virtually with the final nod of his head that Regal grasped victory by a neck from the bravely determined Congress, with the equally resolute Shifnal three lengths back in third place. Chimney Sweep was fourth, in front of Rye, Jackal and Master Mowbray.

If denied a winning favourite, the vast crowd had at least been treated to a finish as exciting as they were ever likely to witness anywhere and the relationship between the winning owner and jockey in the winner's enclosure was considerably more congenial than when Machell had last stood there.

Having supplied three National winners in the last four years, it was a surprise to find Captain Machell without a runner for the 1877 race. With his customary aplomb he had bought Congress in time to win Liverpool's Grand Sefton Steeplechase in November 1876 with him, then sold both Regal and Congress to Lord Lonsdale.

Most fancied of the 16 contestants was Shifnal, topping the betting ahead of Chimney Sweep, Reugny and Regal, while at more generous prices came Congress, The Liberator, Gamebird and Zero.

One of the most likeable characters in jumping circles around this time was Fred Hobson of Baldock, Hertfordshire. His father, George, won the Oaks with the filly Rhedycina in 1850, six years before seeing his colours carried into third place in Freetrader's National by his outsider Minos. Fred was to attain even greater turf fame, not only as a most successful owner but at the sharper edge of the sport, in the saddle. Already an accomplished horseman to hounds, Hobson was just as adept on the racecourse, topping the list of amateur riders in 1867 at the age of 25, when his nearest rivals were George Ede and his close friend Arthur Yates. At the beginning of 1877 he bought the five-year-old entire Austerlitz, with the intention of having a useful partner in the Grand National. Bred by Lord Scarborough, the chestnut showed little ability in two seasons on the flat, yet took well to jumping and had it not been for Fred Hobson insisting on riding the horse at Aintree, Austerlitz would have been at much shorter odds than his starting price of 15/1. The reason for this was a somewhat unusual habit the rider had when taking a horse over a fence. In mid-air Fred would grip the back of his saddle, a practice frowned on by most observers, yet Hobson believed that by doing so he took his weight off his mount's shoulders and forelegs.

From a good start Austerlitz made the running to the first fence where, after landing safely, he relinquished his lead to Zero who raced on at a terrific clip. With hardly any fallers in the early stages of the race, all eyes stayed with the leaders which at Becher's consisted of Citizen, Zero, Chimney Sweep and Congress, and with Austerlitz close up people in the vicinity chuckled at the sight of his rider clinging to the cantle of the saddle. Having galloped himself almost into the ground, Zero refused at the fence before the second Becher's and Mr Hobson took Austerlitz to the front. Trying to match strides with the leader after jumping the Brook, Arbitrator lasted until falling at Valentine's and Austerlitz maintained his advantage all the way back to the racecourse. The Liberator was travelling so easily under the impeccable riding of 'Mr Thomas' that, as he surged into the lead, the crowds were convinced he was on his way to victory. But the man whose riding techniques had brought smiles and laughter from those watching, had merely given his mount a breather. Sitting down tight in the saddle, Fred Hobson gave Austerlitz some magical signal that the end was in sight and his horse simply sprinted away, over the last and on to a comfortable four-length victory. Last year's winning jockey, Joe Cannon, rallied Congress in the final yards to snatch second place from The Liberator by a neck and Chimney Sweep stayed on well to be fourth.

The genial Fred Hobson was the toast of Aintree that afternoon, many congratulating him while considering his methods somewhat audacious. Yet the praise he valued most came from his fellow riders, who to a man declared he had ridden a most judicious race and thoroughly deserved his victory. Neither Mr Hobson nor Austerlitz ever took part in the Grand National again.

Another great rider bidding farewell to Aintree after the 1877 race was Tommy Pickernell, alias 'Mr Thomas', who, having steered home three winners from a total of 17 rides in the National, decided to hang up his boots. He became the first National Hunt Inspector of Courses, a duty he performed most admirably until retiring in 1885. He passed away peacefully near King's Heath, Birmingham, in 1912.

From an original entry of 63 subscribers, the 1878 race disappointingly cut up badly, to leave but 12 runners contesting the prize at Aintree in late March. Favourite at 9/2 was His Lordship, with Boyne Water at 5s, Pride of Kildare on 6/1 and favourite last time, Shifnal, now a 7/1 chance.

A brown entire by Saccharometer, Shifnal was bred by Mr J. Eyke and was bought when quite young by John Nightingall out of a selling plate, the owner training him for jumping at his South Hatch yard in Epsom. A reliable, staying 'chaser, Shifnal was making his third attempt in Aintree's big race, having finished a good third two years before and sixth in the most recent running. John Jones, the Epsom jockey, partnered Shifnal in what was to be his fifth Grand National ride.

Right from the start Shifnal bounded into the lead, taking them along when it became apparent that nobody else was prepared to make the running. At the first fence Miss Lizzie, Jackal and Martha landed just to the rear of Shifnal, while Northfleet came down and almost in the same moment the field was reduced still further. Martha led into Becher's Brook, jumping it well, if slowly, and at the next fence Jackal was lucky to survive a bad mistake which saw him on his belly before recovering to continue a long way behind. As they came over Valentine's, Shifnal regained the lead with a super jump, Miss Lizzie was second and Martha a close third. In this order they returned to the racecourse, Shifnal increasing the pace as he took them over the water jump. Once back in the country, Martha went on again ahead of the improving Pride of Kildare, with Shifnal and Jackal well placed and Miss Lizzie and Curator starting to find the contest a struggle. All the way back over Becher's, the Canal Turn and Valentine's, Martha was foot perfect and maintaining such a good pace that those following were being raced off their feet. As Martha landed over the final flight of hurdles, her stride shortened for a brief moment and Jones, aboard Shifnal, was close enough to notice this and immediately set his mount after the mare. Riding a brilliant finish, John Jones brought Shifnal past the Irish amateur Tommy Beasley and the brave Martha to win rather cleverly by two lengths, with the outpaced Pride of Kildare ten lengths back in third place.

It was a most fitting result, Shifnal winning at the third attempt under a jockey who in four previous bids had finished second once, fourth twice and fifth once. Like Shifnal's owner-trainer, Mr Nightingall, John Jones was to father a son who would preserve the excellent reputations of their forbears.

Five

1879-1888

In 1879 Britain faced a succession of problems at home and abroad, not least of which was the formation of the Irish Land League, instituted to secure independence for Ireland. Further afield an uprising against the British by Afghan tribesmen led to the murder of the British envoy, Sir Louis Cavagnari. By far the biggest embarrassment for the British Empire came at Isandhlwana, South Africa. In the worst defeat ever inflicted on a modern army by natives without firearms, a Zulu force wiped out over 1,400 British soldiers who were part of Lord Chelmsford's incursion across the Buffalo River. Within 48 hours a large measure of British military prestige was restored through the heroic defence of Rorke's Drift. In this single action, 11 Victoria Crosses were won when 140 men of the South Wales Borderers fought off continuous attacks by over 4,000 Zulu warriors.

At Liverpool, the field for that year's National was not much bigger than its predecessor, numbering just 18 competitors. Captain Machell made a determined effort to win the race for a fourth time by buying back Regal, who started the 5/2 favourite.

There was a powerful Irish contingent, particularly in the form of amateur riders, with four brothers named Beasley taking part and each of them holding reputations as outstanding horsemen.

A last-minute absentee from the 1878 Grand National, The Liberator, made it this time, fully fit and the second best backed horse in the race at 5/1. Now ten years old, he first saw the light of day at Annendale in Ireland, where he was bred by Mr Stokes. After a fruitless period racing on the flat, The Liberator developed into a useful 'chaser, winning the important Galway Plate in 1875 and, after falling in his first National 12 months later, ran well to finish third behind Austerlitz in 1877. John Hubert Moore eventually bought the huge gelding and set about training him at his establishment, Jockey Hall, the Curragh. Originally owned in partnership by Moore and a Mr Plunkett Taaffe, this arrangement was apparently dissolved some time in 1878, with The Liberator remaining the property of John Moore. However, shortly before the 1879 Grand National, an injunction was sought in the Dublin courts by Mr Taaffe to restrain Moore from running the gelding at Aintree. Fortunately for John Moore, judgement was given in his favour, but still concerned he ran the animal in the name of his eldest son, Garrett. A perfect, natural horseman, Garry Moore, and his brother Willie, had benefited from being around good-class 'chasers from their earliest childhood as well as having the tutelage of that legendary rider Alan McDonough.

From a first-time start, Bacchus, Regal and Jackal rushed into the lead, but at such a frenzied gallop mistakes were quickly made. The Bear, together with Bellringer, refused, Bacchus fell and Regal lost a tremendous amount of ground through a succession of blunders. Over Becher's The Liberator was lying third, some six lengths behind the leaders, Lord Marcus and Bob Ridley. With the two in front still racing freely, Garry Moore took a pull on his mount, allowing Marshal Niel, Jackal and Martha to pass and in this order they galloped back onto the racecourse. Bob Ridley was first over the water jump, half a length in advance of Lord Marcus, with Regal a long way behind the leading group. Running back to Becher's, The Liberator took closer order and with Marshal Niel falling at the Brook and Victor II calling it a day, Garrett Moore began to ride his race. Quietly moving into third place jumping Valentine's, The Liberator kept well in touch as they came towards the second last and as Lord Marcus ran out of steam, he shot to the front. The Liberator raced home to win in a common canter by ten lengths. Jackal stayed on to pass some very tired horses and take second place, with Martha again running a brave race to finish third.

It was a most popular victory, not just for Irishmen, who had backed The Liberator to a man, but for everyone who admired the stylish riding of that exceptionally tall rider named Garrett who had made a procession of the Grand National.

Although still suffering from a shortage of runners, the big Aintree showpiece attracted countless thousands of spectators still and with three former winners of the race among the 14 hopefuls in 1880, the racecourse was packed to capacity.

The Liberator shouldered an impossible 12st 7lb, yet was still attractive enough a proposition to start the 11/2 second favourite. The strongest betting choice was again Regal, this time at 5s, whereas Shifnal was 20/1.

Students of form at this period would have found much to confuse them, especially if tracing the racing record of a chestnut mare called Empress. In the *Racing Calendar* for 1880 no less than four of that name appeared, all mares, though apart from the subject of this narrative, the others were bay coloured and slightly older than she who found herself at the start for this year's Grand National. Bred in Ireland by Mr Thomas Lindesay, she was raced on the flat as a three-year-old in the colours of her trainer, Henry Eyre Linde, without attracting much attention. Linde was originally a farmer from County Kildare who, after a spell with the Royal Irish Constabulary, decided to seek his fortune on the turf. Setting up training quarters at Eyrefield Lodge on the Curragh, he rapidly made his mark as a veritable genius in the preparation of racehorses. So thorough was Linde in his endeavours to produce winners, that he built a private course on his land featuring every kind of obstacle to be found on any Irish or English racecourse. A regular visitor to Henry Linde's stables was the Empress Elizabeth of Austria, and it was in her honour that he named the chestnut mare Empress. Having won four of her five races prior to Aintree, she was a well-fancied 8/1 on the day and with Mr Tommy Beasley in the saddle carried the confidence of Eyrefield Lodge.

After one false start, the small band raced to the first fence where Gunlock and Sleight of Hand refused and at the next St George also dug his toes in and a gasp of horror signalled the fall of Regal. Downpatrick was clear up to and beyond Becher's, followed by Victoria, Shifnal, Woodbrook and Wild Monarch. Jupiter Tonans moved up smartly as they rounded the Canal Turn, gaining the lead with a splendid leap at Valentine's and with a sustained gallop he quickly opened up a long gap as he came back to the racecourse. Jumping the water, Downpatrick almost came upsides the leader but once back in the country Jupiter Tonans drew clear again. As he came to Becher's once more, he was all of a furlong in front and, with Shifnal, Wild Monarch and Woodbrook losing ground after clearing the Brook, the leader appeared uncatchable. As Downpatrick made a determined run after jumping Valentine's, so too did The Liberator and Empress. Tommy Beasley had lost a stirrup halfway round the first circuit but now, in perfect harmony with Empress, saw himself for the first time with a chance in the race. On the turn to the final hurdles, Jupiter Tonans at last began to tire, fading rapidly before the second last and being passed with ease by both Downpatrick and Empress. With these two racing neck and neck, it was the very last flight which put the result beyond issue. Galloping flat out, Empress put in a spectacular leap, estimated at 30 feet, landed in full stride and left Downpatrick as if he was standing still. Displaying the courage of a truly great racehorse, The Liberator battled on resolutely up the long run-in, outstaying Downpatrick at the end but, conceding every ounce of 28lb, unable to catch the beautifully ridden Empress. The winning margin was two lengths, with Downpatrick a head away in third place and runaway Jupiter Tonans a further two lengths back, a gallant fourth.

Any pre-race critics were silenced by the performance of Empress and her rider Tommy Beasley, who was pleased to discover after the race that his brothers, Harry and John, had also completed the course. To his credit, Henry Linde paid tribute to his winning rider and once again the Irish had a riotous journey back across the Irish Sea.

From a disappointing entry of just 34, only 13 stood their ground for the 1881 Grand National, resulting in the smallest prize money for many years.

Regal was back, though after two sad experiences as favourite, he was allowed to start on 11s. Of the remainder, most were newcomers and of them Mr Leopold de Rothschild's young horse, Thornfield, had been spoken of with confidence for many weeks.

Last year's winner, Empress, had been retired to stud, where she was to prove a highly successful brood-mare, and in her absence Linde relied on the seven-year-old gelding Woodbrook. Named after the place of his birth, Woodbrook, near Boyle, the Irish chestnut was bred by Captain Kirkwood, in whose colours he competed on the turf. Standing up well to the demands of the master of Eyrefield's rigorous training schedule, Woodbrook had on two occasions already proved his ability over Aintree's notorious fences. In November 1879 he had jumped perfectly to win the Grand Sefton 'Chase by four lengths, only to forfeit the prize in the stewards' room through a technical omission. Behind his stable companion, Empress, in the most recent National, Woodbrook was staying on at the end when finishing fifth in the care of Harry Beasley. Now ridden by that man's brother, Tommy, it was a combination of his rider's ability and the reputation of his trainer which found favour with the majority of gamblers.

Despite the weather, which consisted of heavy rain and snow, the crowds were as usual numbered in many thousands, among them being some very distinguished personalities. Edward, Prince of Wales, was once more present and, probably at the urging of Henry Linde, the Empress of Austria took her place among the spectators.

The veteran of the party, The Liberator, went to the front as soon as the starter let them go, jumping the first with joint favourite Thornfield in close attendance. Still going well up front, The Liberator took Becher's with the flamboyance of his younger days but misjudging his take-off at Valentine's he paid the penalty. In the fall, his rider, Garrett Moore, injured his shoulder badly when Cross Question kicked him when passing, but still this did not prevent the plucky Irishman from remounting and chasing the rapidly disappearing field. The Liberator's fall had left Woodbrook in the lead, possibly sooner than Tommy Beasley would have wished, but so well was his mount travelling that he decided to let him go on. Entering the racecourse some six lengths in advance of the rest, Woodbrook continued in good style over the water ahead of Montauban, New Glasgow and Fair Wind. Regal at this stage was a very distant last, having even been passed by The Liberator. Fair Wind called it a day when refusing at the second fence back in the country, and Woodbrook still held a commanding lead as he jumped Becher's brilliantly. Tommy Beasley went into Valentine's with Woodbrook, seemingly once more about to make a procession of the affair and racing on his own, most of the excitement was played out to his rear. Regal had made an enormous amount of ground since the halfway stage, now striding boldly just behind Montauban, New Glasgow and Cross Question, and to everyone's surprise The Liberator, after his mishap, had also fought his way back into the fray. Returning to the racecourse for the final time, Woodbrook was well clear with a terrific struggle being enacted behind him. Captain Machell's outsider, The Scot, suddenly added to the excitement, appearing from nowhere to range alongside Regal, New Glasgow, Thornfield and Abbot of St Mary's. With these four in a line across the course, they came to the final hurdle some six lengths to the rear of Woodbrook, who jumped it cleanly and raced home to win unextended by four lengths from Machell's old champion, Regal. Labouring on in third place Thornfield finished a very tired horse, in front of New Glasgow and The Scot. The Liberator was last of the other four which passed the post.

The winner's enclosure that wintry afternoon could well have been mistaken for the capital of Ireland, the lilting brogue of excited expletives rising above the staid English congratulations showered on the winning connections. Tommy Beasley was, for the second year running, the toast of the hour and Henry Linde was treated to the reverence more in keeping with that reserved for the Pope. The very next day Linde saddled his own horse Seaman for the inaugural running of the Liverpool Hunt Steeplechase over four and a quarter miles of the National course. Ridden by Mr Harry Beasley, Seaman followed the example of his stablemate 24 hours before by making an absolute procession of the event to win by 30 lengths.

Yet again, in 1882, British military might was put to the test when Egyptian nationalists attempted to take over the Suez Canal. Sir Garnet Wolseley eventually settled the situation by defeating the Egyptians at Tel El-Kebir. The St Gotthard Tunnel was opened, providing the first railway tunnel through the Alps, and that inspiring musical masterpiece, the *1812 Overture* by Tchaikovsky, was performed for the first time.

Little had changed at Aintree though, at least in terms of the shortage of runners and, equally important for those present, the atrocious weather. But with 12 contestants, the pundits freely declared that the race was at the mercy of that wizard from the Curragh, Henry Eyre Linde. There appeared very little to prevent his achieving a third successive victory, with both his five-year-olds,

Mohican and Cyrus, in splendid heart and with recent winning form. The former went off favourite at 100/30, while Cyrus, successful over Aintree's big fences the previous November, held third position in the betting on 9/2. The Scot divided the Linde horses, on 4s, with the now 13-year-old The Liberator, again expected to hump 12st 7lb around, at 20/1.

As events would soon prove, Henry Linde had uncharacteristically made an error of judgement concerning one of his former champions, the small yet perfectly proportioned Seaman. In the circumstances it could well be seen as an understandable error, for Seaman had been unsound almost from birth, yet at the time which mattered most it was to result in the costliest mistake the famous trainer ever made. Bred at Knockany, County Limerick, by Captain Gubbins, Seaman never grew above 15 hands 3in and from his youngest days suffered almost constant sickness. His sire, Xenophon, also produced Cyrus, possibly the better of Linde's pair that year. After being bought by the Curragh trainer, Seaman responded well to the usual harsh methods employed in getting a racehorse ready to compete on the track. In only his second year of life, so bad were his legs that Seaman had to be fired on both hocks, yet despite his fitness problems, proved a valuable servant to Henry Linde. As a five-year-old he gave one of the finest exhibitions of jumping ever seen in the Conyngham Cup to record a fabulous victory and, as well as proving his ability over Aintree, took Paris by storm with a brilliant performance in the premier French hurdle race when winning the Grand Hurdle at Auteuil. Believing he had achieved all that could be expected from the little son of Xenophon, Linde readily accepted the £2,000 offered him by Lord John Manners for what was very obviously an unsound horse. The third Baron of Foston, Manners was educated at Eton before serving in the Grenadier Guards and, although without experience of race-riding, was an excellent man to hounds, being the Master of the Quorn Foxhounds. Placing Seaman in the care of Captain James Machell, who was to prepare the horse for Aintree, Lord Manners set about conditioning himself to partner his new purchase in the National. Exactly three weeks before the big race his lordship rode his own horse, Lord Chancellor, in Sandown's Grand Military Gold Cup and gave his confidence a tremendous boost by winning quite easily. Unhappily the news concerning Seaman was far from promising, Machell declaring that he was only able to get the horse three-parts fit for the National.

As the tiny band of hopefuls milled around awaiting the starter's orders, a heavy downfall of snow made matters more uncomfortable than ever and it was a relief to all when the race began. Wild Monarch was the first into the country, taking the first fence in advance of Eau de Vie and Cyrus, and as Ignition refused at the second the people in the stands lost sight of the runners as the swirling snow impaired their visibility. In the treacherous conditions the runners were soon well spread out, with Eau de Vie the clear leader over Becher's, a position she occupied still when racing back in front of the stands. After leaping the water with space to spare, Eau de Vie charged back out towards Becher's, still full of running and with Zoedone making a determined effort to get on terms. Fate dealt a cruel blow to Dan Thirlwell, the rider of Eau de Vie, as they touched down safely over Becher's, for whilst in mid-air one of his stirrup leathers broke. To the alarm of those watching, Eau de Vie veered away from a true line and dashed headlong into the crowd. This sudden departure of the leader left Zoedone with a clear advantage but after rounding the Canal Turn the little mare came under pressure from the only others left in the race, Fay, Cyrus, Seaman and The Scot. With the blizzard raging to a peak, just three horses came back towards the stands, with Cyrus leading Seaman, leaving the tired Zoedone before jumping the second last. The prospect of Tommy Beasley winning his third successive Grand National appeared a certainty as he landed on the flat a length to the good over the unfit Seaman and his titled if novice rider, Lord Manners. On closer inspection, the large crowd were able to recognise that Seaman was in a distressed state, his hind leg having broken down in the last fateful leap. Then, to the amazement of everyone, Seaman somehow hung on; the gap between Cyrus and Linde's cast-off failed to lengthen and unbelievably it narrowed. Seaman, running on heart and instinct, came back, inch by inch until, with barely 100 yards left, they drew level. In the finest example of equine bravery ever seen at Aintree, a place which is itself a by-word for courage of the highest order, the little lame Seaman got his noble head in front in the very last second to win by that head. A long way behind came Zoedone, the only other survivor of a gruelling, yet unforgettable, race.

Neither horse nor rider ever competed in a race again, Seaman being honourably retired to Lord Manner's home, where he became a much-loved family pet.

So concerned had the National Hunt Committee become regarding the reduction in the number of horses bidding for National glory, they had established a committee to investigate the problem. One of the criticisms of owners had been that in recent years Aintree's fences had become smaller, placing more of an emphasis on galloping as opposed to jumping. In time for the 1883 Grand National, the Liverpool executive restored their obstacles to more substantial proportions only to end up with the smallest number to face the starter in the history of the race.

Only ten runners went out for the 1883 National, seven of them ridden by amateurs, which prompted some journalists to proclaim that the race had reached its lowest ebb. With the previous year's tremendously exciting event still fresh in the public's mind though, Aintree continued to attract many thousands and although the going was heavy for the race, clear skies ensured good visibility.

In the absence of a previous winner, the punters once more looked to Henry Linde's charge, Zitella, as the probable winner, making the mare 3/1 favourite. Almost ignored in the betting was the six-year-old mare Zoedone at 100/7, who when finishing third 12 months before had been unable to maintain the pace in the final half mile. Since then she had been bought for £800 by the Hungarian, Count Charles Kinsky, who agreed to pay a further £200 should she carry him to victory in the National. An excellent horseman, Kinsky had accompanied the Empress of Austria to Ireland and England on a number of occasions and since being posted to the Hungarian embassy in London spent whatever free time he had riding to hounds. A chestnut mare by New Oswestry, out of Miss Honiton, Zoedone was not in the General Stud Book but had proved she was a game, safe conveyance, if somewhat short of speed. A little over three months before the National she carried Count Kinsky to victory in a three-horse race over four miles at Sandown Park, whereupon her trainer, Jenkins, laid her aside for Liverpool.

The first to show at the start was Montauban, who took them over the first at little more than a canter. Jolly Sir John refused at the second, by which time Montauban was four lengths in front of Zitella, with Zoedone going well on ground she obviously preferred. As the leader fell by the wayside, Zitella assumed command, clearing Becher's well, as did Zoedone who had been foot perfect at every fence. Still racing together up front, the two mares took the water some way ahead of Montauban, Black Prince and Eau de Vie. Taking up the running from Zitella as they approached the second Becher's, Zoedone cleared the Brook majestically and after another fine leap at the Canal Turn, Kinsky kicked on. Twelve lengths to the good over Valentine's, Zoedone, with no serious danger to her appearing, returned to the stands side still going strong. Between the final two flights of hurdles, Black Prince and Mohican battled gamely on, hopelessly trying to get on terms with Zoedone but there was no catching the little mare and her astute Bohemian rider. Even taking liberties with the last hurdle, which she knocked out of the ground, could not prevent Zoedone racing clear to a most impressive ten-length triumph from Black Prince, who was followed home by Mohican, Downpatrick, Zitella, Montauban and Eau de Vie.

So far as the public were concerned, it was almost a repeat of the previous year's race, with both successful riders amateurs and noblemen, teamed up with two very brave horses considered to be of little account. In each case also, Lord Manners and Count Kinsky were taking part in the National for the first time.Needless to say, the delighted Hungarian diplomat was more than happy to pay Zoedone's former owner, Mr Clayton, that extra £200.

Although the weather didn't match the occasion, the ground being very heavy and with a thick mist hiding much of the action, Grand National day in 1884 was a right royal juncture in the annals of Aintree. For the first time a member of the British Royal Family had a runner in the race and in a flurry of patriotic fervour the public supported it with enough money to make it favourite for the race.

Edward, Prince of Wales, had developed a keen interest in steeplechasing, attending Liverpool several times in the past to sample the thrills of the big race and, having liked what he'd seen, instructed Lord Marcus Beresford to find him a jumper capable of tackling the National. The eventual choice was The Scot, once the property of Captain Machell and a gelding with a measure of class about him, for his sire was the winner of the 1864 Epsom Derby. On the recommendation of Lord Marcus, The Scot was placed with trainer John Jones, successful as a jockey in the National with Shifnal and whose duties would include riding the royal representative at Aintree.

With the field this time consisting of 15 runners, there was also improvement in the quality of the participants. Zoedone was attempting a double. Regal, an ageing former winner, and Black Prince, Cyrus, Zitella and Cortolvin were others who had been here before. Most fancied of the newcomers were Frigate, Roquefort and a six-year-old gelding named Voluptuary.

That Voluptuary was well to the fore in the betting at 10/1 could only have been because he was bred truly in the purple by no less a personage than Her Majesty Queen Victoria at the Royal Stud. Later sold to Lord Rosebery, he won three decent races on the flat in his second season and led the field around Tattenham Corner in the Epsom Derby before finishing unplaced. Two years later Voluptuary came up for sale at Newmarket, where he was knocked down to Mr H.F. Boyd for the bargain price of 150 guineas. Set with the task of teaching the flat-race cast-off to jump, the Warwickshire brothers, William and Edward Wilson, spent countless hours patiently putting the bay through his paces at their Ilmington quarters. As one of the finest amateur riders ever to sit astride a 'chaser, Mr E.P. Wilson, or Ted as he was more affectionately known, had taken part in nine Grand Nationals before taking the leg-up on Voluptuary for the 1884 event. Now aged 38, Ted Wilson had the dubious 'chance' of attempting to put the record straight with a horse which had never jumped a fence in public in its life.

From a first-time start, The Scot brought a mighty roar from the stands as he bounded straight to the front, jumping the first fence in lively style. At a fast pace, Cortolvin showed the way over Becher's Brook and remained in this position until approaching the water jump. Coming with a powerful run, Regal snatched the lead with a great leap over the water. As Cortolvin regained his former position up front on the approach to Becher's, Zoedone, Voluptuary and Tom Jones all began making progress from the rear. The Scot totally misjudged

Becher's, jumping into the fence instead of over it, and shortly after the loss of the favourite Regal fell lame and was pulled up. Harry Beasley was enjoying a perfect ride aboard the mare Frigate, still going very easily as she went to the front jumping Valentine's, where Tom Jones came to grief. Striding to the second-last flight, Frigate was still in command as Zoedone gave Count Kinsky a moment of hope by sprinting up to the leader's quarters. The effort was short-lived, however, as the weight told and Zoedone faded, but in her place came Voluptuary, produced with perfect precision by Ted Wilson to challenge Frigate going to the final flight of hurdles. Hitting the obstacle, the Irish mare lost some momentum, which gave her no chance of staying with Voluptuary, who jumped beautifully, landed running and raced away to a four-length victory. Roquefort stayed on well to finish third and Zoedone passed the post fifth of the six who completed the trip.

It was an outstanding performance by Voluptuary, to win the toughest steeplechase in the world at his very first attempt over fences, and many were of the opinion that only Mr E.P. Wilson could have won the National with a novice. Voluptuary was subsequently sold to the famous actor, Leonard Boyne, finding himself in a new career as he appeared nightly on the stage of the Drury Lane Theatre in the play *The Prodigal Daughter*. Ted Wilson, meanwhile, remembered a horse which had impressed during his victorious National ride and set about discovering if it were for sale. The name of the animal was Roquefort.

A splendid day, a thrilling race and a result which all who witnessed it could relish the memory of. All of these were embodied in the 1885 renewal of Aintree's great 'chase. And yet, one infamous act of treachery would sadly remain the major incident concerning that year's Grand National; all the more so as it involved a very brave horse who through consistent courage had captured the hearts of everyone who knew of her. The Aintree management proudly announced shortly before the weights were published that for the first time the National would be run entirely on grass.

Ted Wilson had noticed with extreme interest, while concentrating on winning with Voluptuary last year, the superb jumping ability of Roquefort, as well as that vital element so essential at Aintree, enthusiasm. Having persuaded the previous owner to part with Roquefort, Wilson cajoled Mr Cooper to buy it, ably supported in his coaxing of the owner by the trainer Arthur Yates. Bred by Mr J. Gretton, it was claimed that the brown gelding had at one time been reduced to the indignity of pulling a dog-cart, yet under the ownership of Captain Fisher, Roquefort won events on the flat, over hurdles and across fences, at which he proved especially proficient. Realising there was little to teach his new charge about jumping, Arthur Yates concentrated on keeping the gelding fit, with the Grand National solely in his mind avoiding the risk of injury by ignoring other races on the run-up to Liverpool. The man who had first recognised potential in Roquefort, Mr E.P. Wilson, was the obvious choice as rider and the pair started a raging 100/30 favourite.

It was somewhere between the paddock and the parade that the villainy, which was to cast the darkest of shadows over British sport for years, took place. It had been a regular practice, after the parade of runners in front of the stands, for them to jump a preliminary or warming-up hurdle on the canter back to the start. This time, as the second most heavily backed horse, Zoedone, performed this tradition, she stumbled and caused her owner-rider Count Kinsky such concern that he dismounted to examine her. Even before inspecting the mare which had become such an important part of his life, the nobleman knew something was amiss, for he noticed a large amount of blood on his breeches. In an instant he realised, with a combination of anger, disgust and sadness, that the lovely, brave mare he cherished had been 'got at'. Zoedone had been coupled in countless ante-post bets with the winner of the Lincolnshire Handicap, Bendigo, leaving the bookies facing a financial hammering should Zoedone win her second National. Had it not been for the fact that the public had supported the mare heavily with their money, Charles Kinsky would have withdrawn her from the race, for it was clearly apparent that a hypodermic syringe had been used to administer some noxious substance to the unsuspecting animal. Staying loyal to the many thousands who had put money on Zoedone, Count Kinsky took his place in the line-up, but right from the start the mare was lifeless beneath him. It was Black Prince who made the early running, ahead of Candahar, Frigate, Redpath and Axminster. To the concerned onlookers at each fence, the saddest sight was the obviously distressed Zoedone, struggling well to the rear. Going into the Canal Turn the order was Black Prince, Roquefort, Albert Cecil, Axminster and Ben More. A new leader appeared as they came across the road onto the racecourse, Belmont and Willie Canavan snatching a few moments of glory as they neared the stands, closely tracked by Dog Fox, Black Prince, Albert Cecil and Red Hussar. Still toiling on a long way behind came Zoedone, and back in the country she finally fell at the fence before Becher's, causing great concern as she lay prostrate in the hands of the anxious Count Kinsky. Gamecock had come on the scene seemingly from nowhere and with a fine leap at Valentine's took command, only to fall three fences later at the final jump before the racecourse. Rarely had anyone seen a Grand National in which the lead had changed so many times but with just two left to jump, the final moments of truth arrived. Dog Fox, Roquefort, Redpath and Frigate were almost abreast of each other, as the crowds tried to guess which would break first, for at this stage each of them appeared capable of winning. Mr

Wilson though, in his 11th National and having taken the time during the strongly run gallop to size up his opponents, knew exactly when to strike and set Roquefort loose. Resisting the determined challenge of the Irish mare Frigate, Ted Wilson brought Roquefort home a very worthy winner by two lengths from Harry Beasley with Frigate and the front-running Black Prince.

It was hard to imagine a more popular winning combination than Roquefort and Ted Wilson for, quite apart from the fact that the favourite had won, the horse had succeeded on merit alone and his partner was a great horseman in the truest sense of the word as well as being a thoroughly decent person.

A dejected and disillusioned Count Charles Kinsky immediately retired his dear Zoedone and he himself never rode in races again. The disgusting perpetrator of the crime against an innocent animal was never brought to justice.

It is interesting to note that of the last 15 Grand National winners, 11 had been partnered by members of the unpaid brigade.

With these statistics in mind, it was no surprise to find in the betting on the 1886 National the first three in the market all paired with amateur riders.

Captain Lee-Barber teamed up with the 3/1 favourite, Coronet; Ted Wilson was trying to repeat his success with Roquefort; and the Irish wizard Harry Beasley took the mount on the Henry Linde-trained Too Good.

Among the less fancied having their first sight of Aintree there appeared a seven-year-old with the quaint name of Old Joe, who had been bred among the rugged hills of Cumberland by a Mr Briscoe. Purchased for £30 from his breeder by the huntsman to the Dumfriesshire hounds, Joe Graham, it was this man after whom the horse was named. After being passed on to owner Mr A.J. Douglas, it was soon discovered that the gelding was something much more than merely a safe ride to hounds. Sent a little up the coast from his birthplace, Old Joe quickly established himself as a 'chaser of considerable ability in the care of trainer George Mulcaster at Burgh-by-Sands, Carlisle. Such was the substance of Old Joe that in a single day he won two races at Whitehaven and from his three outings prior to the National had visited the winner's enclosure twice. His companion in the big race was Tommy Skelton, a jockey considered by many as more familiar with hurdle racing, although known to be able to hold his own over fences.

On a bright and clear afternoon, the starter wasted no time getting the 23 away at the first time of asking, Roquefort immediately setting the pace. At the first fence Frigate fell when trying to match the stride of the leading bunch which consisted of Roquefort, Old Joe, Sinbad, The Badger, Too Good and Coronet. With no casualties at Becher's, they raced on, sustaining the fast gallop, and at the Canal Turn Lady Tempest assumed command from The

Badger, Coronet, Jolly Sir John and Gamecock. Fighting for his head all the way down the canal side, Coronet took up the running shortly before reaching the racecourse and, running on strongly, jumped the water with a clear advantage. Vigorously pursued by a host of horses, Coronet returned to the country three lengths ahead of them. Before reaching Becher's Roquefort fell heavily, as did the following Belmont, and at the Brook itself Limekiln also came to grief and Billet Doux was pulled up. It was still the favourite, Coronet, showing the way over Valentine's closely attended by Old Joe, Savoyard and The Badger. Sensing that Coronet was coming to the end of his stamina, Tommy Skelton sent Old Joe forward, only to find that The Badger would not easily be shaken off, his rider Arthur Nightingall, in this his first Grand National, sharing the same intention as Skelton. Settling the issue at the second last with a fine jump, Old Joe sprinted away with a remarkable turn of foot. Clear over the last, he increased the gap between himself and the others to win by six lengths from Too Good, with Gamecock staying on to take third place.

Winning owner Mr Douglas was delighted, as one would expect, especially since he benefited from a sizeable bet on Old Joe, whose starting price was a favourable 25/1. In a magnanimous display of generosity, the owner presented his trainer with £1,000 and rewarded jockey Skelton with the prize money from the race, a handsome figure of £1,380.

Ever mindful of the apparent ceaseless power of the Irish in producing quality steeplechasers for tests of stamina, the public rushed forward with their money in the 1887 National to make Henry Linde's six-year-old Spahi 9/2 favourite of the 16 runners. It was a tremendous vote of confidence for the trainer and his brilliant rider, Tommy Beasley, but a bewildering choice in light of the fact that until appearing at Aintree, Spahi had never faced up to a hurdle or fence in public before.

Of the two former winners competing again, Roquefort carried more support than Old Joe, holding second place in the betting at 7/1, with Savoyard, Magpie and Frigate also among the leading fancies.

For the inhabitants of Liverpool, however, there was only one horse with any genuine chance and although such an opinion was biased, it was strongly felt. The horse was Gamecock and the reason for it being the hope of Merseysiders was that it was owned by a Liverpool man. In racing circles he was known as 'Mr E. Jay', though copying the practice of some amateur riders, this was an assumed name and in reality he was really Mr Thornewill. Incredibly tough and most consistent, Gamecock was trained by James Gordon at Tarporley, Cheshire, and had indicated a liking for Aintree's unusual fences by running third in the most recent National, finishing in the same position in the Grand Sefton 'Chase and second in the Hapsburg 'Chase also at Liverpool. An eight-year-old gelding, Gamecock was ridden in the big race by William Daniels, a jockey who was not only making his first appearance in the National, but was also making a return to racing after a suspension.

After a few unruly mishaps, the starter, Lord Marcus Beresford, dropped the flag and the race began. Setting a furious gallop, which was to be maintained throughout, Savoyard charged towards the first fence, where Gamecock landed in front of Savoyard and a column of horses which included Old Joe, Magpie, Roquefort and Frigate. A familiar anxious gasp came from onlookers at the third when the favourite, Spahi, crashed to the ground. After jumping Becher's, Old Joe struck the front in advance of Frigate, Magpie, The Hunter and Gamecock, and with very little between any of the leading group the foremost positions changed frequently. The Hunter dropped out before reaching the first hurdle on the racecourse and it was Spectrum who landed first over the water, with a tightly packed group hard on his heels. As Spectrum faded running towards Becher's again, Savoyard sped to the front and with Chancellor at his quarters cleared the Brook and began to draw away from the main group. Staying in touch with the leader over the next two fences, Chancellor took it up with a fine leap at Valentine's and Johnny Longtail relegated Savoyard to third position. Still showing the way as they came back to the racecourse, Chancellor was pounced on rounding the bend to the penultimate flight of hurdles. It was Savoyard, ridden by the previous year's winning jockey, Tom Skelton, who regained the lead, looking all over the winner, so easily was he travelling. Rising at the final hurdle, Savoyard was joined by Gamecock who, once safely over, outstayed Savoyard to win rather cleverly by three lengths. A very long way to the rear Johnny Longtail was third.

It was a splendid result for the local community, Gamecock being at 20/1, and for that matter even the bookies had no cause for complaint. Yet those who enjoyed the victory the most were the owner, trainer and jockey, whose confidence in their robust gelding had been amply rewarded.

As if emphasising his durability, Gamecock came out 24 hours later to carry 12st 12lb to a resounding victory over one circuit of the National course in the recently instituted Champion Steeplechase.

Four years after making his first bid to win the Grand National, His Royal Highness the Prince of Wales tried again and on this occasion the sun shone, the crowds turned out in their thousands and a major alteration to the course added to the excitement.

Following intensive discussions, the decision had been taken to dispense with flights of hurdles and from the 1888 Grand National onwards all the obstacles would be fences. In general the changes were accepted as improvements, in particular those concerning the final two flights, which not only became true steeplechasing obstacles but were resited. Instead of continuing around the outer edge of the course after returning from the country, the runners would now veer gently left-handed along a new approach to the finishing straight.

Irish trainer Henry Linde again supplied the leading fancy for the race, this time the unbeaten Usna, who headed the market jointly with last year's fourth-placed Chancellor. Most of the attention on the day, however, centred around the royal representative, Magic, who barely a month before had carried the Prince of Wales' colours to a 50-length victory over three miles at Sandown Park.

Almost unnoticed in the betting at 40/1 was a lop-eared gelding called Playfair, which many people felt had no right being in the line-up, having only won a humble farmers' race and a couple of hunter 'chases. Trained by Tom Cannon at Danebury, the seven-year-old ran in the colours of Mr E.W. Baird, a subaltern in the 10th Hussars, and was ridden by the little-known jockey, George Mawson.

From flag-fall Trap and Ringlet at once went to the front, with Old Joe close up and a group including Savoyard, The Fawn, Bellona and Jeanie. A magnificent leap at Becher's took Ballot Box straight into the lead from Ringlet, Old Joe, Aladdin, Trap and Chancellor and in this order they continued over the Canal Turn and Valentine's. The first of the 'new fences' brought its very first casualty when Bellona crashed to the ground just to the rear of the main group, which were led by Aladdin, Frigate and Usna on to the water. Clearing it well, a whole bunch of horses chased the three front runners and in the middle of them, recognised for the first time in the race, was Playfair. Aladdin retained his position a few lengths ahead of Ballot Box and Usna and, as they jumped the Brook in this sequence, it could be seen that Playfair was making ground on them. For George Mawson, aboard Playfair, it had so far been anything but a comfortable ride. His mount had been jostled and knocked about almost from the first fence onwards by loose and falling horses, and at the fence after Becher's their effort very nearly came to nought. Mistiming his take-off, Playfair straddled the top of the obstacle, pitched forward at a sharp angle and dislodged Mawson from the saddle. Clinging to his mount's neck for dear life, at the very moment he was about to hit the ground a hand reached out and pulled him back into the plate. In an act of customary care, common among jump jockeys, Arthur Nightingall, alongside with The Badger, had literally dragged the stricken Mawson back into the race. Aladdin was still in front at Valentine's and, just behind Usna, suddenly decided he'd had enough, swerving to run off the course and colliding with Frigate, almost brought the mare to a standstill. Ballot

Box, Ringlet and Playfair raced back towards the stands with just two fences left and making ground rapidly behind them Frigate could be seen bravely putting in a final dash. As Ringlet and Ballot Box tired, Playfair came into the final fence still challenged by the fast-finishing Frigate, and it was the latter who actually landed first over the last. Her sustained effort from the interference she endured at the second Valentine's Brook had taken too much out of the gallant mare though, and on the long run to the post she was unable to withstand the run of Playfair. At the post Playfair won by ten lengths from a very brave and most unlucky Frigate. Ballot Box was third just ahead of Ringlet and Aladdin.

In what proved a most eventful race, an almost unknown combination had won the day, the royal runner had finished eighth and the bookies made a killing.

Playfair had one subsequent race at Sandown, during the course of which he proved somewhat stubborn by running out. He was never seen on a racecourse again. The owner, Mr Baird, continued his military career with tremendous success, eventually retiring with the rank of brigadier-general.

Six

1889-1898

The year 1889 brought designers' plans to create landmarks in three European capital cities which would raise people's eyes to the heavens, provide luxury accommodation and transport them over a great expanse of water. Messrs Fowler and Baker gave Scotland the Forth Bridge; Gustave Eiffel enriched Paris with a futuristic tower; and London could proudly boast the most modern hotel with a name befitting it, the Savoy. In America, Benjamin Harrison was sworn in as the 23rd President; plans went ahead to build more skyscrapers across the nation; and John Philip Sousa first played his 'Washington Post' to a foot-tapping audience.

Increased money for the Grand National attracted a field of 20 runners which were acclaimed as the finest 'chasers to be found anywhere. The Prince of Wales, encouraged by his horse completing the course last time, again ran Magic, although its price of 25/1 indicated the chance it was thought to have.

Making her sixth attempt to capture the prize which had so narrowly eluded her on three occasions was Frigate, the small Irish mare who had so emphatically demonstrated that stature is no indication of bravery or spirit. Slightly over 15 hands high, she had been bred by Matthew A. Maher at Ballinkeele, County Wexford, from excellent blood-lines. Her sire was Gunboat and through her dam, Fair Maid of Kent, she was a granddaughter of that legendary giant of thoroughbreds, the incomparable Gladiateur. Adding to this strain of brilliance within her pedigree was the indelible mark of jumping excellence provided by her sire Gunboat, who was directly descended from the stallion responsible for producing that first Aintree hero, Lottery. Avoiding the temptation to run Frigate on the flat, Henry Linde brought her along gently, though regularly hunting her before choosing the right time to introduce the mare to competition 'between the flags'. In only her second race Frigate gave a sparkling performance when winning the Conyngham Cup over four miles at Punchestown while still just five years of age. Shortly after finishing second for

72

the second time in the National in 1885, Mr Maher sold the mare but she was back bearing his colours when again runner-up in the 1888 race, and 12 months on Frigate started joint second favourite with Et Cetera at 8/1. Curiously, it was only when ridden by somebody named Beasley that Frigate had completed the National course, twice when piloted by Harry and with Willie on board in her most recent effort. For the 1889 Grand National Frigate was prepared by her owner, Matthew Maher, at her birthplace in County Wexford, with Linde generously allowing the use of his Curragh gallops when required. The man partnering her this time was none other than Tommy Beasley.

After two false starts, the runners finally began in earnest with Voluptuary going into an early lead with Why Not, Hettic, Kilworth, Frigate and Magic in close touch. Ahead of the field still over Becher's, Voluptuary kept up his strong pace, followed now by M.P., Roquefort, Why Not and Gamecock. Coming into Valentine's Great Paul, The Fawn and Gamecock rushed past Voluptuary and with Frigate well to the fore, these five presented a fine sight jumping the lesser brook with only a couple of lengths between them. A great roar rose from Irishmen in the stands as two of their compatriots joined issue leaping the water jump, Willie and Harry Beasley bringing The Fawn and Battle Royal upsides Why Not as this trio led at the end of the first circuit. A terrific duel ensued between Why Not and The Fawn back out in the country, first one, then the other going to the front, and over Becher's there was little to choose between the two. Voluptuary bowed out at the next fence, as M.P. again joined the leaders, taking command with a fine jump over Valentine's. Still three lengths clear over the second last, Why Not was being cheered home prematurely when the patiently, yet skilfully, ridden Frigate was brought with a perfectly judged assault on the leader. Within seconds the little mare took command, drawing away from Why Not and jumping the final fence a couple of lengths to the good. The race was not yet over though, Why Not rallying well on the dash to the line and only a very brave horse like Frigate could have withstood the determined effort Why Not produced. In the worthiest manner, however, Frigate deservedly received the accolades so often denied her in the past as she held on by a length from Why Not, in a finish which had everyone on their toes. M.P. came in a long way back to take third place and that game old Aintree performer, Gamecock, finished last of the ten which got round.

The victory of Frigate was a triumph of perseverance and determination which was acknowledged and admired by all who respect the bravery of total commitment. Providing the peerless Tommy Beasley with a third win in the race was just another reason why the courageous little mare Frigate had secured a revered place in racing history.

If racing pundits are to be believed, the 1890 Grand National was a case of 'after the Lord Mayor's Show'.

In terms of quality, the runners were considered well below standard and with only 16 taking part there arose disputes regarding the present appeal of the race.

To many the principal interest that year revolved around the previous year's winner, Frigate, making her seventh and possibly final appearance, and Prince Edward's ongoing involvement. This time he relied solely on the mare Hettie.

Favourite at 4/1 was the six-year-old Ilex, a chestnut gelding bred in Ireland and now the property of a man renowned for his heavy gambling, Mr George Masterman. It was, in fact, largely due to the owner that his horse was so feverishly bet on, for he made no secret of his conviction that at the weights Ilex was a 'certainty'. Appropriately, the man who rode Ilex, the inimitable Arthur Nightingall, was the person who first detected a spark of promise in the horse when winning a humble hunters' selling plate with him at Leicester. In the furtherance of time the jockey persuaded Mr Masterman to buy Ilex and the gelding was sent to be trained at Epsom by John Nightingall, Arthur's father. Having prepared Shifnal to win the National 12 years before, John knew just what was required at Aintree and sent Ilex there fit to run for his life.

Away at the second time of asking, Gamecock was the first to show on the gallop to the first, with Brunswick and M.P. closely tracking him, and Ilex, Pan and Baccy also well to the fore. Over Becher's Gamecock was still in the lead but with Battle Royal falling at the next and then the ditch at the Canal Turn causing havoc as Frigate, Hettie and Baccy all departed, the contest was rapidly being reduced to a handful of horses. Bellona went out at Valentine's and when two fences later Gamecock fell, Braceborough and M.P. found themselves in front. M.P. led over the water with a clear advantage, Braceborough having come down at the previous ditch, and with Ilex now in second place, excitement rose in the packed stands. Moving alongside M.P. at the second fence back in the country, Ilex jumped fence by fence in unison with M.P. all the way to Becher's where both landed safely. As the others started to feel the strain, Ilex was going well within himself, taking the lead over Valentine's and setting sail for home in confident style. Back on the racecourse Ilex looked invincible, going so easily it was hard to believe he was at such a late stage of the Grand National, but to his rear distress signals were coming from long-time leader M.P., whose stride had shortened appreciably. Racing clear of all opposition, Ibex won unextended by 12 lengths from Pan, M.P. coming home a remote third in front of Brunswick, Why Not and Emperor.

In what had proved the easiest winner of the race for years, Ilex recorded a very popular victory indeed, his owner becoming a very popular individual for the way he had advised so many of the ability his horse possessed. As was his due, Arthur Nightingall also came in for volumes of praise, having given his mount a masterly ride and an indication of the winner's popularity was that so many already attempted to back him for the next National.

Of the 21 runners bidding for Aintree glory in 1891 no less than four of them had tasted the delights of victory before and opposed by such notable jumpers as Grape Vine, Roman Oak, Cloister and Cruiser, the purists among the many thousands attending the race were delighted with the quality of the field.

Ilex had, of course, been at cramped odds for many months, such was the esteem he had earned, but with 12st 3lb to carry this time it was understandable that many sought elsewhere for the possible winner. With the exception of the most recent winner, the top of the market consisted mainly of newcomers and of these one in fact became a very warm favourite at 4/1.

The animal in question was a seven-year-old bay gelding named Come Away and for once it could truly be claimed that if ever a horse deserved to be favourite for the National, this was it. First distinguishing himself when only four years of age, Come Away confounded the experts by winning the Conyngham Cup when then owned by Matthew Corbally. Off the racecourse the following year, he came back with a vengeance in 1890, in the colours of his new owner, Mr W.G. Jameson, to win four of his five races. These included a second victory in the Conyngham Cup and, perhaps more importantly for those with the Grand National in mind, the Valentine Steeplechase at Aintree. By the time the Irish-bred, owned, trained and ridden Come Away made his way to the start of the National, he had become an extremely popular steeplechaser to all supporters of the sport. His trainer also shared the popularity, being Harry Beasley, recently recruited to the ranks of trainers, although nobody ever rode Come Away in races except Harry.

From a perfect start the scene was like a cavalry charge, with so many horses attempting to make the running, but as they neared the first fence Ilex was marginally in front. As they came to the Brook it was Cloister maintaining the hot pace ahead of the rest. Following him over were Grape Vine, Gamecock and Roquefort, these four being a few lengths clear of Ilex, Roman Oak, Voluptuary and Dominion. In this order they rounded the Canal Turn and proceeded over Valentine's. Racing down the side of the canal on their way back to the racecourse, Roquefort had secured the lead, galloping well some eight lengths in front of Cloister who, in turn, had opened up a gap between himself and Gamecock. As they approached the halfway stage, Roquefort was joined by Gamecock and Cloister as they jumped the water in line. Cloister put in a superb leap at Becher's, taking the breath from nearby onlookers and galloping on in front, while Gamecock began to feel the strain as he dropped away. As they ran to Valentine's with the race now settling into its final pattern, Come Away took command from Veil, Ilex, Cloister and Why Not, and with Veil failing to leap high enough at this brook, Cloister went up to join the leader. Come Away and Cloister, both the pride of Ireland, coming back to the penultimate fence with the race between them, when they were suddenly challenged as Why Not produced a blistering run. Almost abreast of the two leaders as they rose at the fence, Why Not hit the top hard and fell heavily, sending his rider, Mr Cunningham, crashing onto his head. With only Cloister to beat, Harry Beasley rode the finish of his life, taking the last fence well and inching Come Away over to the rails as he rode out his race in a style more associated with a flat-race jockey. Never headed by Cloister, Come Away held on gamely and as Captain Roddy Owen on the challenger tried to squeeze through a narrow gap, Beasley quite rightly refused to pull over. Come Away passed the post half a length in front of Cloister, then a long way back came Ilex third.

Roddy Owen immediately lodged an objection to the winner on the grounds of 'jostling' but the stewards overruled it without needing to deliberate long and the celebrations were given the go-ahead. Everyone was agreed that in what had developed into a highly thrilling race, the best horse had won and once again the ferries back to Ireland rocked without any assistance from the sea. The one sad note to come from the splendid performance of Come Away was that in winning a glorious victory he had lamed himself and despite intensive treatment was never able to race again.

A good indication that steeplechasing was by 1892 more popular than it had ever been was demonstrated that year at Aintree, when of the 25 competing riders in the Grand National, no less than 15 of them belonged to the unpaid ranks.

It was no surprise to find the runner-up to Come Away as favourite this time, particularly with the previous year's winner unable to compete, and Cloister, now the property of Charles Duff, went off heavily backed down to 11/2.

As a result of Cloister being sold, Captain Owen was not aboard him this time, taking the mount instead on the seven-year-old bay gelding Father O'Flynn. Contrary to popular belief, Father O'Flynn was not a product of Ireland but was, in fact, bred in Shropshire by Mr E.C. Wadlow, and in his short life had been owned by a variety of gentlemen, most of them amateurs who rode him in hunter 'chases. A small, though good-looking horse, Father O'Flynn was very robust and apparently needed to be, for in 1891 he took part in 13 races, of which he won six. Before his final victory that year, he was bought by Mr G.C. Wilson who, to his credit, treated the gelding with more consideration, running him only twice in his National preparation. Father O'Flynn's 36-year-old rider, Captain Edward Roderic Owen, was born at Bettws, Montgomeryshire, entered the army as a young man and when 20 years of age was stationed with his regiment, the East Devonshires, which afterwards became the Lancashire Fusiliers, in Halifax, Canada. A fine horseman, Roddy Owen as a professional soldier was naturally limited in his race-riding in Britain due to his regular service abroad, but if one delves deeply enough Roddy can be found partnering winners in many faraway places. Having already ridden Father O'Flynn to his two victories on the run-up to Aintree, Captain Owen felt confident they would give a good account of themselves.

At the second attempt the starter despatched them to the gloom and hazards of a National few could see the progress of and as in the past the only reliable accounts of events originate from the jockeys' reports after the race. Nap led the disappearing group out into the country with Cloister, The Primate, Jason and Bagman close up and in this order they took the first. Cloister had assumed command ahead of a large number of horses, taking Becher's in fine style followed by Flying Column, The Primate, Nap, Father O'Flynn and Ardcarn. As the viewers in the stands were at last able to see some action, Cloister gave them something to shout about by taking the water jump brilliantly to regain the foremost position. Flying Column was a close second, with Lord Arthur and The Midshipmite third and fourth some way in arrears. On the second circuit the field was reduced through a succession of accidents, with Tenby, The Primate and Billee Taylor exiting before the fourth fence, and with Cloister still clear jumping Becher's, Meldrum came down here. Over Valentine's Cloister held a comfortable advantage over The Midshipmite, Flying Column, Ilex, Ardcarn and the improving Father O'Flynn. The Midshipmite fell on the run back to the racecourse at the exact moment that Captain Owen decided to make his move. Sending Father O'Flynn to the front, the gelding came right away from his rivals, well clear of them by the time the second-last fence was reached. His two jumps at the final fences were as good as any seen at this late stage of the race and still full of running Father O'Flynn romped home the easiest of winners by 20 lengths from Cloister and Ilex. Of the 11 which finished, remarkably, Father O'Flynn looked not only the freshest but capable of going round the course again.

Having won the Grand National at his sixth attempt, Roddy Owen rested for three days after his victory before travelling to London and volunteering for active service. Over the next four years he attained the rank of major, was awarded the Distinguished Service Order and served in the Gold Coast, Uganda, India and, finally, Egypt. It was in this last location that Major Roddy Owen was laid to rest, buried in the desert by faithful Arabs who so respected the brave, quietly spoken British officer. Whilst a member of the Dongola expedition he contracted cholera and died less than 12 hours later. His greatest steeplechase achievement is recorded in letters of gold on the roll of honour at Aintree while several thousand miles from there, the Owen Falls in Kenya bears the name of this very gallant gentleman.

If ever a Grand National favourite deserved to be considered unbeatable, that horse was Cloister in 1893. Making his third attempt in the race after twice finishing as runner-up, the nine-year-old bay gelding became a red-hot 9/2 favourite despite carrying the maximum weight of 12st 7lb.

Bred in Ireland by Lord Fingall, Cloister was by that outstanding stallion, Ascetic, regarded so useless as a racehorse that he was used to collect the mail from the local village. As a sire of jumpers, however, Ascetic was the leading stallion of his generation and in Cloister he produced not only his greatest offspring but a steeplechaser who was to become a legend in his own time. Purchased when three years old by Captain J.A. Orr-Ewing, a British officer stationed in Ireland, Cloister carried his owner to victory within the year in a regimental meeting 'chase at Punchestown. Three weeks later, at the same venue, when partnered by a brother officer of the owner, the son of Ascetic caused a minor sensation when running away with the Irish Grand Military Steeplechase. When posted with his regiment to India, Captain Orr-Ewing was forced to part company with Cloister, selling him to the Earl of Dudley, whose colours he carried into second place in the 1891 National. In the autumn of that year he was resold, this time to Mr Charles Garden Duff, for whom in 1892 the gelding ran in seven races. Quite apart from finishing runner-up for the second time in Aintree's blue riband of steeplechasing, Cloister won five of these events, most significantly the final one being the Grand Sefton 'Chase over one circuit of the National course. Now trained by former rider Arthur Yates, at Bishop's Sutton in Hampshire, the transformation in the horse's form was a revelation to racegoers everywhere and even the most critical had to admit that Cloister possessed every requirement needed for the toughest race of the year. For his third attempt in the National he was for the first time to be partnered by a professional jockey, William Dollery, who started his working life as a shepherd before becoming a stable lad at trainer Yates's yard.

Fellow Irish-bred Why Not featured as second choice in the market to the favourite, with Aesop, The Midshipmite and Father O'Flynn the only others considered capable of causing a threat to Cloister.

In beautiful sunshine, with good fast ground, the crowds were bigger than ever to see if Cloister could live up to his reputation as the greatest steeplechaser in the nation. Away to a first-rate start, the gallop was fast into the first fence where Aesop held a narrow lead from a group consisting of Cloister, Joan of Arc,

The Primate and The Midshipmite. Falls were few on the run to Becher's, Golden Link refusing at the second and The Primate coming down at the first ditch, but even at this early stage Cloister was well in command. Striding out boldly, at a furious pace, his jumping appeared to gain him ground at every fence and his leap at Becher's Brook brought a gasp of amazement from the spectators. Another fantastic jump over Valentine's further increased Cloister's lead and nearing re-entry to the racecourse Dollery checked his mount's progress with a pull, allowing his pursuers to close up. Thrilling the people in the stands with a classic leap over the water jump, Cloister was four lengths ahead turning back to the country for the final circuit. Golden Gate and Choufleur were pulled up before reaching Becher's again, their riders realising the impossibility of trying to catch the runaway favourite, who jumped the Brook ten lengths in front of The Midshipmite, Why Not and Aesop. In the same order they crossed Valentine's with Cloister not merely stretching them but making the contest into a one-sided procession. Looking incredibly fresh, Cloister took the final fence as fast and true as he had the previous 29 and, to thunderous applause from the crowds, romped past the post an unbelievable 40 lengths in front of Aesop. Why Not plodded on a long way back in third place, with Tit for Tat fourth and Father O'Flynn sixth of the eight who finished.

When the announcement was made, as Cloister made his triumphant way to the winner's enclosure, that the time record for the course had been shattered, the roar from the adoring throng was deafening.

Not unexpectedly, the handicapper treated Cloister very harshly when framing his weights for the 1894 Grand National, setting the champion a massive task by allocating him 12st 12lb. It still came as an enormous shock, though, when Cloister was withdrawn from the National just days before the event. Said to have injured himself in one of his final gallops at Sandown, the owner, naturally furious and suspicious that foul play was involved, instructed detectives to investigate. Their findings were never divulged and the big race field was now down to 14 runners.

The five-year-old mare, Nelly Gray, came in for a good deal of support, eventually winding up joint favourite at 5/1, and with Father O'Flynn the only former winner in the race he received his share of supporters. Ardcarn and Aesop were also well backed and a large section of Irish visitors were vociferous concerning the chances of one of their newcomers, the 40/1 shot Wild Man From Borneo. Sharing favouritism with the youngest runner in the race was the oldest contestant, Why Not, now 13 years of age and making his fifth attempt.

Bred at Donore in County Meath, by Miss Nugent, Why Not began his racing career in Ireland when four years old, passing through a number of hands before becoming the property of Captain C.H. Fenwick in the spring of 1892.

Entering the Weyhill yard of trainer Willie Moore, whose elder brother Garrett won the National on The Liberator, Why Not progressed to such an extent that he was successful in his final four races of 1893. More recently, in his final race before returning to Aintree, Why Not gave a splendid weight-carrying performance to trounce the opposition over three miles at Kempton Park. His partner in the National was Arthur Nightingall, who would be going to the start of the big race for the eighth time and by now had developed a fine working relationship with his mount.

With perfect sunny weather and excellent going the runners got away well in line, with Aesop and Schooner showing in front after the first fence. After taking the Canal Turn, Nelly Gray challenged for the lead, passing Aesop with ease as she took a long leap over Valentine's, but within seconds she was out of the race, falling at the very next fence. With Aesop back in command, they ran on towards the racecourse, Trouville, Why Not, Lady Ellen II and Musician all going well just to the rear of the leader. Dawn joined the leaders approaching the water jump, ranging up alongside Aesop and Lady Ellen II, with Musician and Wild Man From Borneo also well in contention. Former hero Father O'Flynn came a cropper at Becher's, where upon landing safely Lady Ellen II moved smoothly past Aesop. It was at this point that Arthur Nightingall brought Why Not into the race, still going well within himself as they secured second place, while Wild Man From Borneo and Carrollstown also took closer order. Over Valentine's Lady Ellen II retained her position and by the time the second-last fence was in sight the mare, together with Why Not and Wild Man From Borneo, had gone well clear of the remainder and had the race to themselves. Saving valuable ground on the inside rail, Nightingall took Why Not ahead as they rose at the fence, landing clear and galloping on to the final obstacle. Measuring up for the jump, Wild Man From Borneo suddenly streaked past Why Not, landing first on the flat. In an exciting tussle to the line the veteran Why Not bravely came back at Wild Man From Borneo, stride by stride gaining on him until going past, seemingly with his race won. With less than 200 yards to go, Lady Ellen II issued a fresh challenge, storming up on the outside in one final brave attempt to snatch victory. Sticking to his task Why Not pulled out that little bit extra to win by a length and a half. A mere neck away in third place came Wild Man From Borneo.

Even with the dreaded Cloister a non-runner the bookies had taken a bashing on the day, but of course, as was cynically pointed out, they were well in hand from the ante-post losses of so many people. It was generally agreed that the result was a most worthy one for an old horse displaying such unflinching courage and for a jockey whose ice-cool nerve in such a nail-biting finish was a delight to survey.

The miracles of science were very much brought to mind in 1895 with Wilhelm Rontgen discovering the X-ray, an apparatus which was to revolutionise medical diagnosis in the future. Of a more leisurely interest was the opening of the world's first motion picture theatre in Paris and author H.G. Wells stretched the imagination of his readers with the publication of his science-fiction masterpiece *The Time Machine*. The sinister activities of Russian politics came to the attention of the world when Vladimir Ulyanov, otherwise known as Lenin, was arrested for alleged plotting against Tsar Alexander II.

Now trained by Harry Escott at Lewes in Sussex, who also doubled as his jockey, Cloister won again by a lengthy distance at Sandown Park in December and was then declared bang on target for the Grand National, a little over three months away. With the publication of the weights for the race Mr Duff's champion received 13st 3lb yet, his reputation still intact, many thousands of pounds were wagered on Cloister at ante-post odds. Mysteriously, though, the behaviour of certain bookmakers followed an almost identical pattern to the previous year, as they lengthened the odds against Cloister in the final weeks up to the race. With just days remaining before the National, Cloister yet again was scratched from the race, having this time collapsed in pain after a winding-up gallop.

Aesop now became the 5/1 favourite of the 19 runners, which included the two former winners Why Not and Father O'Flynn.

The section of Irishmen who last year sang the praises of Wild Man From Borneo had swelled to an army this time round, all insistent that The Wild Man, with or without Cloister to contend with, was sure to win. Nor was it just Irish money which made their hero third in the betting at 10/1. Since his impressive début 12 months earlier, the story of the team behind Wild Man From Borneo so stirred the imagination of sportsmen everywhere that support for the horse was good on both sides of the Irish Sea.

Mr G. Keays bred Wild Man From Borneo at Nenagh, in southern Ireland, from reliable jumping stock, the sire being a stallion called Decider and the dam Wild Duck. Purchased as a foal by James Maher of Clonsilla, a breeder and trainer of some distinction, in 1892 he won three of his six races. The following season, when still only a five-year-old, his work rate was stepped up, making 11 appearances, of which he again won three. Strangely, it wasn't his victories which attracted the Widger family, but two races at Aintree within the space of 24 hours in which Wild Man From Borneo was runner-up in each. Before the year's end he passed into the ownership of Mike and Joe Widger for £600, promptly rewarding them by winning twice.

The Widgers of Waterford were well-known and highly respected horse dealers, with a successful business supplying cavalry remounts to the armies of a number of European countries. Of the five sons born to Thomas Widger, the youngest, Joseph, set himself a task when still only a boy. That task, to ride the winner of the Grand National, became a fervent obsession when his brother Tom finished fourth in the race on Downpatrick in 1883. Joe by then was already an excellent rider, having won a pony race on the sands of Woodstown when barely ten years of age. The following year he was successful again, this time at Castletown astride a mare belonging to his father. Shortly after being sent to school at Mountrath, his parents received the shock of their lives when, reading a sporting newspaper, they discovered that young Joseph, having absconded from school and somehow made his way across the Irish Sea, had ridden the winner of a steeplechase at Bangor in North Wales. It was obvious to all that Joe Widger lived solely for horses and race-riding, his prowess in the saddle becoming a source of pride, not just to the family but to the whole of County Waterford. It was typical of Joe that he blamed himself for not winning the National in 1894 when, with his first ride in the race, he finished third with Wild Man From Borneo. Uncertain then of his mount's staying ability, he believed he had failed to make proper use of the horse and pledged there and then that he would be better prepared in 1895. For the previous year's event Joe and his brother Mike had trained the horse themselves, but this time they had placed their faith in trainer James Gatland and both brothers moved to his yard at Alfriston in Sussex to assist in the preparation.

As Aesop broke well from the start, a great cheer went up from the stands. Taking the first two fences well, he was followed by Horizon, Manifesto, Cathal, Fin-Ma-Coul II and Father O'Flynn and despite the atrocious going all the runners were coping extremely well. Jumping Becher's, Dalkeith joined Aesop as they landed, the pair racing together over the Canal Turn and on to Valentine's, which again was taken safely by every competitor. Closing up nearing the water jump, Aesop was joined by Dalkeith and Horizon but as the three landed together the latter was barged into by a loose horse and brought down. Close on the heels of the leading pair back in the country came Father O'Flynn, Manifesto and Cathal, while ahead of them jockey Jimmy Knox struggled to stay aboard Dalkeith when his stirrup leather broke. In what must have been a nightmare for the rider, Dalkeith rose at Becher's just half a length in arrears of Aesop and, coming down steeply, blundered badly on landing, losing a lot of ground, yet miraculously the partnership remained intact. Holding a clear lead, Aesop totally misjudged his take-off at the Canal Turn and crashed to the ground, joined moments later by the very tired Prince Albert. With the race now wide open, the Irish horse Cathal, ridden by Cloister's trainer Harry Escott, struck the front, closely attended by Manifesto, Lady Pat and Wild Man From Borneo. Once on the run-in, however, Joe Widger produced his horse at exactly the correct moment and riding a masterly finish brought Wild Man From Borneo past the winning post a length and a half in front of Cathal. Coming late on the scene, Van Der Berg was a bad third, just ahead of Manifesto and Why Not.

Amid a throng of cheering Irishmen, a very proud Joe Widger guided his winner to the winner's enclosure and after weighing-in joined his family to receive their congratulations. His one regret on the glorious day of triumph was that his father was not able to witness Wild Man From Borneo's success, Thomas Widger having passed away ten months before.

From an original entry of 63, 28 runners formed the line-up for the 1896 Grand National, the biggest number to contest the event since 1873. Top weight of 12st was the price Wild Man From Borneo was asked to pay for his victory in the previous year's race, while the runner-up, Cathal, carried just 1lb less. Tom Widger rode Wild Man From Borneo this time, as brother Joe elected to team up with Mr Irving's Waterford. A third brother, Michael Widger, also had an interest in the proceedings as the owner of the Terry Kavanagh-ridden Miss Baron.

Principal choice of the punters rested with the mount of Robert Nightingall, Rory O'More, at 7/1, and at 8/1 came Ardcarn, making his fourth attempt to win. Having made such a promising début 12 months earlier, Manifesto returned, along with Van Der Berg and The Midshipmite.

Sharing the same starting price of 40/1 as the most recent winner was another product of Ireland, the seven-year-old gelding The Soarer, who provided a great deal of local interest. By Skylark out of Idalia, he was bred by Pat Doyle and when four years old was bought very cheaply by David Campbell, a subaltern with the 9th Lancers, then stationed at the Curragh. Liverpool-born Campbell rode his horse to seven victories the following season before discovering early in 1896 that The Soarer was proving difficult to train. Barely two months before the Grand National, David Campbell was approached by Liverpool businessman William Hall-Walker, resulting in the gelding becoming the property of Hall-Walker for £500, including the condition that the vendor be allowed to ride The Soarer in the big race at Aintree. Consigned to trainer Willie Moore's Weyhill yard, Mr Hall-Walker's new purchase hardly inspired confidence in his final race before Aintree when falling at Hurst Park.

From a good start, the big field raced to the first fence in a tightly packed bunch, with some jostling among the runners inevitable and just as certain was the upset which occurred at the first obstacle. Bundled off his stride by Redhill, Manifesto fell, together with the culprit and a very good horse was out of the race through no fault of his own. Wild Man From Borneo came down at the fourth, while Alpheus went four lengths clear lining up for the Brook, which he jumped superbly. Next in line came Clawson, Cathal and the favourite Rory O'More, and in this order they rounded the Canal Turn and went on to Valentine's. Rory O'More came upsides Alpheus at the water jump, the pair jumping it together in the lead, while in mid-division The Soarer was making swift progress through the field. As Rory O'More landed in the lead over Becher's, The Soarer put in a splendid leap which brought him almost abreast of the favourite and with Father O'Flynn, Biscuit and Why Not also well to the fore, an exciting finish already seemed likely. Putting Valentine's Brook behind them, Biscuit now showed in front by the narrowest of margins from The Soarer, whose rider had not moved an inch yet. The Soarer was in command over the final fence, still going strong, and although the game Father O'Flynn challenged tenaciously over the last 200 yards, David Campbell rode his mount out well and The Soarer held on to win by a length and a half. Biscuit was the same distance away in third place.

Having ridden the winner of the National at his first attempt, David Campbell became the first cavalry officer to succeed in the race and competed only once more in the event. Then concentrating on his military career, he served with distinction in South Africa and the Great War, received a knighthood and retired from the army with the rank of lieutenant-general. He passed away peacefully in 1936, 40 years after his greatest victory on the turf.

Mr Hall-Walker remained associated with racing for many years and in addition to his family business commitments became Member of Parliament for Widnes. He was himself a fine amateur rider and having purchased an expanse of land at Tully in County Kildare, established a stud which achieved tremendous success. In 1915 he most generously presented the stud, together with its stallions and brood-mares, to the British nation, whereupon it became known as the National Stud. In 1919 he became Lord Wavertree and until the mid-1920s was hardly ever without a runner in the Grand National.

Britain and its Empire enjoyed a year of patriotic ardour and rejoicing in 1897, as 78-year-old Queen Victoria celebrated the diamond jubilee of her reign. Having rarely been seen in public for many years, Her Majesty attended and was warmly welcomed at the numerous civic functions held in her honour. In literary circles the newly published *Dracula* by Bram Stoker and H.G. Wells's *The Invisible Man* were popular subjects of discussion. And once more the American 'march king', John Philip Sousa, put rhythm into the step of fellow countrymen with his latest composition, 'The Stars and Stripes Forever'.

Miss F.E. Norris, of West Derby, Liverpool, was the registered owner of former winner Wild Man From Borneo, who was again to be ridden by Joe Widger, soon to become the husband of Miss Norris. As a result of the local connection, the horse was backed to 9/1, placing him third in the market. The favourite, and to many the ideal horse for the race, was nine-year-old Manifesto.

Bred near Navan in County Meath, by Mr Harry Dyas, he was by Man of War out of Vae Victis and was allowed ample time to mature by Mr Dyas. Although lightly raced in his younger years, Manifesto recorded an impressive victory when only four years of age in the Irish Champion Steeplechase at Leopardstown, after which he was again treated with extreme patience. Competing only twice in each of the next two seasons, the son of Man of War caused a major upset when winning the valuable Lancashire 'Chase at Manchester in 1894, and the following year, in his first Grand National, ran splendidly to finish fourth. His unfortunate early departure from 1895's race could in no way reflect on his ability and with Irish-born Terry Kavanagh riding, Manifesto was the most popular choice on the day at 6/1.

Identifying the horses in the paddock was made much easier through the ingenuity of the racecourse executive, who provided white rugs bearing the names of the runners.

Over the first fence the order was Timon, Westmeath, Manifesto, Red Cross and Clawson. Manifesto put in a spectacular leap at the Brook, taking him into second place behind Timon, and with all of the original contingent still on their feet, they continued towards the Canal Turn still tightly grouped. Timon and Manifesto led the way back to the racecourse, closely followed by Nelly Gray, Cathal and Red Cross, and further back it could be seen that Mr Campbell was encountering difficulties as The Soarer took chances at some of the fences. Timon and Manifesto cleared the water well, following the loose horse Goldfish round the turn back to the country, while they in turn were chased by Cathal, Nelly Gray and Gauntlet. Almost stride for stride Timon and Manifesto took Becher's with the following group closing on them as the tempo increased. Valentine's saw the end of The Soarer and at the third from home Greenhill came down after colliding with another runner. Back on the racecourse, Timon and Manifesto were still together in front but at the penultimate fence Timon blundered and, losing his jockey, left Manifesto well clear with the race at his mercy. In a desperate attempt to catch Manifesto, Cathal fell at the final fence, leaving the favourite to come home the easiest of winners by 20 lengths from Filbert and the fast-finishing Ford of Fyne. In sixth place of the ten to finish was the remounted and most unlucky Timon.

There was a tinge of sadness for winning jockey Terry Kavanagh amid the congratulations and champagne, when he reflected on the absence of the one person he would most have wished to be present. Henry Eyre Linde, the trainer who had given him his first chance to become a jockey, had died the previous week of Bright's disease.

It wasn't just the arctic conditions which threatened to ruin the 1898 National but also the angry suggestions that the late withdrawal of Manifesto too closely resembled the mysterious affairs surrounding Cloister to be merely coincidence.

The well-being of the previous year's winner had been clearly demonstrated at Gatwick as recently as February, when he had comfortably won a two-mile 'chase, and being purchased after that victory by Mr J.G. Bulteel for £4,000 only further endorsed the people's confidence in Manifesto. As things turned out, nothing more sinister than a stable lad's carelessness was the reason behind Manifesto being absent from that year's race. With his change of ownership, the horse had also been sent to a new stable, that of Willie Moore, and while there, hardly a week before his Aintree appointment, the door of his box was left open in error. With natural curiosity, Manifesto took himself for a walk, during which he damaged his fetlock when jumping a gate.

Reduced to 25 runners, with The Soarer the only previous winner of the race among them, it was the previous year's third-placed Ford of Fyne which found most favour in the ring, ending up as 11/2 favourite. Others considered likely to run well included Prince Albert, Gauntlet and Barcalwhey. Of the outsiders, Filbert knew his way round, Dead Level had the assistance of a superb jockey in Algy Anthony, and there was a quiet mention of an Irish horse called Drogheda.

Named after the town near where he was bred by Mr G.F. Gradwell, Drogheda was by Cherry Ripe, the winner of the 1887 Irish Grand National, and after winning three small races in his homeland as a five-year-old was bought jointly by Richard Dawson and a former officer in the 14th Hussars, Mr G.C.M. Adam. Dawson, the son of an Irish trainer, attended Dublin University before following his father's footsteps, training in conjunction with the breeder, James Maher. Somewhat disgruntled with his lack of success at home, Richard Dawson moved to Fawley House, Whatcombe, in Berkshire, in 1897, taking with him of course the rather plain-looking Drogheda, and plans to conquer Aintree were put in motion. Jockey John Gourley took the mount on the six-year-old Irish horse, it being only his second ride in the race after an early departure from Manifesto when they were knocked over in 1896.

A powerful wind blowing across the racecourse swirled the heavily falling snow into the faces of jockeys and spectators alike. Greenhill was the first to show, bravely attempting to set the pace from Cushalee Mavourneen, Gauntlet, Swanshot, Cruiskeen II and Athelfrith. Even before reaching Becher's the field was well strung out, with Greenhill still at the head of them as they jumped the Brook, followed by The Soarer, Nepcote, Cushalee Mavourneen and Gauntlet. There was a brief moment of anxiety as Barcalwhey fell at the open ditch, directly in front of the improving Drogheda, but with commendable reflex action Gourley and his mount side-stepped the rolling horse. Reaching for the water jump Drogheda struck the front, landing clear of Gauntlet, Nepcote, Greenhill, Cathal and Dead Level, but it was the end of the line for The Soarer, whose exit from the race was a very damp one. Disappearing from view again as they went back down towards Becher's, Nepcote headed Drogheda. Drogheda landed just behind Nepcote at Becher's Brook, the pair proceeding on to the Canal Turn where Nepcote began dropping back, a tired and beaten horse, and with Drogheda now clear, the final slog home began. With owner Reg Ward on Cathal trying desperately to get on terms with Drogheda, they brought appreciative applause from the crowds as Drogheda passed the post three lengths clear of Cathal, with Gauntlet running on well to secure third place. Each of the ten finishers deserved a medal that day, for rarely in any sporting endeavour have the participants been expected to compete against the worst of nature's elements as well as their opponents.

In a wonderful gesture of appreciation, the winning owner presented jockey John Gourley with a pension for life, a most generous recognition of a brave and determined ride through the worst conditions in living memory.

Neither Drogheda nor his jockey, John Gourley, ever took part in the Grand National again and Richard Dawson had experienced for the first and last time the joy of saddling a Grand National winner.

Seven

1899-1908

In the final year of the 19th century, Britain faced, yet again, that which now seemed an inestimable part of its ongoing history: conflict, turmoil and military confrontation. British attempts to seize the Transvaal and its gold mines led to the outbreak of the Boer War and, although the Boers were derisively considered nothing more than 'angry farmers', by the end of the year the towns of Mafeking, Kimberley and Ladysmith lay besieged by them. It was a problem Prime Minister the Marquess of Salisbury and his Conservative government would struggle with for some time to come.

At Aintree, in that year of 1899, racegoers rejoiced at the prospect of seeing again the mighty Manifesto. Faced with an impossible task, Manifesto topped the handicap with 12st 7lb, giving 14lb to the next one to him in the weights and an impossible 3st to some of his 18 opponents. The regard he was held in by the public still resulted in him starting second in the betting at 5/1, just one point behind the favourite, his half-sister and former stable companion, the mare Gentle Ida.

After winning her second race of the current campaign, Harry Dyas sold the mare to Horatio Bottomley but remained as trainer, firmly believing that Gentle Ida had the beating of Manifesto, especially in receipt of a stone from his former National winner. Another recently purchased contender was Ambush II, a five-year-old entrusted with the hopes of the Prince of Wales.

When the starter lowered his flag Sheriff Hutton jumped off first, but was passed by Corner and Pistache as they landed over the first fence. There was little change in the order into and over Becher's, though Electric Spark had moved into contention and close up followed Elliman, Gentle Ida and Ford of Fyne. Moving well in the centre of the field, Manifesto hadn't put a foot wrong so far, giving jockey George Williamson as smooth a passage as anyone could wish for in the National, but at the Canal Turn they stared disaster in the face. Putting in another fine jump, Manifesto landed on some hay and, momentarily losing his footing, slithered to the ground, causing his jockey to lose both stirrup irons. With the gasp of despair from the crowd still hanging in the air, Manifesto miraculously recovered. Valentine's Brook brought another groan from the spectators as the favourite Gentle Ida fell, and with the runners bunching up as they approached the Anchor Bridge, the leading positions altered regularly. Passing the stands Mum was in front and just to her rear a serious accident looked certain to result in tragedy. The French horse, Pistache, crashed straight through into the open ditch, throwing her owner-rider, Count de Geloes, directly into the path of the oncoming runners. As the leading group took the water jump, Manifesto lay a good distance behind but once back in the country George Williamson decided it was time to progress. Barsac and Mum jumped Becher's together in the lead, ahead of Ambush II, Elliman, Ford of Fyne and Manifesto, and as Mum fell victim to exhaustion Barsac went clear over the Canal Turn. The cheers which had begun when Manifesto simply flew Valentine's accompanied him all the way back to the stands, increasing in volume with every stride that took him nearer to victory. Sailing majestically over the final two fences, Manifesto was greeted to an ear-shattering reception of cheering, the like of which had never been heard on a racecourse before. Looking remarkably fresh as he passed the winning post five lengths in front of Ford of Fyne and Elliman, Manifesto was hailed by an ecstatic crowd as the greatest horse ever to win the Grand National.

The royal colours were carried into seventh place by Ambush II, giving the Prince of Wales reason to believe that he had at last found a horse to provide him with the victory at Liverpool he longed for.

With the tide of war in South Africa turning in Britain's favour in 1900, the new century brought hope that the future would provide a lasting peace and a better way for nations to resolve their disputes than that of resorting to military force.

As the Grand National drew near, the wish of everyone was that Manifesto would be able to set the seal on his greatness by winning the race for an unprecedented third time.

Upon publication of the weights it appeared an impossible task, for the dual winner was allocated a daunting 12st 13lb. Most heavily backed of the 16 runners was Colonel Gallwey's Hidden Mystery, with Ambush II, Manifesto and Elliman the next in the betting order.

By Ben Battle out of Miss Plant, the royal representative was bred by William Ashe at Narraghmore, and as Mr Ashe had little regard for the foal he made every effort to sell it. Not alone in his poor opinion of Ambush II, the breeder quickly discovered that nobody wanted him at any price. It was not until the famous amateur rider-turned-trainer, Tommy Lushington, saw the horse that a deal was entered into with Ambush II changing hands for 500 guineas. As an acquaintance of the Prince of Wales, Mr Lushington received, via Lord Marcus Beresford, a request from the Prince to find him a 'chaser with some ability. Passing into royal ownership, Ambush II continued to be trained by Lushington at Eyrefield Lodge, formerly the establishment made famous by Henry Linde, and quickly rewarded the trainer's confidence by winning a four-mile maiden plate at Kildare in the royal colours. Having matured into a fine, strong horse under Mr Lushington's care, developing a flair for jumping which was unique for such a young horse, Ambush II was particularly effective when ridden by Algy Anthony. A very fine jockey, Anthony was born in Cheltenham, although most of his riding was conducted in Ireland where he chose to live and as a result most people believed him to be an Irishman. His services were constantly in demand under both codes of racing and after partnering Ambush II into seventh place in the 1899 National, he had actually gone on to win the Irish Derby aboard Oppressor. Assisting Mr Lushington as trainer at Eyrefield provided Algy Anthony with a greater understanding of the horses he rode, their ratio of winners clear proof of the wisdom of this strategy, and between them they produced the royal horse in perfect shape for Aintree.

From a perfect start Barsac took them along at a fast gallop, leading over the first fence where an early shock came with the fall of the well-fancied Irish contestant Covert Hack. The only change in the positions over the Brook was the outsider Model going up to join Barsac but there was another casualty at the next fence when Alpheus fell. Hidden Mystery and Easter Ogue both moved up to challenge the leader Barsac jumping Valentine's, with a tightly bunched group just behind and racing comfortably in the middle of these were Manifesto and Ambush II. Returning to the racecourse, Hidden Mystery overtook Barsac, bringing a cheer from spectators as the favourite raced towards the 13th fence closely followed by the remainder, but as they rose at the water jump Barsac was back in the lead. The favourite was right on the heels of Barsac as they streamed back into the country but at the first obstacle there Hidden Mystery came to grief when the loose horse Covert Hack barged into him. Ambush II now took second place behind Barsac but there were still a lot of horses going well and not too far off the pace. The tempo increased going to Becher's, with a number of runners now making their bid, and over the Brook it was Breemount's Pride and Lotus Lily jumping to the front ahead of Barsac, Grudon and Sister Elizabeth. Manifesto and Ambush II were still close up also, and with a fabulous jump round the Canal Turn Ambush II struck the front. At the very next fence, Valentine's, the royal horse was joined by Manifesto and the crowds cheered wildly as these two great horses raced side by side down the canal stretch. Surging to the front as they approached the second-last fence, Manifesto brought a loud cheer from the crowds as the impossible seemed about to happen, a third victory for the great horse they thought of as their own. Yet it was not to be, for between the final two fences Ambush II produced a burst of speed and in receipt of 24lb from Manifesto the contest became an unequal one. They both cleared the last fence well and with Ambush II racing to a four-length victory, George Williamson took pity on his game mount and relaxed, content with second place. Right on the line Manifesto was even denied that position when the determined Barsac got up to pip the old champion by a neck, relegating the dual winner to third place.

His Royal Highness the Prince of Wales went onto the course to welcome his winner and congratulate Algy Anthony for giving the horse a perfect ride. It was the beginning of an incredible season of success for the Prince of Wales, his Diamond Jubilee winning the 2,000 Guineas, Derby and St Leger, commonly known as the Triple Crown. The young jockey who partnered Diamond Jubilee to victory in his classic races was Herbert Jones, the son of John Jones, successful on Shifnal in the 1878 Grand National.

Magnificent in defeat, Manifesto shared the plaudits of an adoring public, who realised that day they had seen in their hero a special brand of greatness.

The Victorian era came to an end on 22 January 1901 with the passing of Her Majesty Queen Victoria at the age of 81. She had reigned for 63 years and was succeeded by the 59-year-old Edward VII.

With the Court in mourning, the engagements of His Majesty's horses were cancelled, meaning of course that Ambush II missed the chance to repeat his victory in the National.

Well accustomed to inclement weather at Aintree, nothing could have prepared racegoers for the atrocious conditions they endured at the 1901 Grand National. A raging blizzard swept the course all day, making the possibility of racing taking place extremely unlikely and when all 24 competing jockeys submitted a signed petition to the clerk of the course requesting that the race be postponed, people began making plans to return to the comfort of their homes. Upon inspecting the track, however, the three stewards of the meeting declared that racing would be possible.

Favourite at 5/1 was Levanter, the mount of Liverpool-born Frank Mason, while the previous year's runner-up, Barsac, was the second choice of the punters, with other notables including Covert Hack, Drumcree and an 11-year-old by the name of Grudon.

The product of humble stock, Grudon was bred by Bernard Bletsoe at Denton, Northamptonshire, from a stallion purchased by the breeder, which had formerly pulled a plough. Old Buck, the plough horse, when mated with the mare Avis, produced Grudon who, despite suffering the inconvenience of getting one of his legs caught in his bridle in the 1900 race, still managed to get round. Having finished in that same position during the notorious snowstorm in 1898, Grudon was making a third attempt in the race and could be said to be familiar with adversity. Bred, owned and trained by Bernard Bletsoe, he started third in the market at 9/1 and was the mount of a jockey with two National wins already to his credit, Arthur Nightingall.

There was a 16-minute delay before they at last began the race which virtually everybody believed should never take place. Grudon went into an immediate lead, his jockey no doubt feeling that if they had to race then it was best to get things over with quickly. Within seconds of their journey beginning, they were lost from view and it was not until they had almost completed the first circuit that anyone knew what was happening. Over the open ditch in front of the stands Grudon was still leading the way and he jumped the water jump a couple of lengths clear of Levanter, Covert Hack, Barsac and Padishah. Disappearing again as they raced back to the country through the driving snow, people could but guess at what might be happening to them in these treacherous and dreadful conditions. As the ghost-like figures came into view at last, unbelievably it was still Grudon at the head of a forlorn-looking bunch of weary and bedraggled men and horses. Passing the post four lengths in front of Drumcree, Grudon won what must have been the most unpleasant Grand National in history. A further six lengths back came Buffalo Bill in front of six other sorry-looking but brave survivors.

It was only after the winner had weighed in and the congratulations were in full flow that the secret of Grudon's start-to-finish success became known. Mr Bletsoe confided that while the stewards were making their deliberations regarding the suitability of the ground, he sent a stable lad to the village shop to purchase 2lb of butter. The butter was then stuffed into the hooves of Grudon as a prevention against the snow balling in his feet. Such foresight was worthy of the victory Grudon achieved. Arthur Nightingall celebrated his third win in the race and, all in all, despite the weather it was a popular result. Grudon ran only in two more races, breaking down in the Lancashire 'Chase at Manchester. Grudon, being a full horse, was then retired from racing and sent to stud.

When the entries for the 1902 Grand National were published in January, 'chasing fans were delighted to see that both the King's horse, Ambush II, and their beloved Manifesto were among the 66 subscribers. Ambush II met with an accident in training and was unable to run, but Manifesto stood his ground, although this time he was ridden by the up-and-coming jockey Ernie Piggott.

Now 14 years old, Manifesto was again top of the handicap with 12st 8lb, which meant he was not only once more conceding weight to each of his 20 opponents, but in the case of at least two of them an incredible 43lb.

Joint favourites at 6/1 were Drumree and Inquisitor, with Barsac, Lurgan and Tipperary Boy also well supported.

Among the newcomers was a mare aged seven by the name of Shannon Lass, bred by James Reidy in County Clare who, after winning a steeplechase with her when she was but three years of age, sold her to Mr E.C. Irish. Without ever appearing in this man's colours, Shannon Lass changed hands again, this time becoming the property of Ambrose Gorham, a well-known English bookmaker. The mare was prepared for racing on rented gallops at Telscombe, near Brighton, by James Hackett, Gorham's private trainer. Her gameness was a byword among her connections, who proudly proclaimed that in the whole of her racing career she had never had need of whip or spurs to give of her best. Teaming up with Shannon Lass for the National was David Read.

Away to an even break, they raced to the first fence headed by Drumcree, but a whole group of horses were close on his heels consisting of Barsac, Helium, The Sapper and Matthew. With Barsac now in the lead they took Becher's well, Helium, Matthew, Drumcree and Arnold tracking the leader and Ernie Piggott conserving the energy of Manifesto by holding him up towards the rear. Still at the head of affairs over the Canal Turn, Barsac, competing in his fifth National, was jumping beautifully and even as Inquistor moved up on the outside, the leader repulsed the challenge. At the open ditch Inquisitor got his head in front, taking them on to the water jump, with Barsac and Matthew racing at his quarters, but with a sudden flurry Helium rushed past the three of them to land first over the water. In this order they charged back down towards Becher's again, with Arnold, Aunt May, Drumcree and the improving Manifesto closing the gap on the leaders. Landing over Becher's the foremost positions had changed, Tipperary Boy now holding a slight lead over Aunt May, Matthew and Barsac. Shannon Lass made up a lot of ground going into the Canal Turn and although she was still only lying eighth, some ten lengths in arrears of the leader Matthew jumping Valentine's, the mare looked to have plenty in hand. The lightly weighted Matthew was still in front coming over the second-last fence, pressed strongly now by Detail and Shannon Lass and, to the amazement and joy of everyone watching, Manifesto moved up into fourth place. With all to play for at the last obstacle, Detail was the first to crack as he blundered his chance away, Matthew was flat out but Shannon Lass just romped away in very impressive style to win by three lengths from Matthew. Staying on in the brave fashion which was his trademark, Manifesto came home third, a further three lengths behind the second horse, bringing as much applause as the winner received.

Shannon Lass never ran in the Grand National again, eventually finishing up a brood-mare at stud. Her owner, Ambrose Gorham, donated most of his winnings to the restoration of the church at Telscombe, a most fitting gesture which hopefully is in some way remembered on the Sussex Downs.

The appearance of Ambush II in the 1903 Grand National was an important milestone in the history of the race. It meant that for the first time in the National a reigning British monarch was represented in the toughest steeplechase in the world.

A record attendance was recorded at the race that year, an indication of just how popular racing 'over the sticks' had become, for quite apart from being blessed on this occasion with perfect sunny weather, there was the longed-for rematch of Ambush II and Manifesto.

Once again there was confusion for the bookmakers, Drumree and Drumcree again being in the line-up, and it was the latter who found most favour with punters, going off clear favourite at 13/2.

A nine-year-old bay gelding by Ascetic out of Witching Hour, Drumcree was bred by Mr C. Hope in Ireland, being first bought by Owen Williams, in whose colours he finished second in the snowstorm National of 1901. In the most recent race he ran well enough to finish seventh when representing his new owner, Mr J.S. Morrison, a very wealthy man who paid £2,500 for the horse. Still in the yard of trainer Sir Charles Nugent, Drumcree won all his three races in the run-up to Aintree when ridden by the trainer's son, the stylish amateur, Hugh Nugent. The intention was that the partnership should continue in the National but, unfortunately, Hugh Nugent suffered a riding injury shortly before the race and 21-year-old professional Percy Woodland became the replacement.

At the second time of asking the race began, with Ambush II taking a strong hold to lead into the first fence, where Expert II and Orange Pat came down. Over Becher's Ambush II, Kirkland and Detail jumped in line abreast, closely followed by Drumree, Fanciful, Marpessa and Matthew, while Manifesto and Drumcree were going well in the middle of the next group. Staying in this order, with Ambush II just to the fore, they came back onto the racecourse with only 12 now still in the contest. Still in command jumping Becher's for the final time, Ambush II had jumped perfectly all the way and at this late stage of the race seemed set fair to repeat his triumph of three years earlier. Bunching up as they re-entered the racecourse, the result was still very much in doubt as Drumcree and Ambush II held the narrowest of advantages over Drumree, Detail, Manifesto and the rapidly improving Kirkland. Jumping the second last they sped on, leaving the fallers Dearslayer and Saxilby rolling behind and as Drumree issued his challenge a close finish looked certain. Just yards from the final fence, though, without any warning or apparent reason, Drumree fell flat on the ground appearing to have been stricken by some strange spasm. Within seconds another drama was enacted when Ambush II crashed into the fence, falling heavily in a nasty-looking tumble. Drumcree, left clear, ran on strongly to a three-length victory from Detail, with a terrific struggle between Manifesto and local-owned Kirkland going to the former by a head.

Successful in the National at the third time of asking and when most of the public money was on him made Drumcree a most popular winner, the only regret for the trainer being that his injured son was not part of the winning team. Consoling himself that there was always next year, Sir Charles Nugent joined the celebrations. Tragically, his son Hugh was killed after falling in a hurdle race at Ostend just a few months later.

With Ambush II the 7/2 favourite and his owner, the King, present at Aintree in 1904, the attendance reached near record proportions. They came in their thousands for another reason also, for what they knew must be the last Grand National for Manifesto, the horse which in nine years had become a legend and an inspiration.

Patlander, Detail, Inquisitor and Kirkland came to Aintree this year with the finest credentials, all figuring prominently in the betting and adding an international flavour to the 26-runner field was a much-travelled gelding with the strange-sounding name of Moifaa.

Bred in New Zealand by Natator out of Denbigh, Moifaa was a giant of a horse standing over 17 hands, though very coarse looking with an appearance which brought many derisive comments from observers. One of the least insulting was that he had 'the head and shoulders of a camel'. Handsome is as handsome does, however, was certainly true in the case of this steeplechaser from the land of the kiwi, for he won nine times over timber in his native land for his wealthy Australian owner, Spencer Gollan. Legend has it that when shipped to Britain to be prepared for the Grand National, Moifaa was forced to swim for his life when his ship was wrecked off the coast of Ireland. Discovered some days later on a sandy spit by some fishermen, the horse eventually arrived at his destination. If this story is true, then it is an interesting coincidence that the name of Moifaa's sire, Natator, means swimmer in Latin. Trained at Epsom by Mr Hickey, the New Zealand gelding's three races before Aintree were far from noteworthy and the attention he received in the paddock before the big race was purely the result of curiosity. The little-known jockey Arthur Birch, having only his second ride in the National, first sat on Moifaa when he mounted the horse in the paddock before the race.

As the starter's flag fell Inquisitor went to the front, landing in that position over the first fence, at which the only casualty was Railoff, but there was soon worse to follow. At the third, the first open ditch, Ambush II fell. Inquisitor bowed out at the next, together with Cushendun, leaving Moifaa at the vanguard of the contest. With the bit apparently between his teeth, the huge gelding blasted his way through, rather than over, the fifth. With a much-improved jump Moifaa led over Becher's as the challenging Biology crashed to the ground beside him, and now some way clear of the remainder, the colonial runner seemed most at home in these surroundings. Striding out well, the New Zealander stretched out over the water jump several lengths ahead of the improving Detail, who was now closely chased by Shaun Aboo, Kirkland, The Gunner and Manifesto. Moifaa stretched away again and with Detail attempting to get on terms at the Canal Turn, the pilotless Ambush II knocked into him. Leaving the country at the Anchor Bridge crossing, Moifaa raced towards the stands with a comfortable lead, which was made more secure when his nearest rival, The Pride of Mabestown, fell at the second last. Without being extended Moifaa came home an eight-length winner from Kirkland, who held off The Gunner by a neck. Of the only five others to finish the course, a very special cheer greeted Manifesto, who finished last of the eight survivors to end a fantastic era of equine magnificence.

The victory of Moifaa in the Grand National was the only win ever recorded in Britain by the horse and although purchased by His Majesty in time for the next Aintree spectacular, it was an unsuccessful enterprise. Developing respiratory problems, Moifaa was eventually retired from racing, becoming His Majesty's favourite hack, in which capacity the horse appeared at all state occasions. At the funeral of King Edward VII in 1910, Moifaa carried his late master's boots reversed in the stirrups as he took his place in the funeral cortège behind the gun carriage carrying the coffin of the late King. The last public appearance of the giant gelding from New Zealand was as the mount of Lord Kitchener in the Coronation procession of King George V.

When Ambush II appeared among the 64 original entries for the 1905 Grand National, the public eagerly awaited publication of the weights to see if the royal runner had received the maximum impost. Unfortunately their curiosity remained unanswered for, tragically, Ambush II died after breaking a blood vessel while on the gallops at the Curragh before the handicapper made his decision.

Determined to have a runner in the race, His Majesty the King instructed Lord Marcus Beresford to find a horse qualified for the race to represent him and the animal chosen was the most recent National winner, Moifaa.

As 6/1 second favourite Kirkland was an obvious choice on the book, having run very well in the race in both his previous efforts and now a nine-year-old, he was at peak fitness. Irish bred by a man of the cloth, the Reverend Clifford, at Newcastle West, County Limerick, Kirkland's first owner was Mr T.A. Halligan, for whom he won first time out at Kilmallock when still a four-year-old. After being placed in four other 'chases, he was sold to the wealthy Liverpool industrialist, Mr Frank Bibby, a staunch supporter of steeplechasing who had set his heart on winning the Grand National in his home town. The trainer of Kirkland, Mr Lort Phillips, owned a share in the horse, which he trained at Lawrenny Park, near Tenby in Pembrokeshire, and he had already enjoyed victory with the horse at Aintree when winning the Grand Sefton Steeplechase. Frank Bibby was as concerned about the fitness of his jockey, Frank 'Tich' Mason, as he was about that of Kirkland, to such an extent that as a precaution against injuries he paid the jockey £300 not to ride in any races for two weeks before the National. With a little over a week to go to the big race, the whole team suffered great anxiety when Kirkland received an injury in training and a race against time began to restore him to full fitness. It was only with constant care and treatment that they got the gelding to Aintree fit enough to do himself justice.

All 27 competitors behaved so well at the start that they were actually sent on their way at one minute before the appointed time, with Detail yet again attempting to blaze a trail. Over Becher's it was Detail holding a slight lead from Moifaa and Ranunculus and this trio still held sway over the Canal Turn. Misjudging his take-off, Detail crashed to the ground at the second Brook, joined moments later by Biology, and from this point Ranunculus took command. With the remainder of the survivors now well strung out, Ranunculus and Timothy Titus, accompanied by the riderless Ascetic's Silver, led the way back to the stands, jumping the water jump and proceeding back for the final circuit. Becher's claimed the favourite Moifaa, who was starting to feel the pace at the time, and two fences later the Canal Turn brought the falls of Aunt May and Bucheron. Meanwhile there was little to choose between Timothy Titus and Ranunculus as they sailed over Valentine's in the lead. The fence after Valentine's caught out Timothy Titus who, over-jumping, crashed in a heap, whilst Napper Tandy made ground on the leader, Ranunculus. With the two leaders fighting it out on the gallop back onto the racecourse, Kirkland came with a burst of speed, passing them both and taking the last two fences with only the riderless Ascetic's Silver for company, followed the loose horse past the post a three-length winner. Napper Tandy was second, four lengths in front of Buckaway II.

It was a most popular victory for local people in the crowd, with owner Frank Bibby and jockey Frank Mason both Liverpool-born men, and with Kirkland heavily backed, the winner provided many celebrations.

Moifaa never ran in the National again, His Majesty the King reserving him for more formal and considerably less hazardous duties.

In 1906 the United States of America suffered a natural disaster of horrendous proportions when the San Francisco earthquake destroyed two-thirds of the city and cost the lives of 2,500 people. England was faced with a campaign of women's suffrage, led by Emmeline Pankhurst and her two daughters. Ominously, Germany followed Britain's example by expanding her naval fleet, which included the building of larger battleships.

On the same 20/1 betting mark as the previous year, when he tried to steal Kirkland's thunder by being first past the post though without his rider, Ascetic's Silver on this occasion represented completely new connections. A chestnut entire by Ascetic out of Silver Lady, he shared the same sire as two former National winners, Cloister and Drumcree, and was bred by Mr P.J. Dunne at Carrollstown, County Meath. A fine-looking individual, when put to racing by his breeder, Mr Dunne enjoyed some success with him, most notably when Ascetic's Silver won him the 1904 Irish Grand National at Fairyhouse. Some little time after the 1905 Grand National, Mr Dunne died and at the subsequent disposal sale of his bloodstock, Ascetic's Silver was knocked down to the Honourable Aubrey Hastings for £800. Third son of the 13th Earl of Huntingdon, Aubrey Hastings trained at Wroughton in Wiltshire, one of his principal patrons being Prince Franz Hatzfeldt, a famous international sportsman for whom Ascetic's Silver had been purchased. Taking his pick of his three, trainer Aubrey Hastings chose to ride Ascetic's Silver in what was to be a second attempt at the National for both horse and rider.

After one false start, the field were sent on their way to a great roar from the stands, Dathi and Phil May at the head of the pack as they charged towards the first fence. With all safely over, the next jump brought the downfall of Dathi, leaving Phil May just ahead of the favourite, John M.P., who thrilled the spectators with his brilliant jumping. Blazing a very fast trail, the two leaders swept over Becher's in excellent style. Still racing together up front, Phil May and John M.P. came to the Canal Turn at speed, only for the latter to totally misjudge the ditch. With Drumcree having joined Phil May in the lead, they both blundered badly at the water jump, surrendering their positions to Oatlands and Timothy Titus. By the time they arrived back at Becher's Brook, Timothy Titus had opened up a clear lead from Buckaway II, Ascetic's Silver and Red Lad, but two fences later the Canal Turn proved the undoing of Timothy Titus. Gladiator fell at Valentine's and it was from here that Ascetic's Silver took command, striding out in front comfortably. At the final ditch before the racecourse, he put in such a splendid leap that he landed well clear of his rivals and full of running. With nothing near enough to issue any real challenge, Ascetic's Silver took the last two fences safely on his own and romped on to pass the post ten lengths in front of Red Lad, with Aunt May third, two lengths further back. Of the six others who completed the course, Gladiator and Phil May were both remounted.

The winning time was but two seconds outside the record set up by Cloister 13 years earlier and the proud owner, Prince Hatzfeldt, gave all the credit for the success to trainer-rider Aubrey Hastings and not without good reason. In order to make the weight, Hastings had almost starved himself.

Despite the presence of two past winners of the race, the field of 23 for the 1907 Grand National was condemned by journalists as the most sub-standard in the history of the event.

With no clear favourite it was an unusually open betting market, Ascetic's Silver and Red Lad jointly holding most attention at 7/1, and as these were the first two home last year it was obvious that the punters' were playing safe.

The majority of the runners were making their first attempt in the National and of these one horse stood head and shoulders above the rest, a seven-year-old gelding named Eremon. Descended from the mighty Pocahontas, he was by Thurles out of Daisy, having been bred at Streamstown, County Meath, by James Cleary. Almost unsellable because of a suspicion that he was thick-winded, Eremon was eventually purchased by Mr Stanley Howard for £400 and didn't see a racecourse until he was six years old, when he fell in a steeplechase at Haydock Park. His trainer, Tom Coulthwaite, soon found, however, that Eremon was a quick learner and his progress was something of a revelation to most, for in that first season he won three of his eight races. Coulthwaite, the man in charge of his preparation, was quite a character who before becoming involved with racehorses had trained athletes, only slightly modifying his methods to accommodate his equine pupils. His yard at Hednesford in Staffordshire turned out a steady supply of winners and in 1907 Eremon made a more than useful contribution. On the run-up to Aintree he ran three times, coming second at Birmingham before comfortably winning his next two contests at Warwick and Haydock. Obviously in terrific form, Eremon went to the start of the National a well-fancied 8/1 shot, ridden by 25-year-old Alf Newey, a native of Halesowen in Worcestershire. The first of his family ever to be involved in horse-racing, Alf started his working life as a miner and never sat on a horse until he was 18.

Away at the second attempt, they charged across the road to the first fence with Eremon marginally ahead of the pack and with only Kilts falling here, the gallop remained fast. Alf Newey found himself in trouble when landing in front over the second, a stirrup leather snapped and as he struggled to regain his balance Timothy Titus overtook him. Jumping Becher's, Eremon was upsiders Timothy Titus, these two heading Roman Law, Centre Board, Extravagance and Red Lad, but as they turned to the Canal Turn, Newey discovered his troubles were not yet over. The riderless Rathvale ranged up alongside Eremon and in the most vicious manner began snapping at the neck of Alf Newey's mount. In an attempt to drive the pest away, Alf was forced to use his whip but after the briefest respite Rathvale began attacking Eremon again. When Timothy Titus came down at the twelfth, Eremon was left clear and racing on to the racecourse, Newey spurred his mount on in the hope of shaking off the offending loose horse. The devilish Rathvale was momentarily distracted coming to the water jump as Extravagance moved up to challenge, switching his attention to the newcomer to such effect that Extravagance took a heavy fall here. Out on his own again, except for the annoying company of the riderless nuisance, Eremon raced back to Becher's Brook, with Rathvale swerving from side to side across his path and although his mount was foot perfect at every fence, Alf Newey couldn't relax for a second. With Roman Law and York II falling at the Brook, the leader was now a long way in front of his nearest rivals, taking the Canal Turn at least ten lengths to the good. Still accompanied by the loose Rathvale, Alf Newey kicked for home. Turning into the second-last fence Eremon was still going strong and as he jumped it the nearest challenger was the rapidly improving Tom West. Still making ground after clearing the last, Tom West for a brief moment looked a real threat but, sticking to his task resolutely, Eremon held on to win with something in hand by six lengths from Tom West. A long way back in third place came Patlander, in front of five others including Ascetic's Silver.

Both Eremon and his hard-worked jockey fully deserved their victory and the reception they received from the admiring crowds was never more justified. Ten days later Eremon made a mockery of his 12lb penalty for the Aintree victory by making a procession of the Lancashire 'Chase at Manchester to win as he liked. The critics were made to eat their words, for the 'sub-standard' National field had produced a winner seemingly capable of anything and one could only imagine with eager anticipation just how good Eremon would be the following year. Nobody was ever to find out, for soon after the Manchester win Eremon bolted on the gallops and injured himself so badly that he had to be put down.

Although, sadly, the 1908 National was without its most recent winner, Eremon, Mr Frank Bibby's Kirkland was back as 13/2 favourite and the inclusion in the field of the royal representative Flaxman insured another visit to Liverpool of His Majesty the King.

The previous year's runner-up, Tom West, was strongly fancied to go one better, sharing second spot in the betting with an exciting newcomer called Springbok at odds of 8/1.

The American millionaire sportsman, Mr Foxhall Keene, acquired a keen interest in the Grand National some years earlier and having got steeplechasing off the ground in his own country, set his sights on Aintree's famous race. His two runners that year, Chorus and Prophet III, were both English bred but considered to be racing on behalf of the United States.

It was the reverse way round for rank outsider Rubio, American bred but his connections very much British. By the English-bred stallion Star Ruby out of La Toquera, Rubio was bred at the Rancho del Paso Stud in California by James Ben Ali Haggin, who shipped him as part of a consignment of yearlings halfway round the world to Newmarket. The infant Rubio obviously had little appeal about him, for at the auction he was knocked down for a measly 15 guineas to Major Frank Douglas-Pennant. Turned out to mature, in the hope that he would one day make a hunter, the youngster flourished under the care of trainer Bernard Bletsoe, a man associated with Grudon, the 1901 National winner. As a five-year-old, Rubio won the three 'chases he competed in, then broke down so badly that many close friends of Major Douglas-Pennant suggested the horse should be put down. The owner would have none of it, however, sending Rubio to the landlord of the Prospect Arms Hotel in Towcester. Believing that some hard roadwork may be beneficial to the animal, the instructions were that he should be used to pull the hotel bus to transport the guests. After almost two years of this 'treatment' Rubio was put back into training, this time with Fred Withington at Danebury in Hampshire, and it was soon apparent that he was back to full fitness. As the stable's second string, Henry Bletsoe, son of Rubio's original trainer, took the mount on the 66/1 outsider when the more senior William Blissill elected to partner the better-fancied Mattie Macgregor.

Roman Law was the first to show as they made their way to the first fence, where Prophet III and Seisdon Prince made early exits. A group of horses landed over the second almost together, with Rubio and Johnstown Lad fractionally in front of Flaxman, Roman Law and Mattie Macgregor, while Kirkland only avoided being brought down by the slithering Extravagance. Continuing in this order to Becher's, Roman Law regained the advantage landing over the Brook, at which Lara fell when lying fourth and the nearest to the leader going to the Canal Turn were Tom West, Flaxman, Mattie Macgregor and Rubio. Strung well out as the leading group came back onto the racecourse, Rubio appeared to be revelling in the poor underfoot conditions and he jumped the water ahead of The Lawyer III, Dathi and Springbok. Back at Becher's Rubio jumped it perfectly, still in the lead. Another splendid leap at the Canal Turn brought a roar of appreciation for Rubio from the crowd but just when the King's horse Flaxman seemed to be in with a chance, his jockey, Algy Anthony, lost an iron when his mount stumbled. At the Anchor crossing Mattie Macgregor moved up sweetly to challenge her front-running stablemate and Kirkland suddenly appeared threateningly, having made up an enormous amount of ground. The crowds in the stands were brought to their feet in anticipation of a close finish but the former bus-horse Rubio somehow found a new energy source, for he quickened going to the final fence, cleared it brilliantly and romped home a ten-length winner from his more favoured stable companion, Mattie Macgregor. After a gap of six lengths came The Lawyer III in third place, followed in by the unlucky Flaxman and four others, including the remounted Kirkland who had fallen at the last fence.

Fred Withington, as the first man to send out the first two home in a Grand National, was spoken of as a genius and Henry Bletsoe was also praised for his handling of the horse. But the day belonged to Rubio, who had travelled from the sunshine of California to the mud of Aintree for his date with destiny.

Eight

1909-1921

It was a very happy new year in January 1909 as Britain introduced old age pensions for citizens of 70 and over, with the Chancellor of the Exchequer, David Lloyd George, raising taxes to fund the enterprise. American President William Taft announced plans for a new naval base intended to defend the United States at Pearl Harbor in the Hawaiian Islands. Dover Castle was the scene of the last technological marvel when Frenchman Louis Bleriot landed there after a 43-minute flight across the English Channel to win a £1,000 prize offered by the *Daily Mail.*

The shock result of the previous year's Grand National tempted owners for the 1909 event, resulting in 32 runners lining up on the day, thus equalling the record field of 1850.

In what developed as a wide-open betting race, Shady Girl shared favouritism at 100/9 with the youngest contestant, a fine-looking chestnut named Lutteur III. Bred in France by Gaston Dreyfus, the son of St Damien was bought as a yearling by James Hennessy, of the famous brandy family, for 610 guineas, but proved too slow when raced on the flat as a two-year-old. It was only the trainer, George Batchelor, who dissuaded the owner from selling the horse and, after using him as a hack, Lutteur III did not re-enter training until the middle of 1907. The transformation in the horse when put over fences was remarkable. Of the six steeplechases he competed in as a four-year-old, Lutteur III won five and was beaten only a neck in the other, all of these contests being at Auteuil. His preparation for the Grand National was conducted at Lewes by trainer Harry Escott, who rounded off the countdown to Aintree by saddling him to win the Champion Sweepstakes 'Chase at Hurst Park. Always ridden by the stylish and very strong French jockey, Georges Parfrement, Lutteur III looked an absolute picture of fitness in the paddock and although joint favourite there remained a doubt among many whether, at only five years old, the horse was too young.

With a perfect spring day and the ground ideal, the big field were sent on their way without any problems, Rubio making the pace to and over the first fence, at which there was not a single faller. Touching down over the Brook Rubio was still in command from Shady Girl, Mattie Macgregor, Tom West and Ascetic's Silver. Some way to the rear at this point was Lutteur III. Rubio was still in front, closely followed by stablemate Mattie Macgregor, but as they came to the water jump Rubio broke down and fell at the halfway stage of the race. With Mattie Macgregor leading going back into the country the race now began in earnest and there was a new leader when Mattie Macgregor came down at the open ditch. Tom West assumed command going towards Becher's Brook, with Caubeen, Judas and Shady Girl close up and Lutteur III beginning to make a forward move. Jockey Georges Parfrement brought Lutteur III through with the smoothest of runs, taking up the running the fence after Valentine's and, going well within himself, the French horse had his rivals struggling to keep pace approaching the second last. Barring a fall the race was his and, jumping the last two fences perfectly, Lutteur III stayed on well to win by two lengths from the fast-finishing Judas, with Caubeen and Tom West a long way back in third and fourth places.

A very popular winner on both sides of the English Channel, Lutteur III was a very good winner on the day and a credit to his trainer Harry Escott. Georges Parfrement not only rode a superb race, he took the trouble to find out everything he could about the National beforehand, studying maps and adapting his own style to suit the peculiarities of Aintree's fences. Within a few months of winning the National, Parfrement won his own nation's principal jump race, the Grande Steeplechase de Paris, for the first of three times. He lost his life in 1923 as a result of a fall in a race at Enghian.

Although the assembled runners for the 1910 National had no previous winners of the race among them, it was nonetheless an interesting assortment, with a few familiar names and an abundance of new ones.

While still only seven years old, Jerry M was already being compared with the mighty Cloister, to such a degree that for this his first Grand National, he received the handicapper's dubious accolade of 12st 7lb.

Another bearing the colours of a past winner of the race was nine-year-old Jenkinstown, making his second appearance in the event in an effort to give owner Stanley Howard a repeat of the victory achieved by Eremon. By Hackler out of Playmate, he was bred by Mr P. Leonard in County Meath, and upon being purchased by James Daly won a couple of 'chases for that gentleman before being bought by Mr Howard early in 1908. Trained, like Eremon, by Tom Couthwaite, the gelding was most disappointing in his first four races and after being pulled up in Aintree's Grand Sefton 'Chase was not seen on a racecourse again for over 12 months. Returning after that lengthy lay-off with a victory over two miles at Wolverhampton, Jenkinstown was hardly illuminating in his three runs before Aintree. It was therefore something of a surprise to find Mr Howard's contender fourth in the betting at 100/8, the consensus being that a large amount of stable money was invested on Jenkinstown. His partner was the talented Yorkshire-born jockey Bob Chadwick who with Judas last year had been beaten just two lengths.

After early snow showers the sun came out to greet the runners as they paraded in front of the stands, with most admiring eyes cast in the direction of 6/1 favourite Jerry M, who looked superb at the head of the line. From a good start they charged into the country, with Jerry M showing prominently among the leading bunch. It was his forward position which probably saved the favourite from the chaos which ensued at the early fences, for after the third obstacle almost half the field had been eliminated. Approaching Becher's for the first time, Jerry M was in front with the outsider Odor in close attendance. With no change in the order, they raced on, round the Canal Turn, over Valentine's and back towards the racecourse and by this time quite a number of those still in the race were tailed off. Taking advantage of his light weight, the owner-rider, Mr Hall, took Odor to the front, jumping the water in advance of Fetlar's Pride, Glenside, Jerry M and Springbok, these five being some way clear of the only five others still in the contest. Jenkinstown was at the forefront of the second group. Jumping Becher's in fine style, Springbok now led from Logan Rock, Jerry M and Fetlar's Pride, the quartet being close together but, keeping this order over the Canal Turn, Springbok's jockey, Bill Payne, found himself in trouble when his saddle slipped. He had no alternative but to pull his mount up. With Jerry M now in command it looked as if the race was at his mercy, jumping Valentine's clear of the remainder and still going strong. Even when joined by Jenkinstown as they came back on the racecourse, so well was Jerry M travelling that it appeared he only need stay on his feet to win. Side by side over the last two fences, they landed together on the flat to a crescendo of cheering from the packed stands and only as the two brave horses began that so-long run to the post did the unequal struggle become obvious to all. With every ounce of the 30lb he was conceding to his rival costing him dearly, Jerry M battled on gamely like the great horse he undoubtedly was, but it was to no avail as Jenkinstown gradually inched ahead to win by three lengths from Jerry M, with Odor the same distance back in third place. Carsey and Fetlar's Pride came in at their own time, the only others to finish the race.

Jockey Bob Chadwick, no doubt still on cloud nine after his National triumph, rounded off a memorable Aintree fixture 24 hours later by winning the Liverpool Handicap Hurdle on Indian Runner for Liverpool owner Mr

Hall-Walker. For one other jockey the 1910 Grand National lowered the curtain on an illustrious career which included riding the only royal winner of the race. Algy Anthony retired from the saddle painfully after suffering two broken ribs from his fall with Judas. He would, though, in his new role as a trainer, be seen at Aintree again.

Sadly the same could not be said of the man who so closely shared in Anthony's finest racing moment. His Majesty King Edward VII died on 6 May and having contributed so much to steeplechasing in general and the Grand National in particular, the royal colours would not be seen over Aintree's fences for a great many years.

To the regret of a multitude of racegoers, Jerry M was missing from the National line-up in 1911, rumours suggesting that his owner, being furious at the weights allocated to his champion, sought to teach the authorities a lesson by refusing to let Jerry M compete anywhere that year. What is probably nearer the truth is that the horse needed a well-earned rest after not just his excellent performance in the National but a fabulous achievement in winning the Grande Steeplechase de Paris at Auteuil so soon after Liverpool.

Top weight in the absence of Jerry M was Lutteur III, back after a break from activity and, despite his 12st 3lb, favourite of the 26 runners at 7/2.

Representing Mr Bibby was Glenside, a nine-year-old bay gelding by St Gris out of Kilwinnet, bred in Ireland by Mr W.G. Peareth. He never raced in his native land, first appearing in the record books of 1908 under the ownership of Mr R.H. Harries, for whom he won a small 'chase at Ludlow. For the next 12 months Glenside competed in mediocre events on both sides of the Welsh border, with only limited success, and after winning a three-mile 'chase at Tenby in January 1909 he was purchased by Frank Bibby. At Hooton Park, on his first appearance in his new owner's colours, Glenside won and although that was his only success up to the spring of 1911, he did provide encouragement by finishing second in the Grand Sefton 'Chase at Aintree at the end of his second season. Trained by Captain Robert H. Collis at Kinlet in Worcestershire, Glenside was due to be ridden by Frank Mason, but when that jockey broke his leg shortly before the big day, a substitute was hurriedly sought. It was the trainer, Captain Collis, who made the selection, choosing an amateur who had already ridden Glenside on a number of occasions. John Randolph Anthony was barely 21 years of age, the youngest of three Welsh brothers from Carmarthenshire who while still in their teens were renowned far and wide for their prowess in the saddle. Despite his mount having only one eye and reputedly suffering from respiratory problems, Jack Anthony was delighted with Glenside, diligently setting out his own tactics for his first Grand National ride.

At the very first fence five came to grief and each obstacle down to Becher's claimed at least one victim. As Rathnally led over Becher's there were barely a dozen left in the race. The favourite, Lutteur III, mistimed his jump at the fence after Becher's to finish up stuck on top of it and at the Canal Turn Hercules II fell. Jack Anthony kept Glenside to the outside of the course in order to give the horse a chance to see as much of the obstacles as possible with his limited vision and it had served an extra purpose with them avoiding the chaos about them. Caubeen and the American-bred Precentor II brought the well-strung-out survivors back onto the racecourse, still in front jumping the water. At the nineteenth Precentor II fell and Rathnally moved upsides Caubeen, the pair jumping Becher's together well clear of Glenside and a few stragglers surrounded by a host of riderless horses. The two leaders both made for the gap in the twenty-third fence caused by Lutteur III on the first circuit and in a split-second they paid the penalty. Caubeen and Rathnally collided and both crashed to the ground. Glenside and Jack Anthony found themselves in front, on their own, with seven fences still to go and a veritable quagmire between them and the safety of the finish. Coming to the second-last fence, it was obvious that Glenside was almost out on his feet but his young rider held him together, displaying a skill and understanding rare in one so young. Safely over the final fence, Glenside and Jack Anthony kept on up the straight and to well-deserved applause from the crowds passed the winning post, the only competitor not to fall. Twenty lengths behind came the remounted Rathnally, followed by two others who had also had to be remounted, Shady Girl and Fool-Hardy.

In a little over ten and a half minutes John Randolph Anthony had emerged from comparative obscurity to become a household name, as the youngster who had guided a one-eyed, broken-winded horse through conditions resembling a battlefield to win the greatest steeplechase on earth. It was a certainty he would be heard of again at Aintree.

As the result of a coal miners' strike there was for a while a doubt about the 1912 Grand National actually taking place and although, fortunately, the threat to the race was eventually removed, the disruption to transport resulted in the smallest attendance at Aintree ever recorded. But it was a field of fine quality steeplechasers and the greatest attraction for those who could manage to get to the National was the return of Jerry M.

By Walmsgate from an unnamed mare by the stallion Luminary, Jerry M owed his existence to Miss Kate Hartigan who bred him at Croom in County Limerick, and as a yearling he was sold very cheaply to John Widger of Waterford. Mr Widger named the newly purchased youngster after a local horse-breeder, Jerry Mulcair, and Jerry M won his first two races over fences in Widger's scarlet colours when still only four years of age. Continuing the good work, the gelding won his first two 'chases in 1908, both at Dublin

Metropolitan meetings at Baldoyle, and by now had caught the eye of Dublin-born trainer Bob Gore. A descendant of the Earls of Arran, Robert George Gore came to England in his mid-20s to act as assistant trainer to William Murland and ride as an amateur. In 1887 he branched out as a trainer in his own right, with his yard at Findon in Sussex, and quickly established himself with a steady succession of winners. Among his owners was Mr Charles Assheton-Smith, previously known as Charles G. Duff, the owner of Cloister, and it was on this gentleman's instructions that Bob Gore purchased Jerry M from John Widger for £1,200. The new owner had taken quite a bit of persuading to buy the Irish five-year-old, for the horse had always been a little thick in the wind but the trainer's confidence was soon justified when Jerry M won the valuable New Century Steeplechase at Hurst Park, first time out for Mr Assheton-Smith. Less than a fortnight later, at the Grand National meeting, he was in the winner's enclosure again after a runaway victory in the Stanley Steeplechase. With two further wins from his next three races, including another Liverpool triumph in the Becher 'Chase, Jerry M had set the jumping scene alight. His narrow defeat under an impossible burden in the 1910 National, followed by an outstanding performance in the Grande Steeplechase de Paris, endeared him to the nation, and although incurring an injury in the French race which kept him out of racing for a prolonged period, his record spoke for itself. Once more carrying 12st 7lb and with a new jockey in the form of Ernie Piggott, Jerry M started joint favourite with Rathnally at 4/1. Shortly before the Grand National the owner received a knighthood, becoming Sir Charles Assheton-Smith, and was doubly represented in the big race with the six-year-old Covertcoat carrying his second colours.

Jumping off well at the start, Rathnally led over the first fence, only to fall at the first ditch which also caused the downfall of Glenside, and with Caubeen now taking up the running they raced on to Becher's Brook. Over the Brook, the order of running was Caubeen, Bloodstone, Jerry M, Axle Pin and Sir Halbert. At the Canal Turn the two leaders were almost forced off the course when Ballyhackle ran very wide after landing, while immediately behind Ernie Piggott faced every jockey's nightmare when confronted with a loose horse straddling the fence. To his amazement and relief, Jerry M cleared both obstructions in his stride, the pair going on some five lengths to the rear of the leaders, Caubeen and Bloodstone. Back on the racecourse, Ballyhackle and Sir Halbert were lying third and fourth just behind the leading pair, with Jerry M hard held in fifth place and in this order they swept over the water jump. Even at this stage the stands spectators were thrilled by the precise and powerful jumping of Jerry M, but with still another circuit to cover the weight he was conceding to each of his rivals was daunting. Caubeen maintained his advantage over Becher's and at the next fence Jenkinstown injured himself and was pulled up at once. The Canal Turn saw the last of Ballyhackle when he unseated his rider and with Caubeen still showing the way they turned for home. Tiring rapidly, however, before reaching the Anchor Bridge, Caubeen dropped back through the field, leaving a tightly bunched group to sort out the finish between them. The outsider Bloodstone led into the final fence, followed by Jerry M, Carsey, Mount Prospect's Fortune and Axle Pin but it could be seen clearly that Ernie Piggott had not yet moved an inch on his horse. Once having landed on the flat, Jerry M forged ahead, defying the handicapper and reason to leave the rest toiling in his wake. At the post he was six lengths ahead of the second horse Bloodstone, with Lord Derby's Axle Pin a further four lengths back in third place. Carsey finished fourth, followed home by three others.

Amid scenes of joy, reminiscent of the royal victory 12 years before, Jerry M was led in by his delighted owner. Still only nine years of age, expectations were high that Jerry M would return in a year's time for a repeat of this fabulous victory. As it transpired, Jerry M never ran in a race again. An injury to his back brought about another lay-off, which in turn worsened his breathing malady and he was retired to his owner's estate at Vaynol Park near Bangor in North Wales. Developing a painful wasting disease, Jerry M was put down to spare him further suffering, shortly after the death of Sir Charles Assheton-Smith at the end of 1914.

The 1912 National was also the last race Jenkinstown contested, for he died shortly after the race.

The critics were scathing again in 1913, declaring the Grand National field sub-standard and the quality of the 22 runners undeserving of the prize money.

Favourite at 5/1 was Ballyhackle, something of an erratic character the previous year, though alleged to have improved in the meantime. Another with his share of punters' money riding with him as a result of a recent victory at Hurst Park was Covertcoat, in the colours made famous most recently by Jerry M and before that by Cloister.

Bred in Ireland by James J. Maher, the seven-year-old was by Hackler out of Cinnamon, and after a spell of running for his breeder, won a maiden plate at Punchestown for Mr Maher. When James Maher decided to give up training to concentrate on breeding, Covertcoat was sold to Bob Gore for £1,075. As with Jerry M, the intended owner was Sir Charles Assheton-Smith, but unlike trainer Gore's first selection, Covertcoat proved extremely disappointing. It was only in his last three races before Aintree that the gelding displayed anything like what was expected of him, winning twice and finishing a close second in the other. Jockey Ernie Piggott was due to take the mount in the National but injured his hand shortly before the race and a chance ride fell into the lap of Percy

Woodland. Since riding Drumcree to Grand National glory ten years earlier, Percy had ridden mostly in France, winning the French Derby in 1906 and again in 1910, but now aged 31 he was still an ideal pilot for Aintree.

Away to a fine start, The Rejected IV led them over the first fence, where the American-bred Highbridge was the only faller. The French-bred grey, Trianon III, took them on to Becher's, at which point Blow Pipe became the new leader with a fine leap over the Brook. Followed closely by Ballyhackle, Merry Land, Carsey and The Rejected IV, Blow Pipe galloped on well, over and round the Canal Turn and down to Valentine's. At each fence on the run back to the racecourse, horses fell, lost their riders or refused and it was a greatly reduced number which approached the end of the first circuit. That old Aintree stalwart, Carsey, led over the water jump and raced on back for the final round. With Carsey still leading over the Brook from Irish Mail, the only other within a reasonable distance of these two was Covertcoat. Turning towards the straight with just two fences left, these three were the only runners left in the race and of the trio, Carsey was travelling much the stronger. At the final fence Carsey fell and Percy Woodland immediately shot Covertcoat into a clear lead, racing clear of the weary Irish Mail to win by a distance. Carsey was remounted to finish third and last.

Apart from the winning connections, few found much to celebrate, with the race reduced to just three horses for the better part of the final circuit. The race did, however, prove that Percy Woodland still knew his way around Aintree and nobody could begrudge him his success.

Covertcoat ran in only another three races, never again entering the winner's enclosure, and he was retired after failing to get round in the 1914 Grand National.

It was unusual to find two past winners of the National not only heading the handicap but also in the same position in the betting market, yet that was the situation on Grand National Day 1914.

Covertcoat was 7/1 favourite despite shouldering 12st 7lb, just 1lb more than the 1909 winner Lutteur III who, together with Ilston, was the second-best-backed horse in the race at 10/1. Another French horse, Trianon III, was also well supported, as indeed were Ballyhackle, Jacobus, Bloodstone and Sunloch.

It was Sunloch, an eight-year-old bay gelding, who some little time before the big race caught the attention of Sir Charles Assheton-Smith, the owner of the last two National winners. Sir Charles attempted to buy Sunloch, so lightly weighted at Aintree that he was receiving fully 3st from Covertcoat, but was told emphatically that the horse was not for sale. Bred in Leicestershire by Mr H.S. Blair, he was by the local stallion Sundorne out of Gralloch and developed into such a fine-looking youngster that Mr Blair hunted him and won prizes with him at the local agricultural shows. A sporting farmer from nearby Loughborough, named Tom Tyler, eventually bought Sunloch for £300 on behalf of a client who didn't materialise, so Tyler set about training the horse for steeplechasing. The gelding's first race was in a farmers' plate at Croxton Park in April 1912 when, carrying the colours of a Mr H.S. Black, he was beaten into second place by a neck. Proving a more consistent performer, the following season Sunloch won four times and was second the same number of times from ten outings. In his final race of three prior to the National, Sunloch won by a distance over two miles at Derby when ridden by his big race jockey, Bill Smith. Cheltenham-born Smith was just beginning to be noticed on the turf and, although somewhat inexperienced, had made much of the running on Blow Pipe in the previous year's race.

The 20 runners got away to a good start, with Sunloch going into the lead straightaway and quickly opening up a substantial gap between himself and the rest. Sunloch treated the big fences as if they were an everyday gallop for him and jumped Becher's 20 lengths clear of his nearest rival. Over the water jump Sunloch was a fence in front of the remainder and on the second circuit his advantage was increased to 40 lengths. Completely on his own, he jumped Becher's Brook splendidly for the final time and at this point there were only five trailing him, a very long way behind. Trianon III and Lutteur III both made up an enormous amount of ground from the Anchor Bridge but with Sunloch never slackening, their task was impossible bar a fall by the leader. With another two perfect leaps over the final two fences, Sunloch stayed on, an all-the-way winner, by eight lengths from Trianon III with Lutteur III the same distance away in third place. The only other to finish was Rory O'Moore.

The winning owner-trainer, Mr Tyler, appeared the calmest man at Aintree after the race, leading his winner in as if he'd just taken a farmers' race at his local Leicester track. Jockey William J. Smith was beside himself with excitement, having won the Grand National on only his second ride in the race. The following year he was to win the jump jockeys' championship for most winners ridden in the season.

Sir Charles Assheton-Smith renewed his offer to buy Sunloch and a fortnight after his start-to-finish triumph at Aintree the horse became his property. Sadly, Sir Charles died later in the year, before it became obvious to all that Sunloch was no longer much use in racing.

Less than three months after the 1914 Grand National, a madman assassinated Archduke Ferdinand, heir to the Austrian Empire, in Sarajevo, sparking the flame which led to the ultimate insanity in August, the outbreak of the Great War.

With the war across the Channel at a stage of stalemate, the 1915 Grand National brought a little light relief to a nation still coming to terms with being at war.

Again no previous winner of the race was among the 20 runners and the favourite was Irish Mail at 7/1, from Lord Marcus, Silver Top, Balscadden and Father Confessor.

In the seven and a half months since the beginning of the war, the role of women in the day-to-day practical running of the country had been something of a revelation to certain sections of British society. Their value it seemed could only be recognised in a time of crisis and with almost the entire male population of the country confronting the enemy, the gentler sex came into its own.

Bearing these somewhat feminist views in mind, nothing could have been more fitting than a woman having a runner in that year's race. The horse was the six-year-old bay gelding Ally Sloper and the owner, Lady Nelson. Bred in Lincolnshire by Mr C.J.C. Hill, he was by Travelling Lad out of Sally in our Alley, and as a yearling was sold at Doncaster for a mere 25 guineas to Sugden Armitage. In due course Lady Nelson paid £700 for Ally Sloper and he came under the care of trainer, the Honourable Aubrey Hastings at Wroughton. As a four-year-old gelding he ran 13 times, winning three of his races and showing scope for improvement, which came in 1914. Of his seven contests that season he won three, including the Stanley Steeplechase and the Valentine 'Chase, both at Aintree. This was very impressive form for such a young 'chaser and although he ran a little indifferently on a couple of occasions in 1915, it was surprising to find Ally Sloper at 100/8 in the National, especially with Jack Anthony riding him.

From a good start the field raced into the first fence and although they all cleared this safely falls were again plentiful as the race progressed. At the second, Ally Sloper made a complete hash of the obstacle, shooting his rider so far forward that Jack Anthony was at the point of parting company with his mount when a saving hand pulled him back into the saddle. The hand belonged to Jack's brother, Ivor, racing alongside on Ilston. Some way behind the leaders jumping Becher's Ally Sloper made another dreadful error at the Canal Turn and, clinging to his mount's neck for many yards, this time Jack Anthony found his own way back into the plate. At the head of the field an exciting contest was in progress, involving the American-bred Alfred Noble, Balscadden, Jacobus and Father Confessor, and in this order they jumped the water in front of the stands. Remarkably, the jumping of Ally Sloper improved on the second circuit and steadily he began making up the ground he had lost earlier. By the time he cleared Becher's Ally Sloper was almost in touch with the leaders. At the second last Balscadden fell when in front and Jack Anthony sent Ally Sloper on, touching down after the final fence in the lead. With Jacobus putting in a determined effort on the run to the line, it was a rousing finish but Ally Sloper held on to win by two lengths, Father Confessor coming in third eight lengths behind Jacobus.

As the first lady to own a Grand National winner, Lady Nelson was welcomed with a fondness by all and her praise of her jockey's horsemanship was in the finest tradition of the sport.

After the last race on Saturday, 27 March 1915, Aintree closed its gates and the racecourse was handed over to the War Department. It would be four years before brave horses and gallant men thrilled the crowds here again and in that time the world continued its madness, wiping out an entire generation in the process and destroying the dreams and aspirations of many millions.

Some four months after armistice brought the Great War to an end, Aintree racecourse became the centre of the sporting world once more, with 22 competitors preparing to thrill the huge crowd assembled on 28 March 1919.

Apart from the two former winners, Ally Sloper and Sunloch, the rest of the field were tackling the National for the first time. Far and away the most popular choice of punters was the 11/4 favourite Poethlyn. A nine-year-old bay gelding by Rydal Head out of Fine Champagne, Poethlyn was bred by Major Hugh Peel at Bryn y Pas in North Wales and as a yearling was a very sickly character. A publican named Davenport from Shrewsbury bought Poethlyn for £7 at this period in the youngster's life, selling him back to Major Peel within 12 months for £50. Placed in the care of trainer Harry Escott at Lewes, patient handling brought Poethlyn to maturity and when five years of age he won three of the six 'chases he ran in. It was the breeder's wife, Mrs Peel, whose colours Poethlyn always carried and having developed into a strong, reliable jumper he was unbeaten in four steeplechases in 1918, including a four-and-a-half-mile event at Gatwick referred to as the 'War National'. His regular jockey was Ernie Piggott and even burdened with 12st 7lb the public considered Poethlyn unbeatable.

The snow stopped, the skies cleared and sunshine bathed Aintree as the runners were sent on their way. Keeping Poethlyn handily placed throughout, Ernie Piggott avoided the many falling horses on the run to Becher's and beyond, and after jumping Valentine's the favourite was a close second to Loch Allen. As they cleared the water jump in this order, what was left of the remainder were struggling a long way behind. Taking up the running approaching Becher's, Poethlyn jumped the Brook perfectly and proceeded to dictate the pace from there on, with Ballyboggan and Pollen his only possible dangers. To the delight of the crowds all along the rails, it became a procession from the Canal Turn back to the racecourse, Poethlyn giving a fabulous display of jumping all the way. Still clear over the final fence, Poethlyn romped home the winner from Ballyboggan, with Pollen six lengths behind in third place.

As the shortest-priced winning favourite in the history of the race and only the fourth horse to succeed with 12st 7lb on his back, Poethlyn was greeted home as a 'wonderhorse', the crowds simply agog to get a close-up glance of him. Jockey Piggott also came in for an abundance of praise and rightly so, for he became the only man to partner two Grand National winners encumbered with that formidable weight of 12st 7lb.

With the world returning to a semblance of normality by 1920, the usual annoying squabbles and prejudices arose, suggesting little had been learned from the recent world-wide conflict. For the first time since the Russian Revolution in 1917, the Bolsheviks achieved overall control. In response to attacks by Sinn Fein militants, more British troops were sent to Ireland in an atmosphere of near civil war. At the height of so much international uncertainty, the American composer Jerome Kern released his latest composition, appropriately named 'Look for the Silver Lining'.

Aintree's executive increased the value of the Grand National to £5,000 in time for the 1920 running of the race and immediately the entries were published Poethlyn was installed as short-priced favourite. Among his 23 opponents were some likely prospects, such as Gerald L, Ballyboggan, Sergeant Murphy and Silver Ring, but as far as the bookmakers were concerned the only real threat to Poethlyn was the Irish-bred Troytown.

A seven-year-old bay gelding by Zria out of Diane, he was bred by Major Thomas Collins-Gerrard who put him into training with the former royal jockey Algy Anthony at the Curragh in County Kildare. Troytown made his first appearance on a racecourse on New Year's day 1919, finishing down the course in a humble novices 'chase at Baldoyle. Before the end of the year, however, he had become the pride of Ireland. After winning his next race at Leopardstown, Troytown was sent to Liverpool where, the day before Poethlyn won the revived National, Major Gerrard's gelding was running away with the Stanley Steeplechase, when his jockey took the wrong course. Two days later he rectified the error by scoring a brilliant victory over one circuit of the National course in the Champion 'Chase. Visiting Paris during that summer, Troytown made an absolute procession of the Grande Steeplechase de Paris, winning in the easiest manner imaginable. Acquiring a new rider, Aintree specialist though still an amateur Jack Anthony, for 1920 the son of Zria had two warm-up outings before his National engagement. A reasonable fourth in the Leopardstown 'Chase was followed by a most creditable second in a two-mile 'chase at Lingfield Park, where he conceded 15lb to the winner Silver Ring. At 6/1 second favourite, Troytown was three points behind the principal choice, Poethlyn.

As soon as the flag fell Troytown shot off into the lead and at the first fence Poethlyn brought a groan of despair by falling. Troytown appeared oblivious to the heavy ground, striding out boldly at the head of affairs as if wanting to make every post a winning one. At Becher's he made a prodigious leap which amazed nearby spectators and with half the journey covered the Irish horse was a long way clear of the few still in the race. Try as he may and strong as he undoubtedly was, Jack Anthony was unable to restrain Troytown in any way, being forced to allow his mount to bowl along in front, but so well was the horse jumping he wisely decided to let him have his way. Over Becher's again with another massive jump there came just one anxious moment at the fence after Valentine's, the fifth from home. Measuring his stride for the take-off, Troytown slipped on the treacherous ground and went straight through the top of the fence and it said much for the strength and agility of the horse that he recovered his balance almost at once. From there on Troytown romped home without any further damage to his progress, winning by a 12-length margin which could have been doubled from The Turk II, with The Bore six lengths behind in third place. The only others to finish were Sergeant Murphy and Neurotic.

After passing the post, Jack Anthony had a job pulling his mount up and when interviewed after weighing in, the jockey declared that he felt as if his arms had been pulled out.

Making a return journey to France later in the year, Troytown finished third in the Grande Steeplechase de Paris and after the race a decision was made to run him again six days later in the Prix des Drags. It tragically proved to be a fatal decision, for Troytown crashed at a post and rails, breaking a bone above his knee so badly that he had to be put down.

The horse whose brilliance shone so brightly for too brief a period is buried at Asnieres, where a simple headstone bears the name Troytown.

For a change, although there was no former winner in the race, neither was there the all too frequent criticism concerning the quality of the field for the 1921 Grand National.

In a very open betting contest the favourite at 9/1 was the previous year's third placed The Bore, ridden by his owner, Mr Harry Brown, who in the space of a couple of years rose from an inexperienced amateur rider to become champion of the unpaid ranks.

In such a big field the element of luck was of course greater and with many punters recognising this fact, they confined their selections to those with some proven ability. Among those with such credentials were Turkey Buzzard, Garrvoe, Old Tay Bridge, Daydawn and Shaun Spadah.

The ten-year-old brown gelding Shaun Spadah was bred in County Westmeath, Ireland, by Mr P. McKenna from the humblest origins. His sire, Easter Prize, was once sold for a measly £3 and when Shaun Spadah was purchased as a yearling by Dick Cleary of Mullingar he was sent to be trained by Algy Anthony at the Curragh. Returned by Anthony with the judgement that the horse was useless as a racehorse, he was then passed on to Mr R.G. Cleary who hunted him and taught Shaun Spadah to jump. His next owner was Frank Barbour, for whom he won four races in Ireland when six years of age, and the following year was 'chasing in England in the colours of bookmaker Mr M.H. Benson, who operated under the trade name of Douglas Stuart. By 1919 Shaun Spadah was the property of Scottish contractor Mr Malcolm McAlpine, was trained by George Poole at Lewes in Sussex and failed to get round in that year's National. In the run-up to the 1921 race the gelding was successful in both his races before Aintree and partnered by the recently turned professional Frederick Brychan Rees, was well supported at 100/9. It was the jockey's second ride in the race, having finished fifth the year before when still an amateur.

Away to a good start at the first attempt, they charged across the Melling Road towards the first fence, at which there were six fallers. The casualties mounted at each fence, rapidly reducing the field and with Turkey Buzzard leading from All White, Old Tay Bridge, Shaun Spadah and Loch Allen, they jumped Becher's. The order was the same at the Canal Turn, at which point more than half the original complement had dropped out and racing to the water jump it was Turkey Buzzard still in front of Shaun Spadah, All White and The Bore. Before travelling far onto the second circuit, Turkey Buzzard fell and within seconds All White too crashed to the ground. Just two were left in the race as Shaun Spadah and The Bore jumped Becher's side by side and the duel continued, fence by fence, with neither giving an inch on the long run home. Back on the racecourse they turned towards the penultimate fence with The Bore holding a fractional advantage and seeming to be going the better of the pair. The crowds began shouting the favourite home as The Bore measured up for the fence but he hit the obstacle hard and fell, his rider, Harry Brown, breaking his collar bone on impact with the ground. Shaun Spadah, the only horse to complete the course without falling, came past the winning post a lonely but worthy winner. Harry Brown, suffering untold agonies, remounted The Bore to finish a distressed and weary second, a long way behind the winner and an equally great distance ahead of the other two remounted horses, All White and Turkey Buzzard.

Fred Rees, the triumphant jockey, was presented to the King after weighing in, a most appropriate gesture after his perseverance in such an action-packed and gruelling contest. The victory of Shaun Spadah was a truly all-British achievement, with the horse coming from Ireland, the owner from Scotland, the trainer being English and the man in the saddle from Wales.

Nine

1922-1931

Another large field for the 1922 National once more intrigued the public and had the bookies rubbing their hands, for the more runners, the better the chance of a shock result. In theory at least.

Most heavily backed of the 32 runners was Lord Woolavington's outstanding six-year-old, Southampton, unbeaten in his last six races and with Mr Harry Brown in the saddle considered a good bet at 100/12.

A nine-year-old bay gelding called Music Hall came into many people's reckoning less than a fortnight before the big event at Aintree, when giving a sparkling performance to win over four miles at Hurst Park. He was bred in County Kildare by Mrs Freddie Blacker, who had bought his dam Molly after seeing her run in point-to-points and who subsequently rode the mare to hounds for a number of years. When mated with the stallion Cliftonhall, a winner on the flat of the Northumberland Plate, the first foal Molly produced was Music Hall and with the breeder's husband Colonel Blacker away at the war, Mrs Blacker broke the youngster herself and then hunted him. Sold when six years of age to Mrs Molly Stokes of Market Harborough, Music Hall made his first public appearance a winning one in a two-mile 'chase at Birmingham in January 1920. Before the end of that year he won a further six races for Mrs Stokes, including the Scottish Grand National at Bogside, a wonderful achievement for a horse in his first season's racing. The following year Music Hall was bought by Mr Hugh Kershaw, a Manchester cotton broker, who placed him with the newly licensed trainer Owen Anthony to be prepared at his Lambourn yard for a tilt at the National. Well up in the handicap with 11st 8lb, the gelding was ridden by Lewis Bilbie Rees, the brother of the winning jockey 12 months before.

It was another damp day for spectators when the starter brought the National field under orders but at least the going was decent this time and at flag fall they galloped away into the country. The 1921 hero, Shaun Spadah, fell at the first fence as did the favourite, Southampton, along with a few others, but it was the early loss of two of the most heavily backed horses which brought that all too familiar groan from the crowds. Sergeant Murphy made all the running, putting in a particularly fine jump at Becher's but, misjudging the ditch two fences later, he slipped into it and struggling to extricate himself brought about the downfall of Norton, General Saxham and All White. Back on the racecourse A Double Escape was in front, gamely heading a handful of survivors on to the water jump, where he led from Music Hall, Arravale and Drifter. Back in the country A Double Escape maintained his slight lead but at Becher's Arravale went for a gap in the fence only to stumble onto a prostrate horse on the landing side. With only three holding a realistic chance now, they jumped and negotiated the tricky angle at the Canal Turn, running to Valentine's in line abreast, A Double Escape, Drifter and Music Hall. Drifter badly split the coronet of his foot, to such effect that the hoof was almost hanging off, and Lewis Rees lost one of his stirrups. At the next fence A Double Escape fell, no doubt disturbed by the earlier jostling, and from there on it became a two-horse race. Galloping bravely on three legs, Drifter stuck well to his task, matching strides with Music Hall all the way back to the final fence. Landing on the flat barely a length ahead of Drifter, Music Hall raced away from his injured opponent to win by 12 lengths, with the fast-finishing Taffytus running on into third place, six lengths behind the very gallant Drifter. After a long delay, the remounted Sergeant Murphy and A Double Escape finished the contest to rousing and sympathetic applause.

Music Hall was sent to France three months later to contest the Grande Steeplechase de Paris and, ridden by Jack Anthony, was well clear of all others when he broke down close to home and had to be pulled up. The jockey's elder brother, Owen, was left with the task of restoring the horse to fitness for the next season.

The racecourse executive made an attempt in 1923 to improve the quality of horses competing in the Grand National by doubling the entry fee for each runner to £100. Of 68 original entries, 28 actually faced the starter on a foggy Friday in late March with Jack Anthony's mount, the promising young Forewarned, a warm favourite at 11/2.

Steady in the betting at 100/6 was Sergeant Murphy, once more supported by his constantly loyal followers, for at 13 years of age 'the Sergeant' was trying for the fourth time to win Aintree's great steeplechase. Bred by Gerald Walker at Athboy in County Meath, the chestnut was by General Symons out of Rose Graft and changed hands numerous times before being bought by Mr M.H. Benson and arriving in England. Never a brilliant jumper, he was a brave, dour stayer of the old-fashioned type, who in a long-distance event would be staying on when most of the opposition had called it a day. After finishing fourth in his second National in 1920, Sergeant Murphy was sold for £1,200 to the American carpet tycoon Mr John Sanford, who in turn passed the horse over to his son Stephen. The intention was that Cambridge undergraduate Stephen would hunt the ageing 'chaser but upon discovering that Sergeant Murphy was still somewhat frisky, he was put back into training with George Blackwell at Newmarket. Finishing a remounted fourth in the National 12 months before, he was ridden now by leading amateur Captain Geoffrey Bennet, who was a 28-year-old veterinary surgeon and the son of a racehorse trainer.

At the halfway stage Drifter led over the water from Sergeant Murphy, Shaun Spadah and Arravale, with Max and Punt Gun the most prominent of the labouring stragglers. As if remembering Becher's Brook from the previous year, Arravale came down there again and in so doing knocked Drifter against the improving Conjuror II. Fortunately both Drifter and Conjuror II survived the disturbance. Conjuror II was in the lead two fences from home, closely followed by a loose horse and Shaun Spadah, Sergeant Murphy, Drifter and Punt Gun. Between the last two fences Sergeant Murphy struck the front and racing away from his tired rivals jumped the final obstacle clear and stayed on to win by three lengths from Shaun Spadah. Six lengths behind the runner-up came Conjuror II, in front of Punt Gun, Drifter, Max and Cinders II.

Led in to a hero's welcome, Sergeant Murphy had at last succeeded and in doing so became the first Grand National winner to be owned by an American. There were special congratulations for the rider, Captain Bennet winning the race, like his mount, at the fourth attempt.

At the end of December, having topped the list of winning amateurs with 62 victories, Captain Geoffrey Harbord Bennet smashed his skull after being kicked after a fall at Wolverhampton. Without regaining consciousness, he died 17 days later.

In 1924, through the auspices of the National Hunt Committee a new steeplechase was introduced to the racing calendar which would one day rival the importance of the Grand National. The Cheltenham Gold Cup, over three and a quarter miles at Prestbury Park, was designed, as a level-weight affair, to attract the finest middle-distance jumpers and therefore be classed as a championship.

Despite the new feature event added to Cheltenham's National Hunt Meeting, the high spot of the jumping season remained Liverpool's Grand National fixture and that year, blessed with fine weather and good ground, the attendance was bigger than ever.

In a very competitive field of 30, the red-hot favourite at 5/2 was Conjuror II, who quite apart from courageously coming third in the race last time when injured, had been beaten only a head in the recent Cheltenham Gold Cup.

At 25/1 and making his National début at the rather late age of 11, was the chestnut gelding Master Robert, whose background was straight from the pages of a Nat Gould racing novel. Bred by Robert McKinlay at Castlefin, County Donegal, Master Robert was by Moorside II out of a 22-year-old mare called Dodds. For many years Mr McKinlay had a frustrating time with his young horse, Master Robert being twice sent back from two Curragh trainers as totally useless for racing. With the need to earn a living more important than anything else, Robert McKinlay used Master Robert as a plough horse on his farm, until an offer of £50 was made for the horse from Mrs Pat Rogers. In due course he came to England as the property of Lord Airlie and Mr Sidney Green, who bought him in the hope of Lord Airlie riding him to victory in a soldiers' race at Perth Hunt. Sent to be trained by the Honourable Aubrey Hastings at Wroughton, his lordship's ambition was realised when Master Robert carried him home in first place in the Scottish Military Plate at Perth on 30 September 1922. Hastings worked wonders with the horse in just getting him fit to race, for Master Robert was afflicted with a diseased bone in a foot, which only constant poulticing eased. Frank Cundell, a veterinary surgeon from Swindon, attended the gelding on a regular basis, prescribing hard road work which in time strengthened the foot. Just a week before the Grand National Master Robert pulled up lame after being narrowly beaten over three miles at Wolverhampton, so it was back to poultices and prayers. Another set-back rather late in the day was the decision by Mr Peter Roberts, his amateur rider, to ride something else in the race. At such a late stage most jockeys had their Aintree rides well booked and the substitute they found was Bob Trudgill, a freelance nearing the end of a hard, profitless career who had never been in a position to pick and choose his mounts. Grateful to be offered a ride in the Grand National, Trudgill very nearly lost the mount when just 24 hours before the race, he was seriously injured by a fall in the Stanley 'Chase. With commendable determination, the jockey had his leg extensively stitched up and weighed-out for the ride of his life.

After making his annual inspection of the runners in the paddock, King George V invested £5 each way on Master Robert before taking his place in the royal box and the scene was set for what promised to be another thrilling spectacle. From the start the favourite caused great excitement, galloping at the head of the field and jumping with the brilliance he had displayed in the Cheltenham Gold Cup. Leaving a host of fallen horses behind at each fence, Conjuror II was still in command at Becher's when a loose horse ran into him as he took off and that ominous groan signalled the favourite's exit. Over the Canal Turn at least six riderless horses hemmed the leading group in and at Valentine's the leading positions were held by Silvo, Sergeant Murphy, Eureka

II and Fly Mask. Nearing the stands Winnall moved into a forward position and when Sergeant Murphy almost fell at the water jump, he took up the running. Back in the country for the final round, Winnall came down at the ditch, leaving the race wide open and Old Tay Bridge and Arravale shared the lead approaching Becher's, where for the third successive year Arravale bowed out. Still dogged by loose horses, the four leaders at the Canal Turn were Silvo, Fly Mask, Old Tay Bridge and Sergeant Murphy and no sooner had they made that difficult turn than a posse of riderless horses ran right across the face of the jump bringing most of those following to a standstill. Among the few which did manage to squeeze through were Drifter, Master Robert, Wavetown and Shaun Spadah but these were still some way behind the leaders. A fantastic leap by Silvo at Valentine's brought a roar of approval from the crowd and drawing three lengths ahead, he came back onto the racecourse. Still in front over the second last, his nearest challenger, Old Tay Bridge, fell at this fence and almost at once Silvo shortened his stride on the run to the final fence. Tiring rapidly Silvo was passed before the last obstacle by Fly Mask and Master Robert. Producing a terrific burst of finishing speed at precisely the right moment, Master Robert and Bob Trudgill galloped home very worthy winners by four lengths from Fly Mask, with Silvo six lengths away third. Drifter stayed on to deprive Sergeant Murphy of fourth place.

As he was unsaddling the winner, jockey Bob Trudgill almost collapsed but, his breeches covered in blood from the torn stitches in his leg, he insisted n weighing in like the absolute professional he was. The joint owners were generous to both their heroes; immediately retiring the gallant Master Robert and rewarding the brave Bob Trudgill with £2,000.

Aintree and its world-famous steeplechase took a big technological step forward in 1925 with the introduction of an automatic starting barrier. The Jack Anthony-ridden Old Tay Bridge was 9/1 favourite, being considered unfortunate not to have at least gained a place in the previous year's event and recently showing a return to form with a win at Hurst Park.

There was also Double Chance, a nine-year-old chestnut gelding who, in the truest sense of the word, was a gift horse. Bred by Leopold de Rothschild at his Southcourt Stud, like many before him Double Chance was not very useful on the flat, winning just two small races in the colours of Mr Anthony de Rothschild. His trainer, John Watson, was encountering other problems also and they involved being able to keep the animal sound. Deciding to rid himself of the worry concerning the future of Double Chance, while at the same time giving a helping hand to a former comrade from the Great War, Mr de Rothschild made a present of the horse to Fred Archer, who had just started training at Malton. A nephew of the legendary flat-race champion jockey and grandson of William Archer, who won the National in 1858, Fred Archer had served with de Rothschild in the Royal Bucks Hussars and he proceeded to hunt Double Chance. Finding his 'gift horse' could jump, Archer entered him in 'chases, winning a couple of small events with him before the gelding broke down and had to be severely fired to preserve his legs. Back in action again at the beginning of 1925, Double Chance took a step up in class, yet won his three races before making his first visit to Aintree. Trainer Fred Archer, by now based at Newmarket, sold a half share in the horse some weeks before the race to the Liverpool cotton broker David Goold, and engaged the very talented amateur, Major John Philip Wilson, as his Grand National rider. A Yorkshireman by birth, Wilson had played cricket for that county and Cambridge University and during the war served in the Royal Flying Corps as a pilot. His hair had turned white overnight when becoming one of the first to parachute from a balloon and in action over Hull he shot down a German Zeppelin.

Drifter cut out the early work, setting a hot pace over the fences leading to Becher's and, as in the previous two years, falls were plentiful. Over Becher's Brook, the leader was followed by Silvo, Old Tay Bridge, Double Chance and Sprig but that great old favourite, Sergeant Murphy, fell at the Canal Turn. Fly Mask took up the running coming to the water jump, clearing it ahead of Double Chance, Old Tay Bridge, Sprig and Silvo, with the remainder spreadeagled to the rear. As they approached Becher's Silvo and Double Chance were in the lead and they jumped the Brook together. Of those most affected by interference, Sprig and Max were very lucky to still be in the race when at Valentine's they both received continual jostling from the riderless pests. Double Chance dropped back coming to the final jump in the country, seemingly having reached the end of his endurance and with Silvo making a dreadful mistake at that obstacle, the race was left in the grasp of Fly Mask and Old Tay Bridge. As these two jumped the final fence together, Jack Anthony took Old Tay Bridge into the lead, leaving Fly Mask easily behind. The favourite was still in front with a little over 200 yards left to run, the crowds cheering him on expectantly, but suddenly, with a blistering burst of speed, Double Chance raced up on the inside rails. Passing the post four lengths to the good, Major Wilson and Double Chance won from Old Tay Bridge, with Fly Mask a further six lengths back in third place, just in front of Sprig. Last of the other six which finished was that gallant old-stager, the remounted Sergeant Murphy.

Double Chance never competed in the Grand National again but his was a very popular victory on the day the starting gate was used for the first time in the race.

Of the 30 runners which faced the starter on a misty Liverpool day in 1926, the favourite was the previous year's fourth-placed Sprig at 5/1. Silvo, Old Tay Bridge and the newcomer Koko, fresh from his success in the Cheltenham Gold Cup, were the leading fancies after the favourite.

Interest across the Atlantic in the Grand National was at its greatest during this period, the exploits of such Yanks as Foxhall Keene, Morgan Blair and particularly Stephen Sanford beckoning other American sportsmen to emulate their achievements. One such American sufficiently tempted by the mystique of the famous Aintree spectacular was a gentleman by the name of Charles Schwartz, a wealthy polo player of some renown. Seeking a horse to represent him at Aintree, he searched high and low until, within a fortnight of the race, he managed to purchase the nine-year-old gelding Jack Horner for £4,000 with a condition of sale being that a further £2,000 would be forthcoming should the horse succeed in the National. Bred at the Melton Stud by John Musker in 1917, Jack Horner became the property of Lord Barnby when only a yearling, for many years serving his owner in the Blankney Hunt. Sold on to a Mrs Tate for 160 guineas, the gelding changed hands again and again before the American, Morgan de Witt Blair, bought him and sold a half share to Kenneth Mackay, who was later to become Lord Inchcape. Carrying Mackay's colours, Morgan Blair rode him into a creditable seventh place in the 1925 Grand National after which Mr Mackay bought him outright before making the deal with Charles Schwartz. Trained by Harvey Leader at Exning in Suffolk, Jack Horner was never thoroughly sound and the trainer regularly performed wonders in getting the horse onto a racecourse. Bill Watkinson, a jockey born in Tasmania, was delighted to accept the ride at Aintree, hoping to go one better than when finishing second on the near crippled Drifter in 1922.

Right from the off, Darracq, Bright's Boy and Lone Hand set a cracking pace into and over the first fence, at which two of the most fancied runners, Silvo and Grecian Wave, came to grief. Lone Hand took up the running after jumping Valentine's well, making his way back to the racecourse closely pursued by Bright's Boy, Darracq and Ben Cruchan. Continuing at a cracking gallop, Lone Hand jumped the water just in front of Sprig, Bright's Boy, Jack Horner, Ben Cruchan and Darracq, with Old Tay Bridge making steady progress from the rear. Moving up to challenge at Valentine's, Bright's Boy raced past Darracq after landing safely, to be almost immediately joined by Jack Anthony on Old Tay Bridge. Landing first after the last fence, Old Tay Bridge made his run for home only to be quickly overtaken by the fast-finishing Jack Horner, who went on to win by three lengths, with Bright's Boy staying on just a length behind Old Tay Bridge in third place. Fourth, for the second year running, was Sprig.

The American visitors were over the moon with the result, the more so with

Stephen Sanford's Bright's Boy coming third, but most delighted with the outcome were the connections of the winner, Jack Horner. Charles Schwartz was so pleased with his victory that he made arrangements to reward his jockey, Watkinson, with a gift of £4,000, but was persuaded to change it to £1,000 per year for four years. Tragically, three weeks after winning the National, Bill Watkinson lost his life after a fall at Bogside, the day before poor Sergeant Murphy also met his end at the same track.

A field of 37 added to the historic significance of the Grand National in 1927, as the largest number ever to contest the event on the day the first radio broadcast of the race was transmitted. Among the best-supported horses on the day were Thrown In, Silver Somme, Bright's Boy, Shaun Or and Master Billie. Clear favourite by one point from the youthful Grakle was, however, Sprig again, this time at 8/1.

Bred by Captain Richard Partridge from a mating between Marco and the mare Spry in 1917, while the officer was on leave from service at the front, the breeder's deepest wish was that when the war ended he may one day ride the horse in the Grand National. Sadly it was not to be, for Captain Partridge was killed shortly before hostilities ended in 1918. As a memorial to her lost son, Mrs Partridge put the horse into training with Tom Leader at Newmarket in the fervent hope that Sprig may fulfil at least one part of a brave soldier's dream by running in the National. Trainer Leader, whose father had been head lad to the legendary Tom Olliver, took his time with Sprig, for the gelding was prone to leg trouble, but after winning five hurdle races with the horse the decision was made to send him over fences. The transition to the major obstacles was made comfortably and with much success, as Sprig developed into a brave, fluent jumper, winning Aintree's Stanley Steeplechase when only five in 1924 and the prestigious National Hunt Handicap 'Chase at Cheltenham two years later. Fourth in each of the last two Aintree showpieces, this time he was set to carry 12st 4lb and yet his supporters were loyal enough to make him favourite. Ridden by the trainer's son, 24-year-old Ted Leader, the chestnut Sprig looked a picture of health in the paddock before the race, receiving quite a deal of attention from His Majesty the King on his pre-race inspection of the runners.

On heavy going the starter got them away to a good start, the mare Grecian Wave making the early running to the first fence, where the recent Cheltenham Gold Cup winner, Thrown In, made a premature exit. Rapidly opening up a substantial lead, Grecian Wave was way out in front over the Canal Turn, from Hawker, Sprig, Knight of the Wilderness and Keep Cool, but Grakle finished his race here by landing in the ditch. There were still a lot of horses in the race as they raced past the stands. The favourite Sprig was now left at the head of affairs, racing back into the country and it was from here that falls became plentiful. Less than a dozen horses were still in the contest as they reached Becher's again, the one-eyed rank outsider Bovril III holding the narrowest of leads on the wide outside of the course. Dwarf of the Forest was second from Keep Cool, Master Billie, Bright's Boy, Sprig and Amberwave, but at the Canal Turn Sprig produced such an amazing leap that, having taken off in fifth place, he landed in the lead. Four from home, the final open ditch, Bright's Boy hit the front with Dwarf of the Forest falling just behind and Jack Anthony was still in front with Bright's Boy over the second-last fence. Halfway to the final fence, Ted Leader made his move, taking Sprig past Bright's Boy, with Bovril III at this point a good four lengths behind. The race from the last obstacle was one of the most exciting seen in the history of the event, Sprig striding for home while an unknown, half-blind ex-hunter called Bovril III came, still on the outside, with a devastating run to leave Bright's Boy for dead and get within strides of the favourite. At the post it was Sprig by half a length from Bovril III, with Bright's Boy another length back in third place.

With one of the most popular victories ever in the history of the race, Sprig was greeted back to the winner's enclosure, hardly able to find a way through the packed crowds straining to see him. Mrs Partridge, together with the jockey, Ted Leader, were presented to the King, who congratulated them warmly without commenting on the tears in the lady's eyes.

Nobody could, in their wildest dreams, have imagined the catastrophe 112 subscribers for the 1928 National would result in. All too soon the public were to discover that the 1928 race would become famous for all the wrong reasons.

On that fateful day, 30 March 1928, a record field of 42 runners paraded in front of the stands, with Master Billie the 5/1 favourite and Sprig sharing top weight of 12st 7lb with the twice third-placed, American-owned Bright's Boy. United States involvement in British steeplechasing was reaching fever pitch at this time, solely as a result of the romance and prestige associated with Aintree's supreme test, and besides Stephen Sanford's on-going involvement, Morgan de Witt Blair was again represented, as also was a certain Mr Howard Bruce. As the owner of Billy Barton, Mr Bruce found himself in Liverpool intent on following in the footsteps of his fellow countrymen, Sanford and Schwartz, with a horse which had carried everything before it in his homeland. His starting price of 33/1 belied the interest and emotional support the American challenger aroused.

Of the many outsiders, the least considered was a ten-year-old brown gelding with the somewhat catchy name of Tipperary Tim. Bred by Mr J.J. Ryan near Dogstown in County Tipperary, by Cipango from the mare Last Lot, Tipperary Tim was named after Tim Crowe, the long-distance runner from Dundrum whose many successes included the marathon from Windsor to London.

Bought by James McKenna for 50 guineas at Goff's Sales, he was put into training at the Curragh but after six runs as a two-year-old was declared useless. Arriving in mainland Britain under the ownership of Mr C.F. Kenyon, the flat-race cast-off won a 'chase at the Tarporley Hunt early in 1924 whereupon he became the property of Mr Kenyon's brother for 240 guineas. Trained in Shropshire by Joseph Dodd, Tipperary Tim was by now tubed and as his partner at Aintree had the Chester solicitor Bill Dutton, a most accomplished amateur rider who three years earlier had won the Liverpool Foxhunters 'Chase on Upton Lad.

Getting away to a good start, Easter Hero went straight to the front, leading over the first fence. With a marvellous leap Easter Hero cleared Becher's ahead of the rest, seemingly without breaking his stride, but at the Canal Turn he made a complete hash of things. Hitting the fence hard, Easter Hero toppled back into the ditch, causing absolute mayhem as the following horses baulked at the scampering animal running to and fro in the ditch. In a matter of seconds, at only the eighth obstacle on the course, less than ten runners were still in the race. Of the fortunate survivors, Billy Barton led over Valentine's from May King, Maguelonne and The Ace II, followed by a meagre assortment of stragglers. The forlorn little group was almost further reduced in number when Billy Barton dropped his hind legs in the water, but he recovered to carry on in the lead from De Combat, May King and Great Span, with Maguelonne and Tipperary Tim the only others still continuing. Shortly after jumping Valentine's May King fell and as Maguelonne had been pulled up by then, the contest was reduced to just three with Great Span appearing to be going the best of them. At the second-last fence, though, Great Span's saddle slipped and his 17-year-old jockey, Bill Payne, was deposited on the ground. Rising at the final jump, Billy Barton was on the inside, Tipperary Tim on the outside and the riderless Great Span between them but the American horse hit the fence hard and fell. Tipperary Tim passed the winning post, the first 100/1 winner in the history of the race and although virtually unknown still received the cheers of a shocked and bewildered crowd. Billy Barton was remounted by his jockey, Tommy Cullinan, to gain second place as the only other to get round.

Winning owner Harold Kenyon collected the record amount of £11,255 for his unexpected triumph and in America a statue of Billy Barton was erected outside Laurel Park racecourse in honour of a very brave effort. Giving up the law as a career, William Parker Dutton became a successful trainer and in 1956 saddled Limber Hill to win the Cheltenham Gold Cup.

Before the next Grand National the ditch at the Canal Turn was filled in, hopefully removing any likelihood of a repeat of the calamity which enabled Tipperary Tim to become the greatest surprise winner the race had known.

The financial markets of the world were shattered to their very foundations in 1929 when a run on the New York Stock Exchange brought about the Wall Street Crash. Its effect was far reaching, causing mass unemployment and the Great Depression, which was to last until 1932.

Drastic amendments were made to the conditions of entry for that year's Grand National in an effort to keep the number of runners for the event to reasonable proportions. Publication of the names of 121 entries in January brought anxious warnings from the gentlemen of the press, which increased to predictions of disaster when on the day of the race 66 runners made their way to the start.

In the 12 months since the last National, Easter Hero, the cause of all the trouble then, had undergone a welcome change of behaviour. The American multi-millionaire, John Hay Whitney, bought Easter Hero and sending him to be trained by Jack Anthony at Letcombe, a successful if unusual campaign was implemented to prepare the gelding for another crack at the Grand National. Less headstrong now, Easter Hero ran in four hurdle races, winning them all before making a procession of the 1929 Cheltenham Gold Cup to win by 20 lengths. As a result he became the 9/1 favourite for the big race at Aintree.

The previous year's winner, Tipperary Tim, was one of eight hopefuls on the 100/1 mark, as also was a seven-year-old called Gregalach.

Having the same sire, My Prince, as Easter Hero, Gregalach was bred by Marriot Finlay in Ireland from the mare St Germanie and was bought by trainer Tom Coulthwaite as an unbroken three-year-old to represent his patron, Mr T.K. Laidlaw. In Mr Laidlaw's colours Gregalach won his first race over hurdles at Birmingham and before the end of his first season was successful in three 'chases, including the Stanley Steeplechase at Aintree. When Mr Laidlaw had to leave the country to care for his ailing wife, his horses were sent to Newmarket Sales, where Gregalach was bought for 5,000 guineas by Mrs M.A. Gemmell and put into Tom Leader's Newmarket yard. In his first four races for his new owner, the son of My Prince finished second in each of them and in the fifth, just eight days before Aintree, finished well down the course. He was ridden by Australian-born Bob Everett, who had served in the Royal Navy and only recently become a professional jockey.

With hardly any delay, the barrier rose and like a cavalry charge from the past the 66 runners galloped to the first fence. To everyone's amazement there was not a single faller at the first fence, nor at the second. A perfect leap at Becher's took Easter Hero into a two-length lead over Sandy Hook and Richmond II, with Gregalach some ten lengths further back in about twelfth position. Maintaining his blistering gallop, Mr Whitney's top weight had the opposition well strung out behind him as he swept over the water jump. With no let-up in the pace, the favourite raced on back towards Becher's, jumping the Brook still with Sandy

Hook and Richmond II his nearest rivals and with Gregalach slightly closer lying seventh. It was only after landing safely over the final Brook, with but five obstacles left, that the leader's stride began to shorten and Gregalach came alongside him. Fence by fence, from there on the two raced together and only after landing on the flat with all the obstacles behind them did Gregalach draw away from Easter Hero to win by six lengths, with Richmond II a long way behind in third place.

Only after weighing in was the sudden collapse of Easter Hero explained, when it was discovered that somewhere in the vicinity of the second Valentine's the favourite had twisted a racing plate which, with the sharp edge of it brushing against his other foreleg, had made that last half mile home a very painful one for the brave horse.

Mrs Gemmell, the victorious owner, was not present at Aintree to receive the congratulations of so many people, but in her absence Tom Leader and Bob Everett were more than happy to accept them in her place. During the Second World War Robert Everett returned to the Royal Navy as a Fleet Air Arm pilot, being awarded the Distinguished Service Order before being reported as missing in action.

Although a large field turned out for the 1930 National, consisting of 41 runners, it was considered considerably more preferable than the unwieldy assembly the previous contest produced.

Grakle was favourite at 100/12, ridden by Keith Piggott whose father Ernie had partnered both Jerry M and Poethlyn to victory. Apart from the favourite, the bookies did most business with Sir Lindsay, Gregalach, the mare Melleray's Belle and a locally owned competitor named Shaun Goilin.

The circumstances of Shaun Goilin's conception are a matter of a good deal of conjecture, the actual responsibility for his breeding being down quite simply to nature itself. A mare by the name of Golden Day was grazing in a paddock belonging to a Major Edwardes at Ballyneety in County Limerick, when an unbroken three-year-old colt jumped the fence from a neighbouring field to join her. That the subsequent relationship between the lonely mare and an adventurous passing youngster was a friendly one there can be little doubt, for Golden Day was soon discovered to be in foal and Shaun Goilin was duly born. Sold as a yearling for 22 guineas to Mr F.J. de Sales La Terriere, he raced in Ireland solely on the flat, being placed when four years of age at Thurles and winning just once the following season at Naas. After damaging a leg in training, Shaun Goilin was about to be destroyed when Allen Baker, a veterinary surgeon from Lismacue, stepped in and restored the gelding to fitness. His next owner was the Liverpool cotton broker Mr W.H. Midwood. Sent to be trained by Frank Hartigan at Weyhill in Hampshire, Shaun Goilin was in good hands, as Hartigan was the nephew of Garrett Moore, who partnered The Liberator to victory in the 1879 National. Slow to come to hand, Shaun Goilin won just twice in his first three seasons over the sticks, but in the latest campaign showed tremendous improvement to win his first three races, including Liverpool's Grand Sefton 'Chase. Partnered in the big race by Tommy Cullinan, Shaun Goilin went off second favourite at 100/8.

Away to a good start, two grey horses, Glangesia and Gate Book, set the early pace, leading over the first jumps on the run down to Becher's, with hardly any fallers at this stage. At the Canal Turn Gate Book went to the front as Glengesia lost ground by running wide, and showing prominently behind the leader were Gregalach, Ballyhanwood, Sir Lindsay and Shaun Goilin. At the last ditch before the racecourse Gate Book and Gregalach both fell when sharing the lead, leaving Glangesia in front again and the American-owned grey came past the stands to jump the water two lengths ahead of Shaun Goilin. Glangesia, Toy Bell and Merrivale were among the leading bunch rounding the Canal Turn, but with the pace beginning to tell after clearing Valentine's, they began to lose ground. Approaching the second-last fence the result lay between Sir Lindsay, Shaun Goilin and Melleray's Belle. In a nail-biting race to the winning post, Shaun Goilin just prevailed by a neck from the very brave mare Melleray's Belle, with Sir Lindsay one and a half lengths behind in third place. Glangesia was fourth.

For Tommy Cullinan, winning the Grand National rounded off an incredible hat-trick of important victories, for just 17 days before he had won the Champion Hurdle with Brown Tony and the Cheltenham Gold Cup on Easter Hero. As a private with an anti-aircraft unit in the Second World War, Thomas Brady Cullinan suffered a fit of depression and shot himself.

Due largely to the abandonment of the Cheltenham National Hunt Meeting in 1931, it was another big field which went to post for the National, despite the recent changes to the regulations.

Of the 43 runners, Easter Hero returned, top weight again with the expected 12st 7lb but the undeterred public still made him 5/1 favourite. Three others in the handicap also carried in excess of 12st, the rising star of 'chasing, Gib, and former winners Shaun Goilin and Gregalach.

Making his fifth consecutive appearance in the race was the nine-year-old Grakle, whose waywardness in the past had often ruined his chances. Bred in County Carlow by Mr B.M. Slocock's Hanover Stud, he was by that good stallion Jackdaw from the mare Lady Crank and, like Gregalach, not only came up at the same Newmarket Sales but was bought by the same man, Mr T.K. Laidlaw. It was in this owner's colours that Grakle first ran in the National, when just five in 1927, and shortly after this he changed hands for 4,000 guineas. The new owner was the Liverpool businessman Cecil Taylor, the unsuccessful underbidder when Grakle was sold at Newmarket. Leaving the gelding with trainer Tom Coulthwaite at Rugeley, in Staffordshire, his headstrong tendencies cost him many a race he should have won and although he was placed in the Cheltenham Gold Cup three times, so far only jockey Tim Hamey had managed to control him sufficiently to complete the National in sixth place in 1929. Bob Lyall was back in the saddle this time, attempting to go one better than his brother Frank, who had finished second on Bloodstone in 1912.

There was a delay of several minutes at the start when a number of runners broke the tape when charging it, but once repaired they were despatched to a level break. Remarkably few falls occurred in the early part of the race but Swift Rowland came down at Becher's and at the Canal Turn Gregalach performed wonders in avoiding two fallen horses lying in his path. Gregalach jumped the water a length in front of Great Span, with Easter Hero, Solanum and Grakle next in line and Theras and Shaun Goilin going well. Jumping beautifully at every fence, Gregalach kept up the tremendously strong gallop, landing over Becher's ahead of Great Span, with Grakle now third and just behind these Easter Hero crashed into the fallen Solanum. Plagued by the riderless horse Tamasha, Gregalach and Great Span rose at the Canal Turn almost together but Gregalach was travelling so fast he lost valuable ground by going wide at the bend. At the last ditch Great Span fell and with Grakle easing his way to the front he jumped the second last ahead as exhausted Drintyre refused here. Rallying well, Gregalach came again at the final fence, where Grakle landed a length to the good and in a spirited run to the post held on to win by a length and a half from Gregalach, with Annandale ten lengths away in third place.

Yet another local victory was well received by the huge crowd, with Grakle being well supported on the books, but even those who hadn't backed the winner felt that the perseverance of Grakle deserved the prize.

Ten

1932–1940

The year 1932 saw Los Angeles host the Olympic Games; the BBC open its new headquarters, Broadcasting House; and Adolf Hitler's National Socialists become the biggest party in the Reichstag. The few warning voices raised against the latter were by and large ignored.

At Aintree, the three most recent winners of the race, Grakle, Shaun Goilin and Gregalach, provided additional interest among the competitors and with Grakle sharing favouritism with Heartbreak Hill, the local community were obviously supporting last year's hero.

There was also a 50/1 shot named Forbra, who was very keenly watched by one bookmaker in particular, his owner William Parsonage. By Foresight out of Thymbra, Forbra was bred by Mr H. Glover and when sold to a Mr Hunt, entered the training establishment of Tom Rimell at Kinnersley in Worcestershire. It was while there that Bill Parsonage, a bookmaker and town councillor from Ludlow, first saw Forbra and bought him at once for 1,500 guineas. The gelding's first race in his new owner's colours was at Newbury in December 1931 and although beaten five lengths by Golden Miller, Forbra was awarded the race on the grounds that 'The Miller' had carried the wrong weight. Less than three months later Golden Miller won the Cheltenham Gold Cup, something he was to make rather a habit of doing. Forbra progressed well with Tom Rimell and as the gelding was still only a seven-year-old, it was originally planned to run him in the Stanley 'Chase on the first day of the National meeting. Forbra, however, ruled himself out of this event by winning a race at Taunton and as the trainer had fortunately also entered him for Aintree's principal race, the decision was made to let him take his chance. His jockey in the National was the Lincolnshire-born but Cheltenham-based James Hamey, commonly known as 'Tim'.

Away to a first-time start, Evolution was the first to show, and once again falls were few and far between on the run to Becher's. It was here that trouble began in earnest, when Inverse, Quite Calm and Red Lynch fell and with Egremont and Forbra hot on the heels of the leader they raced on to the Canal Turn. The leader Evolution completely misjudged the bend here, falling right in the path of Heartbreak Hill, who did well to stay on her feet. With Egremont now in command, he jumped Valentine's in splendid style ahead of Forbra, Near East, Heartbreak Hill, Gregalach and Dusty Foot. Two jumps later, the whole complexion of the race changed in a few dramatic seconds. The riderless Pelorus Jack, running just behind the leading group, suddenly veered right across the front of the ditch and in addition to knocking Gregalach right through the obstacle he caused two-thirds of the runners to either fall, refuse or pull up. Coming back onto the racecourse it was KCB in front of Forbra, Near East and Egremont. At the water jump KCB crashed to the ground and from there on the contest was reduced to a duel between Tim Hamey on Forbra and the amateur Edward Paget with Egremont. All the way back in the country it was first Forbra, then Egremont holding the narrowest of leads, but both horses were jumping perfectly and after rounding the Canal Turn, Forbra was never really headed again. Tim Hamey rode a fine waiting race from the front, concentrating on jumping the fences safely before starting to race. Once over the last fence, he let Forbra go and although Egremont put in a spirited effort, he was no match for Forbra, who passed the post three lengths in front of Egremont. A very long way back in third place came the ever-reliable Shaun Goilin.

Amid the many congratulations to Forbra's connections, the critics again emerged to dissect what had happened during the race and to pontificate on what should happen in the future.

Aintree was the place to be on 24 March 1933, and certainly a quarter of a million spectators accepted this. Everyone, it seemed, wanted to see if the champion steeplechaser, Golden Miller, could conquer the National the way he had the last two Cheltenham Gold Cups.

Three former National winners were among the 34 runners: Forbra, Shaun Goilin and Gregalach, with the latter carrying top weight of 12st 7lb.

But by far the biggest attraction, apart from obviously the race itself, was the prospect of seeing the animal now nationally acclaimed as 'the horse of the century'. Still only six years of age, Golden Miller's rise to the top of the steeplechasing ladder was not merely meteoric, it was phenomenal. Even with 12st 2lb in the saddle, the reputation of Golden Miller made him clear favourite at 9/1.

American owners were still represented, Mr Whitney and Morgan Blair by now regular visitors to Aintree and joining them this time were a husband and wife team, Mr and Mrs Ambrose Clark.

A leading supporter of steeplechasing in his own country, Mr F. Ambrose

Clark and his wife had for a number of years taken such a keen interest in British 'chasing that they spent the winter months in England to follow the sport. Extremely wealthy, even by American standards, Mr Clark was the head of the Singer sewing-machine empire and in a better position than most to indulge his passion for horses. In 1927, while visiting Ireland, he came across a yearling, bred by Mr H. Hutchinson at Kellsboro, in County Kilkenny, and taking a fancy to the youngster, bought him there and then. By Jackdaw out of Kellsboro' Lass, the offspring was named Kellsboro' Jack. Kellsboro' Jack was transferred to trainer Ivor Anthony at Wroughton in Wiltshire, who had prepared jumpers for the rich American for a number of years. By the end of 1931 Kellsboro' Jack had proved disappointing, having run seven times without a single victory and it was at this time that Ivor Anthony suggested to the owner that 'a change of owner may bring a change of luck'. Early in January 1932, Mr Ambrose Clark asked his wife, Florence, for a one pound note and upon her complying, announced that Kellsboro' Jack was now hers. Before the end of the season the son of Jackdaw carried Mrs Clark's colours six times, winning three 'chases, including the Stanley Steeplechase at Aintree by 20 lengths. The trainer's suggestion had paid off and he carefully prepared a plan of campaign designed to bring Kellsboro' Jack to the peak of fitness in time for the 1933 Grand National. His rider in the big race was Welshman Dudley Williams.

Once again there was trouble at the start when the giant-sized Remus got his head caught up in the barrier but, free and on their way, it was Remus who made the running. Racing at a tremendous pace they landed over the first with just one faller. Colliery Band was first over Becher's, followed by Kellsboro' Jack, Remus, Gregalach, Delaneige and Slater, and somewhere in the mid-division Golden Miller still going smoothly. As the leading group left Valentine's behind them, Golden Miller moved closer to the front. Spectators in the stands were amazed to see so many galloping back towards them, no less than two dozen still in the race nearing the halfway stage. Remus and Colliery Band led over the water together, closely chased by Kellsboro' Jack, Delaneige, Forbra, Gregalach, Holmes and Golden Miller. Putting in a brilliant jump at Becher's Brook, Kellsboro' Jack landed in front of Remus, with Delaneige and Slater directly behind and Ted Leader made a good recovery when his mount Golden Miller almost fell. Moving back towards the leaders as they jumped the Canal Turn, Golden Miller made his third and final error, stumbling as he landed and unseating Ted Leader. Still racing freely and jumping brilliantly, Kellsboro' Jack led over the fourth from home with Remus now fading and Pelorus Jack still making ground. These two horses with 'Jack' in their names, began to draw clear of the rest on the long run back to the second-last fence and, having jumped it together, galloped flat out to the final obstacle. In the final strides

Pelorus Jack mistimed his take-off and fell, leaving Kellsboro' Jack out on his own. Keeping on at full pelt he raced towards the finish, holding off the late challenge of Mr Frank Furlong on his father's horse, Really True. At the line it was Kellsboro' Jack by three lengths from Really True, with the fast-finishing Slater just a neck away in third place. In all 19 finished the course.

The time record for the race had been shattered by Kellsboro' Jack to an amazing nine minutes and 28 seconds and under the circumstances his starting price of 25/1 had been generous.

Mrs Clark vowed that Kellsboro' Jack would never be subjected to the rigours of the Grand National again and she was true to her word. The horse did, however, win another ten 'chases, including the Scottish National and the Champion 'Chase round Aintree twice. His racing days over, Kellsboro' Jack was taken with his owner to the United States and is buried in the foothills of the Adirondacks.

Impressed by the late flourish which took him into second place in 1933, the public plumped for Really True, making him 7/1 favourite, despite his unimpressive displays in the current season. Forbra was at 100/8 and among the other better-backed contestants were Delaneige, Sorley Boy, Trocadero and Mr Whitney's rising star, Thomond II.

With a new jockey, Gerry Wilson, but the same weight burden as on his first attempt, Golden Miller returned to Aintree the 8/1 second favourite. Although having recently won his third successive Cheltenham Gold Cup, there was slightly less enthusiasm for him in the National this time, the observations being that he had already suffered two defeats that term and that he had committed two serious errors in the previous year's race before parting company with his jockey. His trainer, Basil Briscoe, was confident, however, that the horse would give a good account of himself. Bred by Mr Laurence Geraghty in County Meath, Golden Miller was by the stallion Gold Court out of Miller's Pride, being sold when a yearling at Dublin for 100 guineas to a Paddy Quinn. Still unbroken two years later, an acquaintance of Basil Briscoe's, Captain Farmer, saw the horse grazing in a field and the trainer was persuaded to purchase it for £500. Upon arriving at Briscoe's Exning stables, Golden Miller received scornful glances from many of the yard staff, in such poor condition did he appear, but owner Philip Carr took a liking to the young horse and parted with £1,000 to buy him. After winning three times for Mr Carr, the owner became seriously ill and decided to get rid of all his racehorses and as a result Golden Miller became the property of the daughter of Lord Queenborough, Miss Dorothy Paget. Purchased for £12,000 as part of a pair with that fine hurdler Insurance, Golden Miller stayed with trainer Briscoe, who became delighted with the rapid progress the animal made. His three Cheltenham Gold Cup victories spoke volumes for the gelding's ability, yet the rather eccentric, though extremely wealthy, Miss Paget had a deep desire to see him prove himself in the supreme jumping test.

From a good start Gregalach belied his years by setting off in front at a cracking pace. There were few upsets at the early fences and it was noticeable that Gerry Wilson was allowing Golden Miller plenty of time to settle, well to the rear of the field. Landing safely over Becher's, Southern Hue and Uncle Batt were together from Mr Whitney's pair, Thomond II and Lone Eagle II. It was a marvellous sight for the stands spectators as Delaneige and Gregalach landed together over the water jump, closely followed by Forbra, Golden Miller, Thomond II and Uncle Batt. Striding out beautifully, Golden Miller surged to the front at the start of the second circuit, landing over the 17th fractionally ahead of Delaneige and Gregalach. Without any let-up in the tremendously fast gallop, all the leaders cleared Becher's again safely. There was little in it as four horses jumped Valentine's almost in line abreast, Delaneige, Golden Miller, Forbra and Thomond II each racing flat out while still some way from the finish. Upon returning to the racecourse Delaneige held a slight lead over Golden Miller, but it could be clearly seen that Gerry Wilson was sitting quietly biding his time on Miss Paget's champion. Moving up to join the leader at the final fence, Golden Miller and Delaneige touched down together and from there on it was all Golden Miller. Sprinting away from his rival, Golden Miller passed the post five lengths in front of Delaneige, with Thomond II the same distance away in third place and Forbra fourth.

A detachment of police surrounded the winner as his owner led him through an excited mass of people, all wanting to get close to this incredible horse who had not only won the Gold Cup and Grand National in the space of 16 days, but had shattered Kellsboro' Jack's time record by eight seconds.

Almost exhausted by the congratulations heaped upon her, Dorothy Paget still found time to thank her trainer and jockey and to congratulate her cousin, Mr J.H. Whitney, for collecting third place with Thomond II.

Rarely, if ever, has a sporting event been considered such a foregone conclusion as the 1935 Grand National. Since his record-breaking victory in 1934, Miss Paget's remarkable steeplechaser had won all his five races, the most recent providing a fourth success in the Cheltenham Gold Cup. Not even top weight of 12st 7lb could deter the punters from plunging in unprecedented fashion on 'The Miller' and at 2/1 he became the shortest-priced favourite in the history of the National.

Of the 26 runners opposing Golden Miller, Thomond II was considered the greatest danger at 9/2, with Tapinois, Castle Irwell and Really True also featuring well in the betting.

1934's favourite, Really True, was now ridden by the professional Danny

Morgan, with his former amateur rider, Frank Furlong, the owner-trainer's son, opting to partner the stable's second representative, Reynoldstown, a 22/1 chance. An eight-year-old almost-black gelding by My Prince out of Fromage, Reynoldstown had been bred by Richard Ball at Reynoldstown, near Naul in County Dublin and named after the place of his birth. Major Noel Charles Bell Furlong subsequently bought him and took him back to Skeffington in Leicestershire to begin his training. As members of a family whose roots lay in County Fermoy, the Furlongs had long been involved in hunting and 'chasing, moving to Skeffington Hall on the mainland during the troubles in Ireland, and Major Furlong's son, Frank, was a most accomplished horseman who rode many winners trained by his father. A subaltern in the 9th Lancers, Frank Furlong was an Old Harrovian who, though constantly battling against increasing weight, was very effective both over hurdles and fences. Graduating from a promising introduction over hurdles, Reynoldstown took well to the larger obstacles, winning three of his six 'chases before tackling the National for the first time.

From a good start the race began with Golden Miller holding a handy position near the inside rails and with Theras and Thomond II disputing the lead over the first fence. Really True failed to survive the Brook and Thomond was very lucky to do so, a bad blunder costing him many lengths, and by this time Castle Irwell had taken the lead from Golden Miller and Blue Prince. Maintaining these positions over the Canal Turn, Castle Irwell jumped Valentine's clear, with Golden Miller going easily just behind hard on the inside rail but as they landed two jumps later Golden Miller appeared to hesitate briefly in mid-air as if unsighted and Gerry Wilson was unable to keep his place in the saddle. The gasp from the spectators nearby warned those further afield of some calamity but nobody in the stands could imagine it being anything to do with Golden Miller. They knew differently when the runners jumped the water with the favourite not among them and it was Mr Whitney's two runners, Thomond II and Royal Ransom, which led them back into the country. A brilliant leap at Becher's took Reynoldstown into the lead and with Thomond II challenging all the way, these two opened up a gap between the remainder. As the two leaders galloped back onto the racecourse all attention was on them. Jumping the final fence side by side, Thomond edged over to the right, slightly nudging Reynoldstown, whose rider held his mount together superbly and proceeded to draw away. Reynoldstown ran out a most convincing winner by three lengths from Blue Prince, who outran Thomond II in the final 200 yards to secure second place by eight lengths.

Scenes of happiness greeted Reynoldstown and Frank Furlong, from family, friends and a large contingent of Leicestershire racegoers and the many whose money was to stay in bookies' satchels gave a cheer of admiration for a magnificent family triumph.

After winning his fifth Cheltenham Gold Cup in March 1936, Golden Miller would probably have again started favourite for the forthcoming Grand National, had it not been for Avenger, a young horse from the stable responsible for Forbra's victory. Golden Miller, ridden this year by Welshman Evan Williams, was at 5/1, with the Grand Sefton winner, Castle Irwell, at 8s and Reynoldstown on 10/1.

Reynoldstown had also acquired a new rider this season, Fulke Walwyn, a brother officer in the 9th Lancers of Frank Furlong, who could no longer make the weight. Born in Monmouthshire, Fulke Walwyn was an excellent horseman who topped the list of leading amateurs three times and having already won twice on Reynoldstown during that campaign was the ideal substitute.

A less-experienced but equally enthusiastic amateur, the Honourable Anthony Mildmay was again taking part in the National, this time aboard a tubed entire horse called Davy Jones. Owned by the rider's father, Lord Mildmay of Flete, its starting price of 100/1 was a fair reflection of his chances.

Away to a good start, it was the chestnut Davy Jones who went straight into the lead, pulling hard as he jumped the first. Golden Miller landed but was brought down although, holding on to the reins, Evan Williams quickly remounted and continued some way behind the rest. Opening up a commanding lead going to Becher's, Davy Jones cleared it in front of Kiltoi, Double Crossed and Avenger. Bravely attempting to make ground, Golden Miller was a long way behind when refusing at the open ditch before the Melling Road. Jumping the Chair in front of the stands with space to spare, Davy Jones was two lengths ahead of Double Crossed, with Avenger, Emancipator, Keen Blade and Reynoldstown well in contention. They cleared the water jump, returning to the country with the favourite, Avenger, making a forward move on the outside. At the seventeenth fence Avenger fell heavily and Davy Jones continued to set them all a difficult task in catching him. As the rest began to tire, Fulke Walwyn took Reynoldstown after the front-running outsider, rising at Becher's just a length behind Davy Jones. Still together over Valentine's, Davy Jones then drew away again and with Reynoldstown making errors at each of the last three fences before reaching the racecourse, Davy Jones looked a certain winner barring a fall. Some three lengths clear at the second last, the leader pecked slightly on landing and the impact caused the buckle of Anthony Mildmay's reins to separate. Unable to steer his mount, Mildmay was powerless to prevent Davy Jones from running out at the final fence, scattering crowds standing on the inside of the course. Left with the easiest of tasks, Reynoldstown raced on to win by 12 lengths from the 50/1 shot Ego, with Bachelor Prince a further six lengths back in third place.

Reynoldstown was quite properly applauded in the traditional manner on his way to the winner's enclosure. The first horse to succeed twice in successive years in the National since 1870, Reynoldstown never ran in the race again.

The mid-1930s had proved a most turbulent period for the world in general and Europe in particular. A Fascist dictator in Italy hell-bent on subjugating a small African state in his quest for an empire; the rise of Nazism in Germany and its evil doctrine of anti-Semitism; and the humiliation and hardship brought about by mass unemployment, created uncertainty and mistrust everywhere. The outbreak of the Spanish Civil War in 1936 was recognised by many as a rehearsal for a larger, more widespread conflict.

Aintree welcomed the, as yet uncrowned, King and Queen in March 1937 and it was the first time Her Majesty Queen Elizabeth had attended the race; it was not to be the last.

Golden Miller wound up clear favourite for the National at 8/1. Runner-up last time, Ego was strongly fancied to improve on the showing and among others featuring well in the betting were Didoric, Don Bradman, Pucka Belle, Delachance and Royal Mail.

In view of the recent abdication and the presence of the royal party at the event, Royal Mail was a very appropriate competitor in that year's race, for his owner, Mr Hugh Lloyd Thomas, had been assistant secretary to Edward VIII. Irish-bred by Mr Charles Rogers, Royal Mail was by My Prince from the mare Flying May, and as My Prince was also the sire of Reynoldstown, in retrospect, the jumping blood within Royal Mail had to be respected. Hubert Hartigan bought the all-black son of My Prince as an unbroken three-year-old, passing him on almost immediately to Mr Lloyd Thomas, who sent him to be trained by Ivor Anthony at Aubrey Hastings' old yard at Wroughton in Wiltshire. In his first season Royal Mail won two hurdle races, partnered in the second of these by his owner. From six outings prior to the 1937 Grand National, Royal Mail was never out of the first three and of his two victories, one was in Liverpool's Becher 'Chase where he outran Golden Miller from the last fence to win by two lengths. Apart from a few occasions when his owner partnered the horse, his regular jockey was Evan Williams, an early victim in the 1936 race when aboard Golden Miller. Evan was the son of starter Fred Williams and Royal Mail was providing a third National ride for him.

All except Misdemeanour II got away well and in the dash to the first fence it was Ready Cash, Tapinois, Golden Miller and Ego who landed in front over it. Landing first over the Brook, Tapinois was in front of Ready Cash, Golden Miller and Delachance but Tapinois crashed to the ground at the Canal Turn, together with Spionaud. Just when the crowds began cheering the efforts of the favourite, Golden Miller refused at the eleventh, an open ditch. Led by the riderless Drim, the survivors came back into the area in front of the stands,

Royal Mail, Flying Minutes, Ego and Delachance jumping the water jump with perfection. Royal Mail had not put a foot wrong the whole way and approaching Becher's again, struck the front once more from Flying Minutes and the improving mare, Cooleen. Over the last two fences it was Royal Mail with Cooleen bravely staying on as the only real threat to the leader but with a superior turn of foot Royal Mail raced past the winning post three lengths in front of Cooleen, with Pucka Belle third ten lengths away.

Even though the favourite Golden Miller had again let the majority of the public down, Royal Mail was hailed as a most worthy winner and his jubilant owner made it known that he would ride the horse in the race himself next year. Training hard to achieve this aim, it came as a dreadful shock barely a month before the 1938 race that Mr Hugh Lloyd Thomas had been killed during a race at Derby. Winning jockey Evan Williams subsequently became a flat-race trainer at Kingsclere and in 1951 turned out the winner of the Festival of Britain Stakes at Ascot, Supreme Court.

Upon publication of the 79 entries for the 1938 Grand National, the absence of Golden Miller was taken as being a final admission that the great horse, despite his record-breaking win of 1934, had developed a distinct aversion to Aintree.

Of the 36 runners eventually started this time, the most recent winner, Royal Mail, now owned by Mrs C. Evans, shouldered top weight of 12st 7lb and again ridden by Evan Williams, featured in the betting at 100/8. Considered more likely to win was the mare which finished closest to Royal Mail last year, Mr James V. Rank's Cooleen, ridden by Jack Fawcus and joint favourite with Blue Shirt at 8/1. Among the outsiders expected to make a good showing were the Becher 'Chase winner Airgead Sios, Dunhill Castle and from across the Irish Sea, Workman.

From much further afield came Battleship, an 11-year-old chestnut entire who, at just 15½ hands high, was barely the size of a polo pony. Bred in the blue grass land of America at the Mereworth Stud in Lexington, Kentucky, by Walter J. Salmon, his sire, Man o' War, was acknowledged as the best horse seen in the United States this century, while the dam was the French-bred mare Quarantaine. Lightly raced as a two-year-old, Battleship took part in 22 races on the flat in his first three seasons, of which he won ten, and he was then purchased by a Mrs T.H. Somerville, later to become better known as Mrs Marion du Pont Scott, for £2,400. In his first year over timber, 1933, the diminutive chestnut won four steeplechases and the following year was successful the same number of times before recording a brilliant victory in the American Grand National at Belmont Park. Sent to England in 1936 to be trained for jumping's greatest test, he was put in the care of Reg Hobbs at Lambourn, Berkshire, who had spent many years training racehorses in the United States. Although British obstacles were totally different to anything

Battleship had encountered before, he adapted well enough to win five of his 13 'chases in his first season here and though entered for the 1937 Grand National was unable to run through injury. During the current term, he appeared less dynamic, recording but a single victory from nine attempts before setting off for Liverpool and somewhat foolishly regarded as now past his best, Battleship was allowed to start at 40/1 in the National. Since sending her horse across the Atlantic, the owner had divorced her husband and remarried the famous Hollywood cowboy film star Randolph Scott and the latter received more attention on National day than did his wife's runner in the race. Having his second ride in the National, 17-year-old Bruce Hobbs, the trainer's son, took the mount on Battleship and being a very tall young man appeared out of proportion to his tiny partner.

An untidy start caught a number of the runners unawares and at the first fence the renowned front-runner Airgead Sios landed first from Lough Cottage, Royal Mail, Bachelor Prince, Royal Danieli and Dunhill Castle. Over Becher's it was still Airgead Sios with Royal Danieli almost level and Rocquilla also in close touch but the next fence nearly proved the undoing of Battleship. The horse gauged the angle of the fence perfectly, turning left in mid-air to face up to the Canal Turn, and the sudden change in his mount's direction caught Bruce Hobbs by surprise. Unbalanced for the merest second, the jockey was on his way to hitting the turf when the hand of nearby Fred Rimell, aboard Provocative, reached out and yanked young Hobbs back into the saddle. For such a small fellow, Battleship was coping well with the big fences, jumping them brilliantly though the huge drops to many of them were causing him problems. Airgead Sios came down at Valentine's, leaving Royal Danieli in front but by the time they arrived back on the racecourse, Delachance had passed him and in this order they took the water jump. Jumping with exceptional flair at every fence down to Becher's, Battleship made such good progress that he was a length ahead of Royal Danieli over the Brook, with Delachance third and Lough Cottage and the improving Workman just behind. At the last fence in the country Battleship made a mistake which cost him many lengths but Bruce Hobbs sensibly allowed his mount plenty of time to recover, lying third some way behind the two Irish horses. At the second last Workman blundered and was quickly passed by Battleship who, now fully back into his stride, went in pursuit of Royal Danieli and sensing a rousing finish, the crowds began cheering before the horses reached the final fence. Just two lengths in arrears as he landed on the flat, Battleship came with a storming run on the stands side of the course, and with Royal Danieli racing on the far side, the riderless Takvor Pacha between them was their only companion up that punishingly long straight. Neck and neck they battled it out and with them on opposite sides of the wide track, it was truly a judges' nightmare as they flashed past the post together. The winner was declared as number five, Battleship, by a head from number six, Royal Danieli. Workman stayed on gamely to finish a bad third, with Cooleen fourth.

As Reg Hobbs unsaddled his winner, he noticed a trace of blood on Battleship's nose and at first feared that the horse had broken a blood vessel. Upon close inspection, however, it was seen to be where the tiny fellow had caught his nose on the ground at some of the obstacles.

One of the smallest horses ever to win the race, Battleship was the last entire to win, the first blinkered competitor to succeed and carried the youngest rider ever to triumph in the Grand National.

Whilst on the crest of a wave, Bruce Hobbs suffered a broken back in a race fall before the end of the year and although he eventually recovered, international developments curtailed his future career.

Returning to America, a fabulous welcome awaited Battleship and overnight the tiny 'giant' of the turf became a household name. Based at his owner's beautiful estate at Montpelier in Virginia, he became the founding stallion at Mrs Scott's stud and on five occasions was the leading sire in the United States. One of his many successful sons, Shipboard, won the American Grand National in 1956. Battleship was 31 years old when he died in 1958.

In 1939 the Spanish Civil War ended with Franco being declared President and still the war clouds over Europe grew darker. Hitler's march into the Rhineland and then on to Czechoslovakia brought the danger of a major confrontation ever nearer, so much so that in Britain plans were drawn up to conscript all men over the age of 20.

As if expecting this to be the last Grand National until after the much talked about forthcoming conflict, the crowds flocked to Aintree in their thousands. Favourite on the day was Miss Dorothy Paget's young Kilstar at 8/1. Steady in the betting at 100/8, the same odds as both Royal Mail and Royal Danieli, was the Irish-trained Workman.

Third in the previous year's race, the nine-year-old brown gelding Workman was bred by Mr P.J. O'Leary at Charleville, County Cork, and was by a stallion beginning to make a name for himself as a sire of jumpers, Cottage, from the mare Cariella. As a six-year-old in the ownership of Mr R. de L. Stedman, he made his first appearance a winning one in the four-and-a-quarter-mile La Touche Memorial Cup at Punchestown when ridden by his owner. After finishing second at Naas in March 1937, he was sold to Liverpool-born Sir Alexander Maguire, whose colours he carried into third place next time out in the Irish Grand National. Apart from finishing third in the 1938 Grand National, he won twice that year from five races and prior to making a second attempt in the National, proved his well-being by finishing fourth in the Grand

Sefton 'Chase and winning the Naas Plate over three miles. Trained by the former jockey Jack Ruttle at Celbridge, County Dublin, Workman had an excellent partner in Tim Hyde, who worked his way up from the showring to become a jockey constantly in demand.

From a good start Rocquilla led them towards the first fence where he landed just behind Birthgift, but five of the 37 starters fell here. Lord Derby's horse, Under Bid, moved up with the main group running to Becher's, at which point Royal Danieli completely mistimed his jump to fall heavily, bringing down Epiphanes in the process. Kilstar had moved quietly through to take up the running and racing back onto the racecourse was followed by Under Bid, West Point, Workman, Inversible and Bachelor Prince. In this order they jumped the water jump. With Kilstar still at the head of affairs on the way to Becher's, his closest rivals were Under Bid, Red Hillman, Workman and Dominick's Cross. Landing first over the Brook, Kilstar galloped on as Red Hillman, Montrejeau II and Scotch Wood fell behind him and another to make his exit was Milano at the next fence. Tim Hyde had ridden a patient and intelligent race with Workman and going into Valentine's went to the front. There was a moment's anxiety at the final ditch before the racecourse, when the tiring Black Hawk struck into Workman as they jumped but Workman's strength saw him through. Streaming away from the rest, Workman raced towards the penultimate fence, his race won bar a fall, and jumping both the final fences superbly, held off a strong late challenge of Macmoffat to win by three lengths. A further 15 lengths back in third place came Kilstar, followed in by Cooleen.

Locals and Irish visitors celebrated the victory of Workman in traditional fashion but when making their way home after racing, the huge question in everyone's thoughts was if there would be another Grand National next year.

Workman subsequently lost his zest for racing, competing in his homeland for the next four seasons without once winning.

On 1 September 1939 Germany invaded Poland and two days later Britain and France declared war on Germany and the Second World War began.

With the war well into its seventh month, the crowds again gathered at Aintree and like that last wartime National 25 years ago, uniforms of all colour, manner and style were in evidence everywhere.

Royal Danieli headed the handicap with 11st 13lb and again ridden by Dan Moore was favourite at 4/1, with Kilstar at 5s and Macmoffat an 8/1 chance. Both Lord Derby and Lord Sefton were represented, by Under Bid and Boyo respectively.

Another peer of the realm with an interest in the proceedings was the Right Honourable Hugh Grosvenor, MC, Lord Stalbridge, who both owned and trained the seven-year-old Bogskar. By Werewolf out of Irish Spring and having been bred by Mr C. Roche in County Dublin, Bogskar took quite a time to fully mature and his first owner, Sydney McGregor, sold him at three years to Lord Stalbridge. During his first three seasons Bogskar ran a total of 18 times without success, then like a completely reformed character began the current campaign with a victory in Windsor's Brocas 'Chase. Repeating the process again at Windsor over three miles, Bogskar then put himself truly in the Aintree limelight by winning the National Trial 'Chase at Gatwick and on that performance alone appeared good value at 25/1. His regular jockey was Mervyn Anthony Jones, on leave for the day from the Royal Air Force in which he held the rank of flight-sergeant, as did his brother, Hywel, also taking part in the National aboard Mr Whitney's National Night.

To a rousing cheer from the stands, they raced from the start at a good clip with Royal Danieli jumping fast and well in front over the early fences and still in that position jumping Becher's. Back on the racecourse, there was still a large number left in the race, with little distance between the first and last, but at the fence before the Chair National Night came to grief. Over the water it was Macmoffat, from Royal Danieli, Venturesome Knight, Kilstar, Under Bid and Bogskar and in this order they went out for the final circuit. Leading over Becher's were Royal Danieli and Macmoffat side by side, just ahead of Gold Arrow, Venturesome Knight, Away and Bogskar. Macmoffat had regained the lead over the Canal Turn, where Boyo crashed out in a dramatic manner and, setting sail for home, Macmoffat began to open up a gap. The second-last fence saw the downfall of Royal Danieli and racing to the final fence Macmoffat appeared to have the race at his mercy, despite the unwelcome attentions of the riderless National Night. It was as the leader rose to the jump that Bogskar joined him, being brought with a perfectly timed run on the inside, and as they landed almost together Bogskar cleverly survived the slightest of errors to sprint away to win by four lengths from a very gallant Macmoffat, filling the runners-up berth for the second year running. Gold Arrow was six lengths away in third place. The coincidence of the finish was that the riderless National Night, who had started the race with Hywel Jones in the saddle, passed the post in front of that jockey's brother Mervyn on the winner, Bogskar.

With such an accident-free contest and a popular, if long-priced, winner, the crowds celebrated and cheered Lord Stalbridge, Flight-Sergeant Jones and the horse who found his true form in time for the big occasion, Bogskar.

Mervyn Jones failed to return from a bombing mission in April 1942.

Again turned over to the War Department, Aintree racecourse closed its gates and it was to be six long, agonising years before horses would face the big fences again.

Eleven

1946–1955

On 5 April 1946, well over 300,000 people made the long-awaited return to Aintree for the Grand National, relieved that the war was over but weary and saddened by the heartbreak and devastation those six years of madness had inflicted.

Many who had played such important roles in the Aintree story were missing from the assembled throngs that day and would no more need to enquire on the state of the going. To mention but a few of so many who made the supreme sacrifice were Frank Furlong, Robert Everett, Thomas Cullinan, Mervyn Jones and Sir Geoffrey Congreve.

Of the 34 runners, the Irish champion Prince Regent was a red-hot favourite at 3/1, in spite of carrying top weight of 12st 5lb. The winner of 14 races, including the recent Cheltenham Gold Cup, the son of My Prince was owned by Mr James V. Rank and ridden by Tim Hyde, successful aboard Workman in 1939. Remarkably, the first and second in the 1940 race, Bogskar and Macmoffat, appeared again. Those considered to pose most danger to the favourite included Limestone Edward, Schubert and Dunshaughlin.

With many of those present still awaiting demobilisation, uniforms were again much in evidence and at least one rider made his way to the jockeys' room while yet to have received his demob suit. Captain Robert Charles Petre was on leave from the Scots Guards and he weighed out to ride a horse whose name apparently had a special appeal to many housewives, Lovely Cottage.

Bred by Mr and Mrs Hyde near Fermoy in County Cork, the nine-year-old was by that outstanding sire of jumpers, Cottage, out of a mare who had been a first-class point-to-point performer, The Nun II. Taking well to jumping, Lovely Cottage won the Conyngham Cup and two other races in 1944, following up these promising performances the following year by coming third in the Irish Grand National at Fairyhouse. With such credentials behind him, the decision was taken to sell the gelding at the end of 1945, the asking price being £2,000 with a contingency of another £1,000 'when he wins the Grand National at Aintree'. Such confidence on the part of those who knew the horse better than anyone caught the attention of Mr John Morant, who duly bought Lovely Cottage and sent him to be trained by Tommy Rayson at Winchester.

Away at the first time of asking, Gyppo led them into the first and jumping the obstacle almost the entire field were in a perfect line. At the Brook, Largo was involved in a horrible-looking fall yet mercifully survived without injury, and up to this stage it could clearly be seen that Prince Regent was having difficulty coping with the big fences. He was still well in touch with the leaders though at the water jump, at which the order was Lough Conn, Limestone Edward and Schubert. Soon after beginning the second circuit, Prince Regent went to the front, but as he neared Becher's he was ominously surrounded by at least eight riderless horses. As they closed dangerously towards Prince Regent as he took the bend at the Canal Turn, Tim Hyde was forced to spurt ahead with the top weight in an effort to shake off the troublesome pilotless pack. Obviously tired landing on the flat, Prince Regent was nonetheless still in the lead and there were only five others with jockeys behind him. Beautifully ridden throughout by Bobby Petre, Lovely Cottage had tracked the favourite for the last mile and now sensing that all too rare chance of success, Captain Petre and his mount pounced. Striding past the top weight effortlessly, Lovely Cottage came home four lengths in front of Jack Finlay, who also left Prince Regent trailing to finish third, three lengths further back.

The sympathy heaped on the beaten favourite tended to overshadow the performance of the winner and although Lovely Cottage was in receipt of 25lb from Prince Regent, the race was won on merit alone. It was the highlight of rider Captain Petre's career and a most welcome return to peacetime Britain. Sadly, within months of his turning professional in 1947, Bobby Petre slipped on a breakwater, his leg being so badly mangled that it had to be amputated. This very gallant gentleman and most talented horseman passed away peacefully in August 1996, aged 84.

In the first month of 1947, the weather suddenly turned to be the worst in living memory, bringing racing in England to a total stop until 15 March, barely a fortnight before the date scheduled for the Grand National. From the publication of the weights, even with the maximum burden of 12st 7lb, Prince Regent was an unshakable favourite, going off on the day at 8/1 of the 57 runners, the second-largest field in history.

Almost a quarter of the field were bracketed in the market with the stigma of 100/1 no-hopers and among these was a little Irish gelding named Caughoo. The eight-year-old was bred by Mr Patrick Power at Fethard-on-Sea, County Wexford, from a pairing of the stallion Within-the-Law and the mare Silverdale, which meant that their offspring did not possess an ounce of jumping blood. Despatched to Ballsbridge sales in 1941, Caughoo was knocked down for 50 guineas to a Dublin jeweller, John McDowell. Entrusting his new acquisition to his brother Herbert, who was a veterinary surgeon, the owner was overjoyed when, after his brother's preparation on the sands at Sutton in County Dublin, Caughoo won the Ulster National at Downpatrick in both 1945 and 1946. His partner at Aintree was fellow Irishman from County Meath, Eddie Dempsey, who not only had never ridden at Aintree before, but had never set foot in England until two days before the race.

On the dreadful going and with visibility greatly reduced through heavy rain and a thick mist, the huge field were sent on their way with Lough Conn, a member of the large Irish challenge, immediately going to the front. With Lough Conn still in the lead landing over the Brook, he was followed by the almost white Kilnaglory, Bricett, Gormanstown, Domino, Prince Regent, Tulyra and Silver Fame. Going splendidly up front Lough Conn led over the water and back out into the country, his nearest mounted rival was Musical Lad, but both suffered from the attentions of a pack of loose horses. Jumping Becher's for the final time, Lough Conn was ten lengths clear of Caughoo who had been patiently ridden on the first circuit but was now being brought forward decisively. Crossing the Melling Road back to the racecourse, Dempsey made his move, smoothly cruising past Lough Conn and safely guiding Caughoo over the last two fences to romp home, surprisingly looking fresh enough to go round again. At the post Caughoo was the winner by 20 lengths from Lough Conn with the French-bred Kami four lengths back in third place and Prince Regent fourth.

It was something of a fairytale victory for the McDowell brothers, whose sister actually led in Caughoo, for despite his long price and unorthodox training schedule, both men had made a healthy profit from the bookmakers as a result of their no-hoper. For Eddie Dempsey, his first trip across the Irish Sea was one he would never forget.

Britain enjoyed a surfeit of sport in 1948 as hosts to the 14th Olympic Games, the first to be held since Hitler's propaganda festival in 1936. In a period of austerity and reconstruction, the United Kingdom put on a splendid show with very limited resources and with Wembley Stadium constantly packed for the track and field events, the world became united in friendly competition. That is except for the Soviet Union, Germany and Japan, who failed to take part.

Some five months before Britain's celebration of world sport, Aintree made its own contribution in time-honoured fashion on 20 March 1948, with 43 runners bidding for fame and glory in the Grand National. Lord Bicester's up-

and-coming star Silver Fame, ridden by the brilliant Irishman, Martin Molony, started favourite at 9/1.

At 13 years of age Prince Regent was back one final time, Miss Dorothy Paget's dual effort with Housewarmer and Happy Home was a lively combination and Lord Bicester also had a promising second string to his bow with Roimond. Regarded as the strongest threats to the favourite, at least in the minds of the bookmakers, were Rowland Roy, Cloncarrig, Loyal Antrim and the runner-up from last year, Lough Conn.

Lord Anthony Mildmay of Flete, so unlucky with Davy Jones 12 years before, took the field astride his own Cromwell, whose five wins from nine races that season made a nonsense of his 33/1 starting price.

Former amateur Neville Franklin Crump was making his mark as a trainer at Middleham, Yorkshire, after active service in the Royal Armoured Corps and saddled a rather headstrong mare by the name of Sheila's Cottage. By that great sire of jumpers, Cottage, from the mare Sheila, Sheila's Cottage was bred by Mrs Daly in County Limerick. Sold at Dublin sales for 190 guineas when five years old, the mare changed hands a number of times before becoming the property of Sir Hervey Bruce, in whose name she got as far as the 12th fence in the 1947 National. Early in 1948 Sheila's Cottage was sold again, this time for 3,500 guineas to the Grimsby fishing trawler owner John Proctor. Again entrusted with piloting the temperamental mare was that brilliant jockey from County Carlow, Arthur Thompson, who had demonstrated his powers of self-preservation during the recent hostilities. Captured by the Germans on the retreat to Dunkirk, with typical Irish audacity Arthur stole a bicycle from one of the guards and pedalled his way back to the British lines. It said much for the jockey's nature that he was the only man Sheila's Cottage would respond to.

When the barrier rose on a perfect spring afternoon, all except Musical Lad got away well, with Cloncarrig and Lough Conn cutting out the early work. That all too familiar groan associated with the collapse of a favourite announced the downfall of Silver Fame at Becher's Brook, but the vast crowd were treated to some delightful displays of jumping by Cloncarrig and First of the Dandies. These two led round the Canal Turn from Rowland Roy, Parthenon, Sheila's Cottage and Zahia. Cloncarrig and First of the Dandies kept up the strong gallop as they came back onto the racecourse. A bad mistake at the Chair by Cloncarrig left First of the Dandies in command and he took the water jump followed by the blinkered mare Zahia and Happy Home, Le Daim, Sheila's Cottage and the improving Cromwell. Soon after safely crossing Valentine's Brook the atrocious bad luck which denied Anthony Mildmay of his chance in the race 12 years before, struck again. Only just recovering from damaged ribs,

Lord Mildmay was stricken by a neck injury sustained some time before, which now resulted in his chin being locked in a downward position, severely restricting his vision. At the second-last fence, Zahia put in a determined effort which took her slightly ahead of First of the Dandies, and landing full of running she looked set to record another 100/1 shock victory. Veering from a straight line halfway to the jump, the spectators gasped in amazement as jockey Eddie Reavey took the wrong course, away from the jump, and steered Zahia towards the Chair again. Such a simple error so late in the race undoubtedly cost Zahia at least a placing and possibly the winner's prize. Coming from behind Arthur Thompson set Sheila's Cottage alight at just the right moment, drawing level with the tiring First of the Dandies close home, then drawing ahead to win by a length. Six lengths behind came the unfortunate Lord Mildmay, little more than a passenger on Cromwell, to finish third.

It was a first victory in the race for owner, trainer and jockey and in winning, the bad-tempered Sheila's Cottage had become the first of her sex to do so since Shannon Lass in 1902. Some days later, while being photographed by Baron Studios, Sheila's Cottage bit off the top of one of Arthur Thompson's fingers, as if requiring a special memento of the time she behaved herself sufficiently to win the National.

When unsuccessful as a brood-mare, the owner decided to have Sheila's Cottage put down and it was only the intervention of Neville Crump which prevented this. Instead she was given to Arthur Thompson, returning to her homeland and a life of leisure on her former jockey's farm. Upon her death, Sheila's Cottage was buried at the bottom of Thompson's garden in Wexford.

The dynamism of Aintree's senior executive, Mrs Mirabel Topham, was demonstrated to the full in 1949 when she successfully negotiated the purchase of the entire racecourse from Lord Sefton.

Another large number of runners, 43 again, increased the difficulty of finding the winner, while at the same time ensuring that spectators would not be short of drama or spectacle.

Clear favourite at 6/1 was Cromwell, so unlucky last time but, with his owner-rider Lord Mildmay so popular on the racecourse, considered to have an excellent chance now. Lord Bicester's Roimond was another thought to be likely to give a good account of himself. Twenty-nine-year-old Dick Francis was having his first National ride on Roimond, his brilliant career as a jockey having been interrupted by service as a Royal Air Force pilot during the war.

Much of Dick Francis's early race-riding had been conducted through his association with Cheshire trainer George Owen, himself a former top jockey who that year saddled a gelding called Russian Hero, totally unconsidered among the '66/1 others'.

The nine-year-old had been bred by Mr W.F. Williamson, a dairy farmer living near Chester, and was by the virtually unknown stallion Peter the Great out of the mare Logique and both sides of the pedigree contained strong French thoroughbred blood. A chancy, often erratic jumper, despite having been hunted and competed in point-to-points, Russian Hero was less than spectacular in 'chases, except in the manner in which he too often fell. He was considered to be absolutely useless in any event beyond two and a half miles and since winning a two-mile steeplechase at Leicester in January, had fallen twice in his three races before the National. His partner at Aintree was Leo McMorrow, from Connaught, County Sligo, and like Eddie Dempsey two years before, almost unheard-of in England.

Away to a good start, Monaveen led over the first fence. Over Becher's Acthon Major led from Roimond, Cromwell, Wot No Sun, Southborough, Ulster Monarch, Happy Home and Monaveen, but the Brook claimed Perfect Night and Magnetic Fin. After Valentine's, Roimond and Wot No Sun led the remainder back to the racecourse. The two leaders brought roars of approval as they leapt the water jump in style, closely followed by Royal Mount, Cromwell and Monaveen, and making ground rapidly to join them, Russian Hero in his distinctive black and white check colours. Royal Mount held a fractional edge over Roimond as they jumped Becher's for the final time and Jimmy Power performed a rodeo act to keep his Clyduffe in the race after his mount came down on its belly. Over the Canal Turn, Royal Mount had a three-length advantage over the beautifully ridden Roimond, with Russian Hero making rapid progress from off the pace, and when the leader made a costly error at Valentine's, Roimond and Russian Hero had the race more or less to themselves. Russian Hero took command between the last two fences and with a fine leap at the last, romped home a most impressive eight-length winner from Roimond, with Royal Mount a good third just a length behind the second. The favourite, Cromwell, was an honourable fourth.

A deliriously happy Mr Williamson enjoyed the satisfaction of not merely owning the winner but of breeding it and, coupled with the fact that he backed his long-shot with £10 at 300/1, he had every reason to feel satisfied. After producing one afternoon of brilliance in an hitherto mediocre career, Russian Hero reverted to his more accustomed ways and never won again.

Sadly, winning jockey Leo McMorrow failed to realise his potential as a jockey in this country and took up an appointment with the Smithwick brothers, who were cousins of the Irish trainer Dan Moore in the United States. He met his death in a motoring accident there, far away from the glory and excitement he sampled so briefly at Aintree on Russian Hero.

Within just five years of the end of the bitterest and costliest conflict the world had ever experienced, the Korean War began in 1950 when Communist forces from the North invaded South Korea. The United Nations Organisation, despite its international power and influence, was powerless in its efforts to avoid a major conflict in the Far East. In South Africa, international tension was increased with the tightening of the inhuman apartheid laws, which were to alienate that country from most of the world for more than three decades.

Restoring some semblance of sanity to an increasingly troubled world was the annual contest over Aintree's historic countryside, the 1950 renewal of the Grand National Steeplechase. For the first time in 42 years a representative of the British royal family featured in the event in the form of a nine-year-old bay gelding called Monaveen.

Through the enthusiasm and encouragement of Lord Mildmay and his closest friend, trainer Peter Cazalet, Her Majesty Queen Elizabeth and the Princess Elizabeth jointly embarked on a venture of ownership of a steeplechaser and their recent purchase progressed so well that he took his place among the 49 runners for Aintree's major showpiece.

The principal position in the betting was also a shared one, between last year's runner-up Roimond and the Yorkshire-trained newcomer to the National, Freebooter, both on 10/1.

Although making his début in the National, Freebooter was already twice a winner over Aintree's big fences, having greatly impressed even the most critical observers by carrying off Liverpool's Champion 'Chase and the Grand Sefton in impeccable style. Bred by Mr W.F. 'Paddy' Phelan in Waterford, from the mating of Steel Point and the mare Proud Fury, Freebooter was an immensely strong individual who was bought for 620 guineas as an unbroken three-year-old by that excellent judge of horseflesh, the former jockey turned trainer, Dan Moore. A quick return on his investment was forthcoming when, after winning two bumper races in his native Ireland, Freebooter was purchased for 3,000 guineas by Mrs Lurline Brotherton and duly placed with her trainer, Bobby Renton, at Ripon in Yorkshire. Most astute at placing his horses well, Bobby Renton immediately recognised that in Freebooter he had that rare talent capable of achieving all that was asked of him. The model of consistency in the current season, the son of Steel Point was never out of the frame in his six races. Ridden by stable jockey Jimmy Power, who was also a product of County Waterford, Freebooter carried 11st 11lb and when inspected in the paddock by the royal party aroused great interest from His Majesty King George VI.

As befitting the mood of the moment, the big field were despatched without any difficulty and in good order. The royal runner Monaveen thrilled his connections by going off at a rare old gallop to lead over the first fence, at which

Russian Hero, Cottage Welcome, Tommy Traddles, Ole Man River, Comeragh and Zarter all came to grief. Rising to the Brook at the head of affairs, Monaveen was outjumped with a tremendous leap by Freebooter, who landed in front and running, while Cavaliero, Battling Pedulas, Gallery and Ardnacassa all found the famous obstacle beyond their endeavours. Five more fell at Valentine's and at the next open ditch Cromwell and Lord Mildmay made their exit, leaving the leaders surrounded by a host of loose horses. Monaveen was still in front, jumping splendidly and going strongly ahead of Cloncarrig, Acthon Major, Saintfield, Freebooter and Mr Rank's Shagreen, and in this order they approached the grandstand. The leaders closed ranks coming to the 14th fence and, misjudging his take-off, Monaveen hit the fence hard, shooting his jockey almost over his head and it was only the fine horsemanship of Tony Grantham which kept the partnership intact. Another brilliant feat of jockeyship was displayed at the very next jump, the dreaded Chair, when Freebooter hit the fence so hard it seemed impossible for him to recover. Jimmy Power was left clinging to Freebooter's ears for many strides after the obstacle but jumped the water no more than ten lengths behind the leaders with Power firmly back in the plate. Angel Hill fell awkwardly at the Canal Turn, leaving Freebooter and Cloncarrig matching strides well ahead of the rest. Holding the slenderest of leads, Cloncarrig rose at the penultimate fence but, clipping it with his hind legs, fell in an untidy sprawl sending jockey Bob Turnell rolling for many yards and leaving Freebooter with the easiest of tasks. Taking no chances, Jimmy Power safely brought Freebooter over the final fence with a superb leap and sprinted to the post a 15-length winner from Wot No Sun, with Acthon Major ten lengths away in third place. Rowland Roy was fourth, in front of Monaveen, Ship's Bell and Inchmore.

The crowds went wild with excitement, not just because most had backed the winner, more earnestly because in Freebooter they saw a new and exciting Aintree champion, a true 'Liverpool' horse of the old style. It was the gelding's third victory over the big fences and there appeared no reason to suspect that Mrs Brotherton's champion would not be back to repeat this impeccable performance.

It was a complete triumph for nothern-trained horses, with the first three home all trained in Yorkshire but, most of all, the thrills of the day and the worthy result were a testament to the tremendous appeal of the Grand National held far and near.

Exactly 100 years after Prince Albert's imaginative celebration of British achievements at the Great Exhibition, the nation rejoiced again in 1951 with the opening of the Festival of Britain. An area of 27 acres of derelict, bomb-damaged land near Waterloo in London was restored into an exhibition site with a distinctly futuristic theme, containing such structures as the Dome of Discovery, the Skylon, and a purpose-built concert auditorium, the Royal

Festival Hall. Opened by Their Majesties the King and Queen, the project by and large was a successful one, the chief complaint of the public being that a cup of coffee was priced at ninepence.

The tragic and sudden loss of Lord Mildmay shortly after the 1950 Grand National left a cloud of sadness which lingered still at Aintree when the 36 runners went to the start for the 1951 race. His contribution to National Hunt racing was immeasurable, his example as a sportsman exemplary and the spirit of fair play he exuded an inspiration to all.

As winner of his last three races, the six-year-old Arctic Gold was the subject of many hefty gambles, Mr J.H. Whitney's gelding going off as 8/1 favourite.

Former winner Russian Hero had reverted to his old disappointing ways, which was reflected in his extended price of 40/1. At the same odds was the mare Nickel Coin, plainly at such a generous price because of the poor record of her sex in the event.

By the stallion Pay Up, who as a three-year-old won the Two Thousand Guineas and was fourth in the Derby, her dam was Viscum and she was bred by Mr Richard Corbett. As a yearling filly she was bought by Mr Jeffrey Royle for 50 guineas but, making a decision he was soon to regret, Royle parted with Nickel Coin after a short period. It was Mr Royle's son, Frank, who bought her back for his father when the young man was demobbed from the forces and soon Nickel Coin was distinguishing herself in the show-jumping arena. When it was decided to race her, she was put in the care of trainer Jack O'Donaghue at Reigate in Surrey and developed into a most reliable jumper and thoroughly sound stayer. By the time she made her appearance in the National, Nickel Coin had won six races and, ridden by ex-paratrooper and prisoner-of-war John Bullock, there was some confidence for her among the stable connections.

The usual roar from the crowds when the runners raced away from the start was replaced this time by a gasp of astonishment, for starter Mr Leslie Firth completely misjudged things and pressed the lever with half the runners facing the wrong way. In their haste to make up lost ground, the jockeys went far too fast to the first fence, with the result that 12 came down at the initial obstacle. With the favourite, Arctic Gold, tearing away in front, the thoughts in most minds were just what could possibly happen next? Surprisingly, Morning Cover was the only faller at Becher's, but the next accounted for three more fallers and at the Canal Turn a further five went out, including the favourite Arctic Gold. Approaching the Chair there were only seven horses left in the contest. This was at once reduced to five when the leader, Russian Hero, and his stable companion, Dog Watch, both fell at the Chair, leaving Gay Heather to lead over the water jump from Nickel Coin, Derrinstown, Royal Tan and Broomfield. Landing in front over Becher's, Nickel Coin and Royal Tan came away from the Brook with only

Broomfield following them, for Gay Heather and Derrinstown both fell. Over the Canal Turn there were just the two left in the race, Nickel Coin and Royal Tan, with Derrinstown a long way out of sight behind them. Side by side the two survivors raced back to the racecourse and coming to the final fence Royal Tan appeared to be going slightly the better of the two. But the Irish gelding hit the last hard, losing his momentum and rather lucky to stay on his feet, leaving the mare to race clear and pass the post the winner by six lengths. A very long way behind came the remounted Derrinstown to claim third prize money, the only other to finish.

For the first time in many years, the press slammed the event and the officials connected with it, claiming that a false start should have been declared, or the race rerun. However, it was a simple human error on the part of an official holding a tremendous responsibility and who had obviously been caught up in the extreme tension of the moment.

Nickel Coin became only the third mare this century to win the Grand National and when sent to stud she bred just three foals, of which only King's Nickel was of any use on the racecourse.

His Majesty King George VI died in February 1952, the Court went into mourning and Britain entered a new Elizabethan era.

Two months later there was still controversy concerning the Grand National, which in view of the previous year's unfortunate happenings was bad timing to say the least. This time the trouble concerned a long running dispute between Mrs Topham and the BBC over the copyright of the radio commentary and just who owned it.

In another big field of 47 runners, Freebooter was clear favourite at 10/1, once more carrying top weight of 12st 7lb and with that excellent Irish jockey Bryan Marshall taking the mount. Teal was second in the market, from Dorothy Paget's Legal Joy, Mr Rank's Early Mist and the locally owned and trained Border Luck.

Two complete trainloads of spectators, numbering some 600 people, were attending as guests of their employer, the rather flamboyant Mr Harry Lane, owner of the strongly fancied Teal. A ten-year-old carrying 10st 12lb, Teal was bred near Clonmel in Ireland by Gerald Carroll, the product of a mating between Bimco and Milltown Queen. Purchased by Mr Richard Gough of Tipperary for a mere £35, Teal was subsequently sent to England where he became the property of Mr Ridley Lamb, of the well-known Northumbrian sporting family, for a similar purchase price. It was Mr Lamb who discovered the gelding's potential, riding the horse himself to victory in a number of point-to-points and a hunter chase. Having made the horse into a most reliable jumper, he accepted an offer of £2,000 for Teal from the 22-stone Harry Lane, a construction magnate hailing from South Shields. Under the tutelage of trainer Neville Crump at Middleham, Teal went from strength to strength, winning three of his five races on the run-up to Aintree and with Arthur Thompson as his jockey, his chances were outstanding.

After a delay of some 12 minutes, the runners were sent on their way to a cheer from the stands, but again the first fence exacted a toll of ten fallers, among them Early Mist, Russian Hero and Lord Sefton's Irish Lizard. Through the mist Freebooter and Teal could just be made out making their approach to Becher's in the lead. Teal and Freebooter were jumping brilliantly in front, followed closely by Legal Joy and Wot No Sun and as these four majestically swept over Valentine's they were accompanied by a throng of loose horses. Back on the racecourse there were only 18 left in the race, headed by Teal, Freebooter, Wot No Sun, Legal Joy and Border Luck and with Royal Tan beginning to make ground from the rear. In this order they cleared the water jump and set off back into the country. At Becher's for the final time, Arthur Thompson's brilliance was put to the supreme test when Teal landed almost on his nose but, although relinquishing the lead, the jockey righted his mount and kept him in the race. Jumping upside Freebooter again as they rose at the Canal Turn, Teal landed well but Freebooter pecked badly and crumpled to the ground. Teal was immediately joined by Michael Scudamore and Legal Joy and together they drew clear of the few survivors as they raced back to the racecourse. Stride for stride over the last half mile, Teal and Legal Joy came to the final fence alongside each other but once safely on the flat Arthur Thompson pushed Teal out and he raced away to win by five lengths from Legal Joy, with Wot No Sun a bad third, after Royal Tan had fallen at the last fence.

Both trainer and jockey celebrated a second success in the race and the ebullient owner, Harry Lane, was giving interviews to everyone within hearing distance.

Great things were expected of Teal, who had won his race well and survived with agility the odd mistake, but he was never seen in the National again. In preparation for the 1953 renewal of the race, Teal took part in the 1953 Cheltenham Gold Cup and injured himself so badly that he had to be put down.

In the year of the coronation of Queen Elizabeth II, Britain's senior flat-race jockey won his first Epsom Derby after many years of trying. As it happened, it was also his only one, but being made the first Knight of the Turf by Her Majesty the Queen in that year of 1953, Sir Gordon Richards had little cause for complaint.

The field of 31 for that year's big Aintree race was without a previous winner of the race, but at top weight of 12st 5 lb was Miss Dorothy Paget's former Gold Cup winner, the striking chestnut Mont Tremblant. Trained by the man who had steered Reynoldstown to a second National victory Fulke Walwyn, the French-bred gelding was undoubtedly the class horse of the race.

Favourite at 7/1 was Yorkshire-trained Little Yid, with Whispering Steel, Glen Fire, Cardinal Error and Lucky Dome also attracting a good deal of punters' money. The latter was one of a strong Irish challenge, which also included the grey Overshadow and the eight-year-old Early Mist.

Bred in England by Mr D.J. Wrinch, Early Mist was sired by Brumeux from the mare Sudden Dawn and as the property of Mr J.V. Rank almost all his racing was conducted in Ireland and the gelding had carried that famous owner's colours in the 1952 National when coming down at the first fence. Upon the untimely death of Mr Rank, Early Mist came up for sale and Lord Bicester, who had tried for so long to win the Grand National, was excited at the prospect of buying him. He was, however, outbid at 5,300 guineas by the Dublin businessman Joe Griffin, who was a newcomer to racing and who sent his new purchase to be trained by Vincent O'Brien at Cashel, in County Tipperary. After twice running unplaced for his new owner at Leopardstown and Baldoyle, Early Mist came good with a victory in the Newlands 'Chase at Naas, only to lose the race on an objection. Three weeks later he was Aintree-bound and with Bryan Marshall as his partner he was splendid value at 20/1. Bryan Marshall was born in 1916 at Cloughjordan, Tipperary, was riding at the age of three and rode his first winner on the flat when just 12 years of age, on Cheviotdale at Kempton Park. That rare combination of horseman-jockey, Marshall lost six valuable racing years through service during the war in the 5th Inniskilling Dragoon Guards, attaining the rank of captain and being wounded on the first day of the Normandy landings. An exceptional judge of pace, and particularly effective in a close finish, Bryan Marshall was without question one of the finest National Hunt riders of the immediate post-war period.

From a good start, Ordnance set off at a cracking gallop, leading over the first fence. Out in front still by a clear margin was Ordnance, who put in a superb leap over Becher's, followed by a line of horses which included Little Yid, Parasol II, Knuckleduster, Mont Tremblant, Hierba and Early Mist. Well ahead of the remainder as he jumped the water, Ordnance kept up his strong pace going back into the country but rising at the big ditch before Becher's Early Mist had moved right upsides the leader. At the next fence, the 20th, Ordnance fell, leaving Early Mist in front and maintaining his advantage held over Becher's by three lengths from Mont Tremblant and the tiring Little Yid. Increasing his lead at every jump on the run back to the final fences, Early Mist was well clear at the last, jumped it well and raced home unchallenged to win by 20 lengths from the brave Mont Tremblant, with Lord Sefton's Irish Lizard four lengths further behind in third place.

The owner, Mr Griffin, and his wife led in Early Mist with obvious pride, followed by a modest man who had now won every important race in the National Hunt calendar, Vincent O'Brien.

Shortly before Christmas in 1953 Liverpool staged its first all-jumping fixture over the newly constructed Mildmay course, named after the man who conceived the plan as a less severe introduction for young horses and riders to the big National fences, Lord Mildmay.

It was considered rather appropriate that on the first day's racing over the Mildmay course, the first three events were won by Bryan Marshall, the most recent hero of the National. The final leg of this notable treble was aboard the popular 'chaser Irish Lizard and some four months later Lord Sefton's horse returned to Aintree as the 15/2 favourite for the 1954 Grand National.

There was a very strong Irish challenge that year, making up almost a quarter of the field, with Royal Tan, the giant-sized Coneyburrow and Churchtown the principal contenders from across the Irish Sea. Each of these held prominent positions in the betting.

With Early Mist missing the race, Vincent O'Brien relied on Royal Tan as his main hope, with his wife's Churchtown a very useful second string and it was the former which jockey Bryan Marshall chose to ride. Bred in Tipperary by Mr J. Topham, Royal Tan was by Tartan out of the mare Princess of Birds, and the best he could do for his first owner, Mr P. Bell, was to finish fourth in a hurdle race. When purchased by Mrs Moya Keogh, Royal Tan was placed with trainer Vincent O'Brien who saddled him to finish runner-up in both the Irish and the Aintree Nationals. Passed on to owner Joe Griffin at the end of 1951, the chestnut gelding put up another exciting performance in the 1952 Grand National, only to once more find the final fence a major problem. Bryan Marshall received instructions from the trainer to refrain from using forceful tactics and just let Royal Tan find his own way round Aintree.

From a level break, Coneyburrow, Legal Joy, Sanperion and Triple Torch led into the first fence, where Gentle Moya, Whispering Steel and Alberoni all fell. With the huge Coneyburrow making the running, the race settled into a regular form. For once Becher's presented no problems for any of them and at the Canal Turn it was still Coneyburrow ahead of Sanperion, Royal Stuart, Churchtown and Punchestown Star. A very bad mistake at the water jump cost Coneyburrow the lead as he splashed through the obstacle, only the reflexes of his jockey, Pat Taaffe, keeping him in the race.

Over Becher's it was Sanperion, Churchtown and Tudor Line disputing the lead, with Coneyburrow striving to reach them and Royal Tan steadily making ground. Jumping the Canal Turn, Royal Tan moved smoothly through on the inside. With jockey Marshall obeying his instructions to the letter, Royal Tan outjumped Tudor Line over Valentine's, landing with a half-length advantage and looking full of running. Racing towards the second last the two leaders had the race between them. Tudor Line appeared to be tiring as he jumped to the right at each of the final fences, and as Royal Tan landed three lengths clear over the last it looked a cut-and-dried victory. But then, once safely over that final obstacle, Tudor Line galloped on as if his life depended on it. Tudor Line gained stride by stride all the way up that punishingly long run-in and with both jockeys riding flat out, the packed stands came alive with excitement. Neck and neck Royal Tan and Tudor Line fought out that incredible finish, both horses and their riders draining their very souls to gain a vital inch and at the post they were so close together the judge was to be pitied. The result was Royal Tan had held on by a neck from the courageous Tudor Line, with the favourite, Irish Lizard, ten lengths back in third place, and Churchtown fourth.

Vincent O'Brien was in great demand by pressmen and broadcasters after saddling his second successive Grand National winner. At his third attempt Royal Tan had finally overcome the last fence bogey and placed himself firmly and deservedly in the record books.

On the crest of a wave and at the height of their fame, Vincent O'Brien and Joe Griffin had a reversal of fortune virtually within days of achieving their second National success. The trainer lost his licence for three months and Griffin suffered a more enduring setback leading to him being declared bankrupt.

Under such humiliating circumstances, the two most recent Grand National winners, together with Joe Griffin's other horses, came up for sale at Ballsbridge and his National gold trophies were auctioned in Dublin. Royal Tan became the property of Prince Aly Khan for 3,900 guineas and Early Mist was bought by Vincent O'Brien for 2,000 guineas.

Of the 30 runners set to contend the 1955 Grand National on 26 March, four of them were prepared by Vincent O'Brien, his licence to train by now restored.

Most heavily backed horse at the off was another Irish horse, Copp, from the yard of Paddy Sleator, and as a winner of his last three races, with the champion jockey Tim Molony in the saddle, was 7/1 favourite.

With Early Mist at 9s, Tudor Line on 10/1 and Quare Times figuring at 100/9, the unusual situation arose that three of the first four in the betting were Irish-trained. Her Majesty Queen Elizabeth the Queen Mother renewed her involvement in the race with her gelding M'as-tu-Vu.

Ever the perfectionist, Vincent O'Brien selected four of the finest horsemen available to partner his Grand National team, the very tall, ice-cool Pat Taaffe more than happy to continue his relationship with the nine-year-old Quare Times.

By Artist's Son out of Lavenco, Quare Times was bred by Mr P.P. Sweeney at Thurles and while still a yearling was bought at Ballsbridge sales by Mrs W.H.E. Welman for 300 guineas. Placed with Vincent O'Brien two years later, the trainer laid the horse aside for a further couple of years to allow him to mature, while already entertaining visions of the youngster making a Liverpool horse. Unraced until after his sixth birthday, Quare Times was brought along quietly by the maestro from Cashel and it was not until January 1954, at Gowran Park, that he first entered the winner's enclosure. In the current campaign, Quare Times was aimed at just one objective, the Grand National, and his second place in Cheltenham's National Hunt Handicap 'Chase as his wind-up race before Aintree proved he was cherry-ripe for the major test.

Such was the mud-like state of the ground, with waterlogging in the area in front of the stands, it was ruled that the water jump should be omitted from the contest.

After a reasonable start it was more of a splash to the first fence than a dash, with the big bold Sundew setting a cracking pace to the first fence. Continuing to blaze a rapid trail, Sundew led from Gentle Moya, Gigolo, Tudor Line and ESB into Becher's where the latter made a horrible mistake which also brought down Roman Fire. One of the troublesome loose horses ran directly across the path of Sundew at the Chair but with perfect anticipation jockey Pat Doyle steered Sundew clear of the danger. Safely on his way, Sundew led around the dolled-off water jump from M'as-tu-Vu, Steel Lock, Carey's Cottage, Gentle Moya and Irish Lizard, with Pat Taaffe some way in the rear with Quare Times but jumping cleanly. The exuberant Sundew was still galloping strongly at the head of affairs, seemingly oblivious to the underfoot conditions, as he led over Becher's and still in command at the Canal Turn he was joined by the swiftly improving Quare Times. Closely followed by Gigolo, Tudor Line and Carey's Cottage, the leaders made their gruelling way back towards the racecourse. Once back on the racecourse proper though, Quare Times exerted his authority, drawing clear and full of running, with his only danger a slender one in the form of the persistent Tudor Line. Quare Times came right away from the opposition to win by 12 lengths from Tudor Line, with Carey's Cottage a further four lengths back in third place. Gigolo was fourth.

Winning trainer Vincent O'Brien was hailed as a genius, a super-being, turning out three successive Grand National winners in his quiet, modest way and nobody could deny that his talent was extraordinarily rare.

Quare Times never ran in the Grand National again and Vincent O'Brien turned his attention to flat racing. He remains, however, the only trainer to win three Grand Nationals in successive years with three different horses.

Twelve

1956–1965

The year 1956 saw British troops in action in the Middle East, after President Nasser of Egypt ordered the seizure of the Suez Canal. In a long-drawn-out dispute, an Anglo-French force was eventually involved in retaking the vital seaway and clearing it of the sunken ships the Egyptians had used to block it. In America a young man by the name of Elvis Presley was rocketing up the pop-music charts with such hits as 'Love Me Tender' and 'Heartbreak Hotel'.

The 1956 Grand National drew a field of 29, with the two former winners, Early Mist and Royal Tan, heading the handicap with 12st 2lb and 12st 1lb respectively. Favourite at 7/1 was the proven stayer Must but far and away the biggest attraction for many was the two entries of Her Majesty Queen Elizabeth the Queen Mother.

M'as-tu-Vu had run well for a long way in the previous year's race and was at 40/1, whereas the ten-year-old Devon Loch was making his first National appearance and, partnered by the former champion jockey Dick Francis, received warm support at 100/7.

Another ex-champion jockey, 43-year-old Fred Rimell, was by now a much-respected and most astute trainer and in saddling ESB was attempting to emulate his father Tom, who sent out Forbra to win in the 1932 National. By Bidar out of English Summer, ESB was bred by Miss Sheila Bourke in County Kildare, and as a yearling was sold for 290 guineas to Mr P.J. O'Regan. The son of Bidar was first seen on a racecourse in the colours of Mr R. Oliver at Birmingham in November 1949, running unplaced in a novice hurdle, yet before that season was over ESB had graduated to fences, winning a two-mile 'chase at Cheltenham. The young gelding was demonstrating his capacity for work and by the spring of 1951 had acquired a new owner. Mrs Leonard Carver was herself a first-class horsewoman, who as Miss Pierce became the first lady to ride the winner of the Daily Mail Championship at Olympia, and at

Newmarket sales her husband bought ESB for 8,100 guineas. For a brief period the new owners trained the horse themselves and he got as far as the first Becher's in the 1955 National with Leonard Carver shown in the racecard as his trainer. ESB was returned to Kinnersley and by the time he lined up for the 1956 Grand National the ten-year-old had won 18 races and he had as his partner one of the most likeable jockeys in the game. Thirty-two-year-old David Victor Dick was the son of the Epsom trainer and with his now six-foot frame it was hard to imagine him as a 7st 4lb apprentice flat-race jockey. Yet in 1941 that was how he was when winning the Lincolnshire Handicap on Gloaming.

With the royal party in attendance, the race began eight minutes late and straightaway Madame Hennessy's Armorial III went into the lead, setting an impossible pace from the outset. For a change there were no casualties at the Brook, where Armorial III was still clear from Dunboy II, Sundew, Witty and M'as-tu-Vu and the leaders returned to the racecourse. Still in front and going strongly over the water jump, Armorial III showed no let-up in the pace going back into the country, chased by M'as-tu-Vu, Sundew, Eagle Lodge and Much Obliged. At the 19th, the open ditch, M'as-tu-Vu, Witty and Dunboy II all came down, just as ESB and Devon Loch moved into contention. Rounding the Canal Turn Devon Loch cruised up on the outside, going easily within himself. At the plain fence after Valentine's, the long-time leader Armorial III fell, as also did Much Obliged, leaving Devon Loch in front and hard pressed by Eagle Lodge, Ontray, ESB and Gentle Moya, the royal runner approached the stands for the final time. Galloping on strongly now, Devon Loch measured the last two fences perfectly, landing on the flat a length and a half ahead of the one-paced ESB. The noise from the crowds packing the stands and enclosures was deafening as Devon Loch increased his lead with every stride up the run-in. With barely 50 yards left to run and with his nearest rival well beaten, the inexplicable, the unbelievable and the tragic happened in the blinking of an eye. Devon Loch in perfect galloping motion one second, suddenly assumed a jumping attitude, his forelegs rising as if about to leap some obstacle that only he could see. In the most dramatic climax to a race ever witnessed, Devon Loch sprawled helplessly, his legs spreadeagled along the turf and with Dick Francis still perfectly seated astride him. ESB, seconds before content to be a gallant runner-up, raced past the stricken royal runner to become the luckiest winner ever in the history of the Grand National. From a tumultuous crescendo of noise, in an instant a deathly silence was all that signalled the end of this remarkable event and for many minutes afterwards few people knew the result. ESB won by ten lengths from the mare Gentle Moya, with Royal Tan the same distance away in third place, just ahead of Eagle Lodge.

The Devon Loch mystery remains unsolved to this day, despite countless theories being put forward over the years. A ghost jump, the horse suffering a heart spasm, and the one which jockey Dick Francis now feels the most likely cause: that the tremendous noise from the crowd welcoming home the first royal victory for 56 years so disturbed Devon Loch that he became for the briefest second disorientated.

Hiding her disappointment with charm and dignity, Her Majesty the Queen Mother immediately saw to the welfare of her horse and jockey before graciously congratulating the winning connections.

Neither Devon Loch nor Dick Francis ever took part in the Grand National again.

The field of 35 in 1957 consisted of a mixed bag, including the former winners, ESB and the evergreen Royal Tan, a Cheltenham Gold Cup winner in Four Ten and Peter Cazalet's brightest new star, Rose Park, together of course with the customary assortment of unknown quantities.

Winner of his three most recent races, the Neville Crump-trained Goosander wound up as 5/1 favourite, with his stablemate Much Obliged second choice in the betting at 10/1. Making a third attempt and once more ridden by champion jockey Fred Winter, the 11-year-old Sundew was on 20s.

Having been bred by Mr J. McArdle in County Meath, from a mating between the stallion Sun King and Parsonstown Gem, Sundew was bought as a yearling from his first owner, Richard Quilan, of Fethard, at Ballsbridge sales by Mr P.G. Grey, of Coole Abbey, Clonmel, for 370 guineas. When trained for this owner by Mr J. McClintock, Sundew was successful in the Munster Steeplechase at Thurles when just seven and the following year kept up the good work with 'chase victories at Limerick, Thurles and Mallow. After finishing a creditable second to Copp in the Leopardstown 'Chase in 1955, the gelding was bought by Mrs Geoffrey Kohn for something in the region of £3,000. Trained in Warwickshire at Henley-in-Arden by Frank Hudson, Sundew was the only 'chaser in the trainer's small yard and the huge gelding was thought by many to have used up his chances at Aintree. His partner was the son of a former top flat-race jockey turned trainer, and after serving his apprenticeship, Fred Winter rode some winners on the flat before growing too heavy and being forced to venture over obstacles. After serving in the war, Fred rode his first jump winner on a horse owned by his father, named Carton, but soon afterwards broke his back when falling in a hurdle race at Wye. After a year's inactivity, Fred Winter made a successful return by riding the winners of 18 races and gaining confidence with every ride, Winter in no time at all established himself as a rider possessing rare talent.

With little delay the race began, Armorial III repeating his efforts of last time by charging to the front and leading over the first fence. Armorial III came down at the fourth when three lengths in front, leaving the giant Sundew in command, followed by Athenian, Cherry Abbot and Gentle Moya. Striding out strongly, Sundew proceeded to run the feet off his opponents and although stumbling badly at Becher's, Fred Winter kept his partnership with Sundew intact. Leading something of a charmed life by surviving a number of errors, Sundew remained in the lead. Romping towards the stands, Sundew had a comfortable lead, leaping the water jump four lengths ahead of Athenian, ESB, The Crofter and Tiberetta. Running down to Becher's again, Athenian moved upsides Sundew, who once more pitched badly landing over the Brook and again demonstrating his tremendous strength, the gelding recovered to go clear. Returning to the racecourse with just two fences left to jump, ESB came with a flurry as if about to make a race of it, only to weaken before the final fence and leave Sundew still in the lead. Although very tired, Sundew stayed on bravely passing the post the winner by eight lengths from the Scottish-trained Wyndburgh, with Tiberetta six lengths further back in third place.

That evening a celebration dinner was given at Southport's Prince of Wales Hotel, at which toasts were given many times over to Sundew and the proud Fred Winter, and two days later the victorious pair paraded through the streets of Henly-in-Arden as returning heroes.

After finishing fifth in his second race of the new season, Liverpool's Grand Sefton 'Chase, Sundew appeared just over a fortnight later in the Makerfield Handicap 'Chase at Haydock Park and after blundering badly at the water jump, was struck into by two other horses. A bone had been smashed in his shoulder and Sundew was put down.

Almost eight months to the day of his greatest racing achievement, Sundew was buried at Haydock Park, close to the grave of Fly Mask who, during the 1920s, finished second and third in the Grand National and also sadly met his death at Haydock.

The only former winner of the race able to contest the 1958 Grand National was ESB, now 12 years old and with top weight of 11st 12lb obviously some way down the betting. In contrast, the four years younger Wyndburgh was all the rage, the little horse from north of the border a hot favourite at 6/1.

A late rush of money on the day also elevated a little Irish horse named Mr What to the top seven most-backed horses.

Bred by Mrs Barbara O'Neill in County Westmeath, by Grand Inquisitor from Duchess of Pedulas, Mr What was only just broken when as a five-year-old he was bought for £500 by the Rathcoole, County Dublin trainer, Thomas J. Taaffe, father of the outstanding jockey brothers. His first appearance on a racecourse was in the Slaney Maiden Hurdle at Naas in January 1956, when he failed to catch anyone's eye but a little over two months later, in his second outing, he trounced 21 opponents in the Navan Maiden Hurdle at long odds. Having lost his maiden status, Mr What was purchased by the Dublin businessman Mr D.J. Coughlan. It was in his third season, when put over fences, that Mr What really came into his own, taking to the major obstacles like a duck to water and winning four times before giving a splendid performance to finish second behind Roddy Owen in the Leopardstown 'Chase. This was his last race before the National, in which by any standards he was very much still a novice and up to visiting Aintree had never competed outside his native Ireland. Tom Taaffe senior booked the strong English jockey Arthur Freeman for Mr What. Thirty-two-year-old Arthur Freeman had as a youngster been apprenticed to the great trainer George Lambton and after the war became stable jockey to Peter Cazalet. He had, however, never sat upon Mr What until mounting the gelding in the paddock before the start of the 1958 Grand National.

After heavy overnight rain the going was heavy on the National course and from a good start the runners approached the first fence in a more sedate manner than usual. The Brook itself brought about the downfall of Must, Sentina, Frozen Credit and Comedian's Folly and with the survivors already spread over a wide expanse, Goosander led them back towards the stands. Athenian was lying second, followed by Mr What and these three were the first over the water jump. Back in the country, the number of fallers increased. Striking the front at Becher's Brook, Mr What raced on freely, with Goosander, Tiberetta, Eagle Lodge, ESB, Green Drill and Wyndburgh struggling to keep pace in the bad ground. Jumping the Canal Turn like an old hand, Mr What began to draw clear of his rivals, the further he went the wider the gap between them. Well clear re-entering the racecourse, he popped over the penultimate fence and approached the last still pulling hard and with the race at his mercy. His only error in the whole of the race came when he hit the last fence, almost costing him the victory he had earned but with Arthur Freeman displaying perfect equanimity, the mistake was corrected at once and Mr What came home the easiest winner of the National for many years by all of 30 lengths. The remote second was Mr Edward Courage's brave mare Tiberetta, with Green Drill another 15 lengths away in third place and the favourite Wyndburgh fourth.

The Irish visitors went absolutely wild when Mr What made his way to the winner's enclosure, as did many non-Irish punters whose money had reduced the little fellow's price to 18/1 shortly before the off. Mr What was to grace Aintree with his presence on many more occasions, sometimes figuring prominently in his efforts to repeat that memorable victory. In the remaining

33 races in which he competed, however, Mr What never won another race.

World news in 1959 had a distinctly sombre complexion, with the passing of four leading personalities. British racing driver Mike Hawthorne lost his life in a crash on the Guildford bypass within just months of retiring as world champion. That most popular rock singer Buddy Holly was killed in a plane crash in Iowa, and Billie Holiday, one of the greatest blues singers of all time, passed away aged only 44. The swashbuckling Hollywood star Errol Flynn also met a premature end to a fun-filled life aged 50.

Of the 34 hopefuls competing in the 1959 Grand National, it was unusual to find as top weight with 12st the mare Kerstin. As the most recent winner of the Cheltenham Gold Cup the Northumberland-trained lady provided the degree of class too often missing from recent Nationals.

Although yet to record a win since his runaway triumph in last year's race, Mr What headed the betting at 6/1. Two other Irish challengers, Slippery Serpent and Nic Atkins, were heavily supported. Also making a strong appeal the nearer the race approached was an eight-year-old called simply OXO, who wound up the second most heavily backed contestant at 8/1.

A bay gelding bearing the conformation of the old stamp of 'chaser, OXO was by Bobsleigh out of Patum, having been bred in Dorset by Mr A.C. Wyatt and as a yearling passed into ownership of Mr Geoffrey Mason for 400 guineas. A natural jumper, OXO won two point-to-points for Mr Mason when six years old before being sent to Newmarket October sales. OXO, as yet unraced under rules, was knocked down for the sum of 3,200 guineas to Mr J.E. Bigg. Placed in the care of trainer Willie Stephenson at Royston, Hertfordshire, the owner chose well, for among the many successes Stephenson had achieved since first acquiring his trainer's licence in 1950 were the Epsom Derby of 1951 with Arctic Prince and three Champion Hurdles with that fabulous horse Sir Ken. OXO made his first racecourse appearance at Haydock Park in the Wigan Novices 'Chase at the end of November 1957, when ridden by Tim Molony he finished sixth of 14. Stepping up in distance and class, he next turned out for the three-mile Wollaton 'Chase at Nottingham two months later, jumping superbly throughout to make all the running for a 12-length victory. Another win followed soon after. Somewhat backward in the first few competitions of the current season, OXO revived the promise shown at the beginning when winning over three miles at Lingfield in early December 1958 and on that occasion he was ridden for the first time by that fine jockey, Michael Scudamore. After a good win at Kempton Park on Boxing Day, his final race before the National came in the Trial 'Chase at Leicester in February when he was a worthy second behind the more experienced Hart Royal. Michael Scudamore was back in the saddle with OXO for Aintree and, having already finished second and third in the National, the 26-year-old jockey knew enough about Aintree to make the perfect partner for the young gelding.

With hardly any delay the starter got them off to a good break, Surprise Packet and Tiberetta cutting out the early work and they cleared Becher's perfectly. Approaching Valentine's Surprise Packet led by three lengths from Tiberetta, these two being some way ahead of Mr What and Wyndburgh. Still clear over the water, Surprise Packet began the second circuit maintaining his strong gallop as Wyndburgh and OXO began to improve their positions. Becher's again took its toll, when the long-time leader Surprise Packet fell, along with Irish Coffee, Soltown and Mainstown and from this pile-up the final pattern of the race emerged. Left with the lead between them, OXO and Wyndburgh came away from the Brook well in advance of the remainder, but jockey Tim Brookshaw on Wyndburgh had also become a victim of Becher's. His off-side stirrup leather had broken as a result of the huge drop at the Brook and rather than ride lop-sided, Tim Brookshaw kicked his other foot free and for the rest of the race rode without irons. Rarely has such an epic piece of horsemanship as that displayed by Tim Brookshaw been witnessed and nothing could have been more fitting than that Aintree was the backcloth for such brilliance. Nursing, cajoling and, when needed, urging Wyndburgh to stay with OXO, Tim Brookshaw rode into Grand National folklore that afternoon, aware that his quest was an unequal one. OXO came to the final fence looking all over the winner, but hitting the top of the obstacle in his only mistake of the entire journey, Michael Scudamore conjured an immediate recovery and sped on towards the winning post. Coming with a courageous and sustained challenge in the closing stages of the contest, Tim Brookshaw brought the terrier-like Wyndburgh to get within a length and a half of OXO by the time the post was reached. OXO won the 1959 Grand National on merit and most deservedly the plaudits, but Wyndburgh and Tim Brookshaw won a place in the annals of the race which is priceless. Slogging on into third place, eight lengths behind Wyndburgh, came Mr What, and the only other finisher was that most consistent of Aintree performers, Tiberetta.

A major milestone in the history of the Grand National was reached in 1960, when for the first time the event was televised, attracting the biggest audience the race had yet enjoyed.

With 26 runners going to post, it was the smallest National field since 1920 but what the race lacked in quantity it more than made up for in quality.

Top weight with 11st 11lb was former winner Mr What, always considered reliable over Aintree's big fences, with Wyndburgh making his fourth attempt and with his heroic effort of the previous year still fresh in the mind, second favourite at 8/1 in the betting.

The horse considered to have the best chance of all though, was the favourite, Merryman II, a striking bay gelding by Carnival Boy out of the mare Maid Marion. Bred by the Marquess of Linlithgow, the horse was purchased when five years old by Miss Winifred Wallace for an undisclosed sum and it was Miss Wallace who broke Merryman II and rode him to hounds. She also trained the gelding to win some point-to-points and also a hunter 'chase when he was seven. It was after this that the Edinburgh lady decided to put him in the hands of a professional trainer, despatching Merryman II to Neville Crump at Middleham. Merryman II in no time at all developed into the find of the season, jumping the big Aintree fences boldly for a clear-cut victory in the Liverpool Foxhunters 'Chase and then beating a good field easily in the Scottish Grand National at Bogside but a serious setback arose after he finished fifth in the Rhymney Breweries 'Chase at Chepstow in mid-December. It was discovered that Merryman II had an inflamed foot bone and it became a race against time to restore him to fitness. With that problem almost overcome, just a week before Aintree, jockey Gerry Scott broke his collar bone for the second time in five days and the replacement, Johnny East, was put on stand-by. Twenty-two-year-old Gerald Scott hailed from the north-east and was educated at Barnard Castle School, but anxious to get into racing he became apprentice to Neville Crump when 16 and was quickly established as one of the leading riders on the northern circuit. Determined to partner his best chance yet in the National, Gerry Scott had his damaged arm and shoulder heavily strapped and proceeded to take Merryman II to the start, the 13/2 favourite.

The preliminaries over, they were sent on their journey from a good start and approached the first fence far more sedately than was normal and in consequence only Lotoray failed to continue beyond the initial obstacle. Tea Fiend was prominent over the early fences, striding out well and jumping with precision, ahead of Green Drill, Arles and Sabaria, with Mr What and Merryman II tucked in nicely just behind. The Canal Turn claimed Clover Bud and Dandy Scot and Valentine's proved too much for Jonjo, leaving 20 still in the race as they returned to the racecourse with Tea Fiend still in the prime position. With Tea Fiend still in command the remainder streamed over the water jump and raced back into the country. Going into Becher's for the last time Tea Fiend, Merryman II and Badanloch had drawn ahead of the rest. Landing over the Brook, Badanloch moved into second place, just behind his stablemate Tea Fiend, while just to their rear Mr What fell, together with Team Spirit, Pendle Lady and Aliform and Canonbie Lee refused. For the next couple of fences there was little to choose between Merryman II and Badanloch, although the former always appeared to be racing more easily and at the final ditch Merryman II began to stride clear. Going further ahead after the second last, the favourite jumped the final fence in splendid style and romped away to win by 15 lengths from Badanloch, with Clear Profit third and Tea Fiend fourth.

Miss Wallace, as the first unmarried lady to own a Grand National winner, received a special array of congratulations. Neville Crump, celebrating training his third National victory, was understandably a very proud man, and Gerry Scott's masterful riding under the most difficult physical conditions added yet another memorable chapter to Aintree's history.

Since the earliest days of the Grand National, the race had attracted visitors from all over the world and in 1961 two competitors together with riders made the overland journey from the Soviet Union to Aintree for the first time. It was a most praiseworthy endeavour, though with neither Grifel nor Reljef having raced in this country, they were automatically allocated top weight each of 12st.

Favourite of the 35 runners was the Irish horse Jonjo, recent winner of the Leopardstown 'Chase and the mount of the redoubtable Pat Taaffe. Merryman II was one point behind the favourite in the betting at 8/1. A flood of money on the day reduced the odds of newcomer Nicolaus Silver to 28/1 and trained by Fred Rimell he was a popular choice among housewives because of his striking grey colour.

Bred by James Heffernan in Tipperary, by Nicolaus out of Rays of Montrose, he was a consistent performer in his native land before coming up for sale at Ballsbridge, where he was bought for £2,600 by Fred Rimell on behalf of his patron, Mr Charles Vaughan. Brought along steadily at Kinnersley, Nicolaus Silver won his first race for his new owner at the fifth time of asking, in the Kim Muir Memorial Challenge Cup at the Cheltenham Festival and 17 days later paid his first visit to Aintree. Partnering the handsome grey in the big race was Bobby Beasley, a descendant of the famous Irish steeplechasing family.

The runners began their journey just two minutes after the scheduled time. The locally owned Fresh Winds was the first to show, leading over the first and the leader drew several lengths clear going towards Becher's. Fresh Winds took the Brook well but behind him there was a horrible-looking pile-up when Kingstel fell awkwardly, to be joined on the ground immediately by Brian Oge, Taxidermist, Carrasco and the Russian horse, Grifel. Over Valentine's, Fresh Winds held a ten-length advantage over OXO, the French challenger Imposant and Merryman II, and some way behind the second Russian entry unseated his rider Ponomarenko. On the final circuit Hunter's Breeze fell at the 17th and two fences later the open ditch saw the end of the long-time leader Fresh Winds. With Nicolaus Silver now in command, the race was on in earnest, Jonjo, Imposant and Mr What chasing the leader for all they were worth. Merryman II took up the running after clearing the Brook well. Tracked by

Nicolaus Silver all the way from here, Merryman II still looked likely to repeat his victory of the previous year as he led into the penultimate fence, but timing his run splendidly, Bobby Beasley landed over this obstacle with Nicolaus Silver in front. Foot perfect at the last, the grey romped away to win by five lengths from Merryman II, with fast-finishing O'Malley Point just a neck back in third place. Scottish Flight II was fourth.

Nicolaus Silver became only the second grey horse to win the National in providing trainer Fred Rimell with his second success in the race and for jockey Bobby Beasley it was an especially proud occasion. He had preserved the illustrious tradition of his family by winning the Grand National almost 70 years to the day his grandfather, Harry Beasley, had won the race on Come Away.

It was a day of contrasts at Aintree in 1962, both in terms of the weather and among the principal contestants. For days during race week frost and heavy rain turned the course into a quagmire, while on the day of the race there were brief spells of sunshine amid snow, hail and sleet.

Of the 32 runners, it was the brilliant newcomer Frenchman's Cove who went off 7/1 favourite. Solfen was next in the market on 9s and those favourites from former years, Merryman II, Mr What and Wyndburgh among the outsiders. Another long-shot thought to be past his best was the 12-year-old Kilmore.

Bred at Corolanty in County Offaly, Kilmore was by Zalophus out of Brown Image, his breeder being Mr Gilbert Webb. First owned by Mr John J. Ryan, for whom he won a number of both hurdle races and 'chases over the next couple of years, Kilmore was trained in turn by Willie Cullen, D. Kinane and Mick Browne. He was looked upon in Ireland as a reliable, workmanlike type, who would never achieve star status, but fortunately that most astute of British trainers, Captain Ryan Price, caught sight of him in a snow-covered field. On the look-out for a likely Aintree candidate for his owner Mr Nat Cohen, the film producer responsible for the 'Carry On' series, the trainer took to Kilmore the moment he saw him. For £3,000 the little gelding left Ireland, arriving at his new trainer's Findon yard to begin his preparation for the 1961 Grand National. Jumping brilliantly in that race Kilmore finished a good fifth and so delighted his jockey Fred Winter, that he asked Ryan Price to keep the horse sound for 1962 when he intended winning with him. His five races before that year's National could hardly be described as encouraging, finishing just second in the first of them and as a result Kilmore started at 28/1.

In the dreadful conditions it was a relief for all when the starter sent them on their way without any delay and on very soft going they charged towards the first fence. Already some lengths ahead of the rest was the Irish outsider Fredith's Son. Followed by Dandy Tim, Duplicator and Clear Profit, Fredith's Son led over

Becher's and falls up to then had been few and far between. At the Canal Turn Duplicator moved into second place and from Valentine's back to the racecourse, Fredith's Son and Duplicator became engaged in a duel for the lead. Jumping the water almost side by side the two leaders continued their tussle several lengths in front of Canonbie Lee, Mr What and Frenchman's Cove. Feeling the strain, Duplicator fell at the 19th, bringing down the favourite, Frenchman's Cove, and with a ten-length lead over the Brook, Fredith's Son was starting to take liberties with some of the jumps. Another Irish outsider, Gay Navarree, moved smoothly into contention going to Valentine's upsides Fredith's Son and still some way behind, the nearest contenders were Mr What, Nicolaus Silver, Wyndburgh, Clear Profit and the rapidly improving Kilmore. With Fredith's Son tiring, Gay Navarree came to the second-last fence marginally the leader. Strongly pressed by Wyndburgh, Mr What and Kilmore they jumped this and raced to the final obstacle in line across the course. First to land over the fence was Kilmore and unleashed by Fred Winter he raced home to a ten-length victory over Wyndburgh, with Mr What the same distance back in third place. Gay Navarree was fourth.

With owner Nat Cohen and his two partners absent through illness, it was left to a very proud Ryan Price to lead in Kilmore, and for Fred Winter it was an even more satisfying success than his first National victory with Sundew. For this time he shared the magical moment of triumph with his friend, the man with whom he had achieved so much turf glory, trainer Ryan Price.

Kilmore, despite his advanced years, ran in two more Grand Nationals, finishing sixth in 1963 and falling at the 21st the following year. Retired after this race, the tough little chap lived on in contentment, roaming the Findon Downs with his former trainer regularly supervising his welfare until Kilmore passed away in 1981 aged 31.

By the time the 1963 National came round it had become apparent that the modifications to the fences, introduced in time for the 1961 race, had made a great improvement to the event with more horses completing the course. Springbok was the 10/1 favourite, from Kilmore, Team Spirit, Loving Record and Dagmar Gittell, and some late money for the seven-year-old Carrickbeg, ridden and part-owned by that fine amateur John Lawrence, reduced his odds to 20/1.

Bracketed somewhat ignominiously among the '66/1 others' was a nine-year-old chestnut gelding named Ayala, whose only significant feature in the racecard was that he was trained by Mr Keith Piggott, father of flat-racing's sensational wonder jockey Lester. Bred by Mr J.P. Phillips, Ayala was by the 1950 Ascot Gold Cup winner Supertello from the mare Admiral's Bliss. It was not until his third season 'over the sticks' that Ayala recorded his first win in

November 1960 at Sandown Park, following it up with two further triumphs during that campaign. Sidelined for most of the next term, he ran only twice without attracting any attention and in only the last of his three contests before the 1963 Grand National did Ayala show any signs of a return to decent form. Ridden by Stan Mellor, he beat ten opponents to win the Worcester Royal Porcelain 'Chase. Ayala was owned by the society hairdresser Mr Pierre 'Teasy-Weasy' Raymond and trainer Keith Piggott was the son of Ernie Piggott, who rode both Jerry M and Poethlyn to National glory.

Two famous Hollywood film stars were among the crowds for the big race, the lovely Kim Novak as a mere, if very special spectator, and Gregory Peck, whose Irish-trained grey horse, Owen's Sedge, was a runner in the race at 20/1.

At last they were on their way and Josh Gifford went straight to the front on Out and About, landing clear over the first. Out and About was still in front over the Brook, at which Good Gracious departed and Vivant was caught out by the Canal Turn. Towards the end of the first circuit, Out and About was making them all chase hard, having increased his advantage to some 15 lengths. Although Out and About still led, the most prominent of the remainder were making ground on him. At the Canal Turn, Springbok, Owen's Sedge, French Lawyer and Carrickbeg were within striking distance of the leader and also moving into contention was Pat Buckley on Ayala. Carrickbeg was slap-bang in the shake-up as they came to the second-last fence. Hawa's Song held a slight lead jumping the fence, from Carrickbeg, Springbok, Ayala, Kilmore and Owen's Sedge, but moving swiftly to the front Carrickbeg was first to rise at the final obstacle. Racing away up the run-in, Carrickbeg reached the elbow with a two-length lead over his pursuers, of which the only one to respond to the demands of his jockey was Ayala, but the amateur-ridden Carrickbeg was sticking well to his task. Inside the final 100 yards though, the leader faltered ever so briefly and Ayala seized the opportunity in a flash. Despite bravely attempting to resist the late challenge, at the post it was Ayala by three-quarters of a length from Carrickbeg, with Hawa's Song five lengths back in third place. Team Spirit was fourth.

Unfortunately, the brave Carrickbeg had broken down close home and he never raced again, while shock winner Ayala took part in another ten races without once finishing in the first four.

With the successful owner absent from Aintree at the time of Ayala's victory, it was left to the trainer and jockey to receive the congratulations and for 19-year-old Pat Buckley it was a time for reflection. Twelve months before he had ridden the strongly fancied Springbok in his first ride in the race, only to fall at the first fence, while now he stood in the winner's enclosure after a trouble-free winning ride on a rank outsider.

When the 1964 Grand National came round, the openness of the race was exemplified by the fact that of the 34 contestants, no less than four shared favouritism, all at 100/7. These were Time, Pappageno's Cottage, the grey Irish mare Flying Wild and the Queen Mother's eight-year-old Laffy.

Making a fifth attempt to lift the prize was the small but robust 12-year-old Team Spirit, bred in County Kildare by Mr P.J. Coonan and by that outstanding stallion Vulgan from a mare named Lady Waleska. Meath trainer Dan Moore, who as the leading Irish jump jockey had come so close to winning the 1938 Grand National on Royal Danieli, bought Team Spirit at Ballsbridge sales for 250 guineas when the gelding was aged four and his wife Joan hunted their new purchase for a year. Put into full training the following year, Team Spirit began his racing career in 1957 in the colours of new owner Mrs D.R. Brand, being placed five times from nine outings. In 1959 he won three of his 12 races and the following season began making regular visits to England, where he won the Mildmay Memorial 'Chase at Sandown Park and the Hurst Park National Trial before running in the Grand National for the first time. Over the next two years he failed to win a single race, then in 1963 he began to regain the confidence he appeared to have lost. By this time he had changed ownership, being bought by three men from opposite sides of the Atlantic Ocean. They were Englishman Gamble North and two Americans, Mr Ronald B. Woodward and Mr John K. Goodman, and following a most sporting suggestion by trainer Dan Moore, Team Spirit was transferred into the care of Lambourn trainer Fulke Walwyn. Walwyn was, of course, the man who had ridden dual National winner Reynoldstown to his second victory and now at the top of his profession as a trainer. His faith in the horse was rewarded when Team Spirit made up a good deal of ground to win the Grand Sefton 'Chase in November 1963 and in his three races between then and the 1964 National suggested there was still scope for improvement. His regular partner, Willie Robinson, was the jockey associated with the famous Cheltenham Gold Cup winner Mill House and in 1958, just two years after turning professional, had finished second in the Epsom Derby aboard Paddy's Point.

Away to a good start, Out and About was the first to land over the initial obstacle, at which the only faller was one of the co-favourites, Flying Wild. Out and About and Cheshire-trained Peacetown had secured a big lead and landed over Becher's well clear of the rest. Peacetown was the clear leader jumping the Chair, with Out and About trying to keep pace and some lengths behind this pair disaster struck when the big open ditch proved too much for Lizawake, Ayala and Border Flight. The latter fell in a particularly ugly fashion and when the remainder of the runners had passed, his jockey, Paddy Farrell, was still lying injured on the ground. Peacetown headed back into the country followed by

Out and About, with 12 lengths in arrears Team Spirit, Time, Reproduction, Merganser, Pappageno's Cottage, Purple Silk and Kilmore. Peacetown led well over Becher's, with Reproduction trying desperately to reduce his lead. At the next fence Reproduction came to grief, leaving Peacetown still well in command over the Canal Turn but going into Valentine's five horses set about cutting back the leader. Purple Silk, Springbok, Eternal, Pontin-Go and the little Team Spirit all moved forward as one in line. It was still Peacetown holding the lead which had been whittled away as they came to the final fence, with Purple Silk looking the most dangerous and as they landed it was the latter who now had the advantage. Striding away well, he was two lengths in front at the elbow, with four opponents taking up the full width of the course behind him and the loose horse Lizawake actually slightly in front. With just 200 yards to go, Willie Robinson brought Team Spirit with a devastating run up the centre of the course to catch Purple Silk in the final yards of the race and win by half a length. Peacetown was third, six lengths further back, in front of Eternal, Pontin-Go.

The congratulations for the winner's connections were somewhat muted after the news came through that Paddy Farrell had broken his back in that horrible fall at the Chair.

In training that year's National winner Fulke Walwyn became one of only a handful of men to both ride and saddle the winner of the great race.

The persistence of little Team Spirit was gratefully rewarded by honourable retirement across the Atlantic in the United States of America.

Two announcements within six weeks of Team Spirit winning the 1964 Grand National brought very different reactions, not only from the world of racing but also the general public. The first, that Fred Winter had retired from race-riding and was to take out a licence to train, was welcomed and applauded.

The news given by Mrs Mirabel Topham was far less well received. The racecourse was to be sold to a property developer and the 1965 Grand National would be the last to be run. Lord Sefton immediately sought an injunction from the High Court forbidding the sale and under this distressing cloud of uncertainty preparations went ahead for the running of the 'last National'.

From 112 original entries on the day 47 faced the starter with the Scottish-trained eight-year-old Freddie a roaring favourite at 7/2. The Queen Mother was represented again, this time by The Rip, second in the betting at 9/1. Rondetto, Kapeno and Vultrix also came in for much support on the books, as did a horse called Jay Trump, who had travelled many thousands of miles to be at Aintree.

An eight-year-old bay gelding by Tonga Prince out of Be Trump, he was bred by Mr Jay Sessenich at Lancaster, Pennsylvania, and when raced on the flat was completely useless. Purchased by top American amateur rider Tommy

Crompton Smith, ownership was shared with Mrs Mary Stephenson and the horse was trained for jumping by Smith himself. Rising to the very top as a 'chaser in America, Jay Trump won the famous Maryland Hunt Cup twice before the decision was taken to make an attempt with him across the ocean in the Grand National. So it was that, wisely, Jay Trump was sent to England in 1964 to be trained for Aintree by an Englishman. The trainer chosen was none other than one in his first season with a licence, the inimitable Fred Winter, whose new establishment was at Lambourn in Berkshire. Crompton Smith travelled with his horse and was also involved with Fred Winter in preparing Jay Trump and of course the intention was that he would ride the horse when the time came. Jay Trump won his first race in this country at Sandown Park over three miles and although it was something of a bloodless victory against only two opponents, it was worthwhile experience for both horse and rider. From his next four races before the National, he won twice and went to Aintree as fit as any horse could be. Into the small hours each night the trainer ran old films of the Grand National over and over, pointing out to the young American the peculiarities of the fences, the line of approach to adopt and the pitfalls to watch out for.

The roar from the crowd as the starter sent them on their way was louder than ever, as if in a final salute to the race nobody wanted to lose. Freddie was well to the fore as they jumped the first fence. With Red Tide coming down at the next they raced on to Becher's, with Peacetown, Phebu, Freddie and Dark Venetian almost in line jumping it. Over Valentine's it was Phebu and Peacetown disputing the lead, followed by Freddie, Kapeno, The Rip and L'Empereur and in this order they came back onto the racecourse. Peacetown went on to jump the water in front of Rainbow Battle, L'Empereur, Freddie, Kapeno and The Rip. Approaching Becher's again, Peacetown and Rondetto were together just ahead of L'Empereur, Freddie, The Rip, Kapeno and Pontin-Go and making steady progress from the rear Jay Trump. Freddie moved right on the heels of the two leaders, biding his time before striking. Pontin-Go came down at the Canal Turn, right in the way of Jay Trump, but the American pair cleverly avoided the fallen horse as they moved up into fourth position. As Peacetown tired and faded, Freddie was now lying second and he was suddenly left in front when Rondetto tumbled out at the fence after Valentine's. From here on it lay between Freddie for Scotland and Jay Trump for America, with both horses racing neck and neck all the way back towards the stands and the finish. Crashing through the last fence Jay Trump survived somehow to land a length to the good over Freddie and racing up the straight he increased his lead. Pat McCarron on Freddie conjured a terrific effort from the favourite, gaining ground with every stride, but at the line it was Jay Trump by three-quarters of a length from Freddie. Twenty lengths back in third place came Mr Christopher Collins on his own horse, Mr Jones, and Rainbow Battle was fourth.

Both the first and second received a wonderful reception from the crowds and the winning owner and rider were almost speechless with delight. Fred Winter smiled quietly, but with obvious pride and satisfaction, having saddled a Grand National winner in his first season as a trainer.

In a most ambitious plan, Jay Trump was sent across the Channel to Paris to take part in the Grande Steeplechase de Paris and ran an outstanding race to finish third, just two and a half lengths behind the winner, Hyere III.

Thirteen

1966–1975

At the sharp end of the market, it was Freddie again as favourite on the crazy price for the National of 11/4, but having recently given a sparkling display to win the Great Yorkshire 'Chase and with no Jay Trump to worry about this time, his prospects looked sound.

Others with good credentials included What a Myth, Highland Wedding, Forest Prince, Vultrix and Kapeno, while The Fossa, Flying Wild and Rough Tweed were considered the best of the longer-priced runners.

Although Jay Trump had retired and was back in America, Fred Winter was still represented, though this time with an eight-year-old named Anglo, which would have been at much longer odds than the 50/1 he started at if it had not been for the reputation of his trainer.

Bred by Mr W. Kennedy at Downpatrick, he was by Greek Star out of Miss Alligator and was first sold for just £140. Changing ownership for 460 guineas the chestnut became the property of Major-General Sir Randle Fielden, running in his colours on the flat under the name of Flag of Convenience. A total failure on the flat, he changed hands again when bought out of a seller at Leicester, after finishing third, for the paltry sum of 110 guineas. Mr J. Nichols, a farmer from Huntingdown, was the new owner and wisely he left the horse to mature for 18 months, in which time there was a transformation in the gelding's appearance at least, to such effect that Captain Ryan Price paid 2,500 guineas for Anglo on behalf of Mr Stuart Levy. In his first season 'over the sticks' Anglo won two hurdle races from eight attempts, being partnered in the latter victory by his future trainer, Fred Winter. The following term he graduated to the major obstacles, quickly stamping his mark as a jumper with a future by winning four novice 'chases on the trot. When Fred Winter began training at the start of the 1964–65 season, Anglo joined his team at Lambourn still under the ownership of Stuart Levy and from eight runs during that campaign was successful four times. During the current season, however,

Anglo appeared to have lost his zest for the game, winning only once from his nine races before the National. His jockey at Aintree was 21-year-old Tim Norman, who had begun race-riding as an amateur before joining Fred Winter's stable.

From a good start they raced to the first fence where all 47 runners safely cleared it, and again at the second there was not a single faller. Rough Tweed was the first casualty at the open ditch and by this time Forest Prince was setting the pace in flamboyant fashion, landing over Becher's clear of the rest. With Forest Prince holding a good lead, they came back to the racecourse with 43 runners still in the race. Jumping the 13th still with a clear advantage, Forest Prince was followed by Kapeno, Gale Force X, Greek Scholar and Freddie. Still in front over Becher's for the second time, Forest Prince looked almost as fresh as when he set out, but behind him the Brook put paid to the chances of Kapeno, What a Myth, Leslie, Valouis, Greek Scholar and Supersweet. Rounding the Canal Turn Forest Prince, while still in front, was challenged by Highland Wedding, Freddie, Anglo and The Fossa and in this order they jumped Valentine's. Three from home Anglo came with a strong run on the inside to tackle Forest Prince and getting the upper hand on the run to the penultimate fence, Anglo jumped that and the last in front and full of running. Ten lengths behind Forest Prince, Freddie was battling on bravely but there was no stopping Anglo, who passed the post the winner by 20 lengths from Freddie, with Forest Prince five lengths away in third place. The Fossa was fourth.

Fred Winter was the toast of Aintree again, having turned out his second successive National winner in only his second season as a trainer, and for Tim Norman, his first ride in the race had been conducted in the coolest of manners.

This third 'last National' attracted 44 runners with the Ryan Price-trained Honey End a very popular favourite at 15/2. As winner of six of his races that term in most convincing fashion, the ten-year-old looked tailor-made for Aintree and with champion jockey Josh Gifford riding, they were a perfect combination for the rigours of the National.

Of the 13 listed merely as '100/1 others' was a nine-year-old named Foinavon, which had been bred by Mr Timothy Ryan in County Limerick. Sharing the same sire as Team Spirit, the outstanding French-bred stallion Vulgan, his dam was Ecilace, also responsible for foaling UMM which won both the Irish Grand National and the Galway Plate in 1955. The young Foinavon was first bought by Mr H.J. Rooney at Ballsbridge sales for 400 guineas in September 1959 and soon after changed hands again when Tom Dreaper purchased him on behalf of the Duchess of Westminster. Woefully unable to live up to the reputation of his ancestors, Foinavon won only three of his 22 races in a 30-month period and was subsequently sold to Mr Jack White of Clonsilla, for whom he finished unplaced in the Dunboyne 'Chase at Fairyhouse in April 1965. Foinavon was sent across the Irish Sea to Doncaster sales. Purchased there for 2,000 guineas by the Newbury trainer John Kempton, Foinavon ran first in the colours of Mr M. Bennellick without distinguishing himself, then becoming the property of Mr Cyril Watkins and remaining with his handler John Kempton, his record continued as unimpressive as before. From 15 outings prior to the National, Foinavon was placed only seven times, although he had led the field for some distance in the Cheltenham Gold Cup in which he eventually finished seventh. Often ridden in races by his trainer, who had also improved Foinavon's jumping with frequent outings in the hunting field, John Kempton intended partnering the horse at Aintree, but it would have meant putting up 10lb overweight. Instead, 26-year-old John Buckingham was engaged to ride the outsider barely three days before the race, presenting the jockey and his brother Tommy with difficulties in finding accommodation near the racecourse at such short notice. Finally making do with the front room of a house in Aintree, their sleeping arrangements consisted of the use of a sofa and two chairs. The young jockey had started in racing as a 15-year-old stableboy with Mr Edward Courage, for whom John's mother worked as a dairymaid and although never destined to be in the top flight of riders, John Buckingham was highly regarded as a reliable horseman who always tried, whatever he was riding. Then as now he is one of the most cheerful and enthusiastic men in racing. Although neither the owner nor trainer attended Aintree for the big race, Foinavon did have one unusual travelling companion, his constant friend, Susie, a goat who shared his stable and went everywhere with him.

The runners began their journey with Penvulgo landing in front over the first, at which the second favourite made an early exit, together with Meon Valley who brought down Popham Down. Up front Penvulgo led by two lengths from Princeful, Barberyn and Kirtle-Lad, with the remainder closely grouped not far behind. Penvulgo still led the way over the Canal Turn, with Princeful, Rutherfords and Dun Widdy tight on his heels. Coming back to the racecourse Princeful, Rutherfords, Kirtle-Lad and Forecastle disputed the lead just a few lengths ahead of Penvulgo, Castle Falls and Kapeno, but the Chair saw the end of Anglo and Forecastle and Dun Widdy pulled up at the water jump. Riderless horses are such a common sight in National Hunt racing that few, apart from competing jockeys, pay much attention to them, yet one who had raced with the leaders since unshipping his jockey at the first fence this time was Popham Down and back in the country he led the field, jumping as well at each fence as those with riders. Rarely have so many still been in the race at the second Becher's and with all of them jumping the Brook safely, a close finish looked on the cards. The next fence though put paid to any prospect of that.

Running loose on the inside of the course going into the 23rd, Popham Down changed direction at the very last moment, running right across the front of the obstacle and in seconds the whole field was engulfed in chaos. Horses fell, refused, were brought down and barged into in the confusion of the mêlée created and jockeys were thrown, catapulted through the air and those who could ran for any shelter that was available. Suddenly from the rear one horse emerged, picking his way sprightly and without the slightest problem through the tangled mass of bodies. Foinavon had been some way behind the main group, though certainly far from tailed off and John Buckingham sized up the situation ahead of him in an instant. Steering a safe path for his mount through the mayhem, Foinavon was the only horse to clear the fence at the first attempt, coming away from it at least 100 yards ahead of the nearest horse and rider to recover from the shambles. With commendable presence of mind, John Buckingham took Foinavon over the Canal Turn and without the slightest panic proceeded to present the horse in copybook style at each remaining fence. Making a lonely yet determined ride back towards the racecourse, Buckingham and Foinavon were soon aware of a host of horses in hot pursuit, racing flat out to catch the unexpected and most unlikely leader. From a lead at one point estimated to be 200 yards, Greek Scholar, Honey End, Packed Home and Red Alligator drew closer to Foinavon but resisting the temptation to risk any errors by pushing his mount out, John Buckingham came to the final fence and jumped it perfectly. Foinavon galloped on up the long straight to pass the post, the greatest shock winner in the history of the race, by 15 lengths from the favourite Honey End, with Red Alligator three lengths back in third place. Greek Scholar was fourth.

With no owner or trainer to welcome in the victors, Foinavon was unsaddled and led back to his box, having finally and in the most unusual circumstances lived up to the reputation of his ancestors. A bemused and modestly delighted John Buckingham faced the television cameras to somehow explain his victory and those lucky enough to have backed the shock winner on the Tote received odds of 444/1.

Whatever was said about the manner of his win, Foinavon jumped every National fence without interruption and when presented with an opportunity of success, John Buckingham seized it and in the coolest manner won a well-earned victory.

The 1968 Grand National took place and for a change the weather was kind with bright sunshine giving Aintree a carnival atmosphere.

Of the 45 runners Different Class went off clear favourite at 17/2, enticing his owner, Gregory Peck, to visit Aintree again with the conviction that they would improve on the previous year's performance. Foinavon figured at 66/1 this time and with John Buckingham out of action with a broken arm, Philip Harvey deputised, but preferred more by the punters was the horse which came third behind him in last year's National, Red Alligator.

Bred like Anglo, by William Kennedy in County Down, Red Alligator was by Magic Red out of the mare Miss Alligator, who also foaled Anglo and as a yearling he was sold at Ballsbridge for 340 guineas. Purchased soon afterwards by Mr John Manners, a farmer and butcher from Bishop Auckland, Red Alligator was put in the care of trainer R. Hall at Newcastle-on-Tyne and in his first three seasons won but a solitary hurdle race from 27 attempts. At the end of this dismal period, the gelding changed stables, to be trained by Denys Smith at Bishop Auckland and that the change of environment suited him was immediately apparent. After winning his first race of the 1966–67 season, a three-mile 'chase at Sedgefield, Red Alligator visited the winner's enclosure a further three times from his ten races that term and of course really placed himself in the limelight by coming third in the National. His preparation for the 1968 race was planned to bring him to peak fitness for the big race and after winning his first race of the campaign, ran well enough in the other three to inspire confidence among his connections. His regular jockey, 20-year-old Brian Fletcher, from the North-east, was again in the saddle and having served his apprenticeship with trainer Denys Smith, felt the perfect way to repay 'The Guvnor' would be to bring Red Alligator first past the post.

Away to a good start, the charge to the first fence was led by a group consisting of The Fossa, Valbus, Reynard's Heir, Princeful and Rutherfords, with the only faller here being Fort Ord. Forecastle and Moidore's Token had joined those at the front as they took the Brook in splendid style, and with Princeful, The Fossa, Valbus and Forecastle still disputing the lead, they returned to the racecourse. As The Fossa, Rondetto and Moidore's Token led over the water, this usually trouble-free obstacle claimed some victims. Champion Prince, Bassnet, Foinavon and Ronald's Boy all came to grief. The Fossa maintained a narrow advantage racing back to Becher's, with a whole host of horses virtually snapping at his heels. Rounding the Canal Turn the final pattern of the race emerged, as the long-time leaders began to tire and Different Class, Rutherfords, Red Alligator and Moidore's Token forged ahead. Four from home Red Alligator struck the front and after a perfect jump at the second last, drew right away from his rivals. Moidore's Token joined Different Class in pursuit and despite a rather dodgy jump at the last, raced stride for stride with the favourite all the way to the line. Their race though was for the minor placings, as Red Alligator won unchallenged by 20 lengths from Moidore's Token, who just got up to take second place by a neck from Different Class. In fourth place was Rutherfords, with The Fossa fifth and 12 others finished the course, among them American grandfather Tim Durant on the remounted Highlandie in 15th position.

Everyone agreed the best horse won, Red Alligator gaining satisfaction for the bad luck he suffered in the 1967 National when, although he had to be put at the 23rd fence three times before putting it behind him, he ran on well enough to finish third.

The year 1969 was a time for jubilation and congratulations, but also one of sadness and regret.

Britain proudly acclaimed the maiden voyage of the Cunard Line's *QE2*, her arrival in New York marking what was stated to be a new era of luxury cruising. American astronaut Neil Armstrong became the first man to set foot on the moon, placing the United States of America well ahead of the Soviet Union in the space race. In London Judy Garland was found dead in her flat; she was only 47 at the time of her death. Sectarian riots in Northern Ireland resulted in British troops being used in an attempt to restore peace, but before long their presence was to be so resented that they became the target of both sides.

The future of the Grand National was as much in doubt as ever, though again there was thankfully another 'last National'.

Of the 30 runners in 1969, Red Alligator was favourite at 13/2, while Aintree newcomer Fearless Fred, from the powerful Fred Rimell yard, was right behind him in the betting on 15/2. Moidore's Token, Bassnet, Rondetto and The Fossa were each trying again and of those appearing in the race for the first time Hove, Arcturus and Liverpool-born Mr Noel Le Mare's Furore II were considered the best prospects.

There was another regular visitor to Aintree, now making a third bid at the National, who always attracted a fair amount of financial interest and Highland Wedding did so again, this time at odds of 100/9. Bred by John Caldwell at Prestwick in Ayrshire, the 12-year-old gelding was by Question out of Princess and although once changing hands for a paltry 90 guineas, Highland Wedding won six point-to-points and finished second in the Royal Artillery Gold Cup when owned by permit holder Peter Calver. Owned in partnership by American Thomas McCoy and Canadian Charles Burns, Highland Wedding was trained by Gerald 'Toby' Balding at Weyhill in Hampshire and had made something of a habit of winning the four-mile Eider 'Chase at Newcastle, having done so three times. His two previous runs in the National had been creditable without bringing success, finishing eighth in 1966 and seventh in 1968. When his regular jockey, Owen McNally, broke his elbow shortly before the big race, the substitute chosen to partner Highland Wedding was 31-year-old Dublin-born Eddie Harty, an outstanding horseman who represented Eire in the three-day event at the 1960 Olympic Games in Rome.

Away to a good start, the first fence was cleared well, without any fallers, and the first to go was Tudor Fort at the third, and with The Fossa again blazing a trail, they ran down to Becher's. The Fossa, Castle Falls and Steel Bridge were prominent. In this order they jumped Valentine's and made their way back towards the stands, followed by Kellsboro' Wood, Kilburn, Flosuebarb and Furore II. At the Chair Highland Wedding was squeezed for room, but Eddie Harty sized up the situation in an instant, to position his mount perfectly for a safe jump and after clearing the water jump they moved into seventh place. Over Becher's it was still Steel Bridge closely followed by Highland Wedding, The Fossa, Rondetto and The Beeches, while behind them Kilburn fell and brought down Tam Kiss. Striking the front at the Canal Turn, Highland Wedding went on from the determined Steel Bridge, who in turn was hard pressed by Rondetto and Bassnet. From Valentine's on Highland Wedding was well in command and, foot perfect at the remaining fences, jumped the last three lengths ahead of Steel Bridge and, staying on strongly, increased his lead to 12 lengths by the time he passed the post. Steel Bridge was second and 13-year-old Rondetto a length further back in third place, with The Beeches fourth.

Highland Wedding's victory was a triumph for perseverance, the gelding making it third time lucky on a day when all went right for him. He was immediately retired and taken in the spring of 1970 to a future of rest and contentment in Canada, a most fitting reward for a very brave horse.

Favourite for the 1970 contest at 13/2 was the consistent Two Springs, with Fred Rimell's French Excuse on 100/8 with last year's Topham Trophy winner Dozo, the mount of Eddie Harty. Of the three Irish challengers, Vulture, trained by Tom Dreaper and owned by American General R. K. Mellon, was thought to have the best chance and was sent off at 15/1 as also was Fred Rimell's other runner, Gay Trip.

Another son of the stallion Vulgan, Gay Trip was bred by Mr F.D. Farmer near Naas, from the mare Turkish Tourist and in the colours of her breeder won one race on the flat before being tried over hurdles when five years of age. Appropriately his first contest over timber was in an event named after a Grand National winner, the Grakle Maiden Hurdle at Gowran Park, which in a hard-fought tussle Gay Trip won by a neck, rewarding his owner Mr Farmer with prize money amounting to £203. Of his seven other races that season the gelding won another hurdle at Baldoyle and during the close season the name Gay Trip had reached the ear of Kinnersley trainer Fred Rimell. Seeking a decent horse for his friend and patron Tony Chambers, Fred sought the advice of Pat Taaffe, who without any hesitation suggested they go to Ireland and take a look at Gay Trip. In consequence the five-year-old son of Vulgan became the property of Mr A.J. Chambers and quietly settled into the everyday routine of

Fred Rimell's yard. In his first race in this country, the Halloween Novices 'Chase at Newbury at the end of October 1967, Gay Trip fell at the water jump but within the month came up trumps with a sparkling display of jumping to win three of his remaining four races that term and in the fourth, the Totalisator Champion Novices 'Chase at the Cheltenham Festival, was beaten only six lengths by the ace Irish novice Herring Gull. After scoring a clear-cut victory in Cheltenham's Mackeson Gold Cup, the decision was made to aim him at the 1970 Grand National. Sixteen days after finishing sixth in the Cheltenham Gold Cup, Gay Trip took his place in the National line-up, top weight with 11st 5lb, without ever having won beyond two and a half miles and with a new jockey on his back. His regular rider, Terry Biddlecombe, having suffered serious injuries, the man chosen to partner him was 40-year-old Pat Taaffe who, together with Josh Gifford, was having his final ride in the National.

Away to a level start, the falls came fast and furious. As they took Becher's the leading group consisted of Assad, No Justice, Vulture and Fort Ord, with Red Alligator bringing up the rear at this stage. Opening up a good lead coming back onto the racecourse, Mr Derek Scott on his own horse Villay was 12 lengths clear of Vulture, with Dozo and Gay Trip both moving well in mid-division. Turning back into the country, Villay still held a substantial advantage over Vulture, Miss Hunter, Gay Trip and Dozo. Vulture led over Becher's but behind him The Fossa and No Justice refused and in a crashing fall The Otter also went out, bringing down Specify as well. Villay began to lose ground after Valentine's, as Dozo moved up dangerously on Vulture and cruising easily on the outside Pat Taaffe kept Gay Trip in a handy position. As they came onto the racecourse Gay Trip moved alongside Dozo to challenge for the lead. Landing in front over the final fence Gay Trip drew rapidly away from the rest to win by 20 lengths from Vulture, with Miss Hunter half a length back in third place. Dozo was fourth in front of Ginger Nut, Pride of Kentucky and Josh Gifford on Assad.

There could have been no finer end to his illustrious career in the saddle than Pat Taaffe's victory on Gay Trip, 15 years after winning the race on Quare Times, and he was cheered long and loud by all at Aintree that day. Fred Rimell also had reason to celebrate, having just led in his third Grand National winner.

If the weights were the only criteria by which the standard of runners is judged, then there could be no complaint about the field for the 1971 National.

Even with his maximum burden Gay Trip started the 8/1 favourite, from Fulke Walwyn's promising Cheltenham winner Lord Jim at 9s, The Laird and The Otter at 12/1 and Money Boat, Vulture and King Vulgan also in the public eye at 16/1.

Making his second appearance in the race, after being brought down at the second Becher's the previous year when on the heels of the leaders, was nine-year-old Specify. Bred in Norwich by Mr Alan Parker, his sire was Specific and he was from the mare Ora Lamae and while still a foal he was bought for £300 by former royal jockey Arthur Freeman. After competing on the flat on many occasions, without setting the racing world alight, Specify had three runs over hurdles in the autumn of 1965 which were similarly unnoteworthy. Twelve months on, Arthur Freeman had improved the gelding enough to win three races on the trot at Leicester, Haydock and Kempton Park, and a rather ambitious final outing of the season in the Champion Hurdle won by Saucy Kit ended with Specify well down the course. His first steeplechase victory was in a two-mile affair at Huntingdon, in the colours of owner Mr F.W. Rogers and over the next couple of seasons Specify developed into a reliable 'chaser, passing into the ownership of Mr P.A. Rackham and the stable of D. Weeden at Bury St Edmunds. After winning the Fairlawne 'Chase at Windsor at the end of February 1970, Mr Fred Pontin, owner of the string of holiday camps, bought Specify to carry his colours in that year's National. He was transferred to the yard of John Sutcliffe near Epsom, who brought him along gently in his preparation for the 1971 Aintree showpiece. Jockey John Cook, who had ridden Specify so well in their first Liverpool encounter, was again in the saddle and at 33 years of age was attempting to pull off a valuable double for Fred Pontin. Less than two months before he had secured the Schweppes Gold Trophy Hurdle at Newbury for the owner on the 33/1 shot Cala Mesquida. Without a victory in the present campaign, Specify lined up for the National a 28/1 chance.

Just one minute after the scheduled start time they galloped on their way to the first fence, where Gay Trip brought dismay to all by falling, along with Craigbrock, Twigairy, Brian's Best and Country Wedding. Irish-trained Gay Buccaneer was setting a merry old gallop, racing freely ahead of Smooth Dealer, Zara's Grove, Miss Hunter, Lord Jim and Black Secret. In this order they jumped Becher's perfectly. Still in the lead jumping the Canal Turn, Gay Buccaneer was carried extremely wide by a loose horse coming fast on his inside. Smooth Dealer led over Valentine's, closely followed by Vichysoise, Miss Hunter, Bowgeeno and Specify and with a great number still in the hunt just a few lengths behind. Miss Hunter crashed out at the Chair when up with the pace and the leaders jumping the water were Smooth Dealer, Vichysoise, Astbury and Beau Bob. Jumping the Brook in copybook style, Beau Bob unseated his rider some yards after landing safely and well to the rear Money Boat fell. At the next fence Jim Dreaper made a remarkable recovery when Black Secret got too close to the obstacle and blundered his way through. First over the Canal Turn was John Buckingham on Limeburner, with Sandy Sprite, Astbury, Black Secret, The Inventor, Specify, Bowgeeno, Two Springs and

Regimental breathing down their necks. Racing towards the second last Sandy Sprite and Limeburner were galloping side by side, but Limeburner crumpled on landing over the fence and as they rose at the final jump there were five horses all with a chance of winning. Sandy Sprite and Bowgeeno were first away from the fence but were immediately joined by Black Secret and Astbury, while John Cook was going strongly on the inside with Specify, waiting for a gap to appear on the rails. Rounding the elbow, the gap opened up for the briefest of moments, but it was enough for Specify to squeeze through and in a desperate race to the post Specify got up in the dying seconds to snatch victory by a neck from Black Secret, with Astbury staying on to finish third, two and a half lengths behind. Bowgeeno was fourth and Sandy Sprite fifth, with eight others managing to get round, including Gay Buccaneer and two remounted runners, Limeburner and Common Entrance.

Wearing a fur hat as alarming as his broad smile, Fred Pontin led in Specify to rousing cheers of appreciation for such an exciting finish. John Cook broke his leg the following season so badly that he was never able to ride in races again and although Specify competed well for some time he never won another race.

In 1972, with the future of the race still under a cloud of uncertainty, the prize money for the National was increased by over £10,000. Once again, though, the executive insisted that this was emphatically the very last Grand National that would take place at Aintree.

Excitement grew when the entries showed the dual Cheltenham Gold Cup winner L'Escargot among their number and there was little surprise when the publication of the weights had the Irish gelding heading the handicap with 12st. Clear favourite of the 42 runners at 17/2, he was trained by Dan Moore and ridden by Tommy Carberry.

Gay Trip and Cardinal Error jointly held second position in the market on 12s, with Black Secret, Fair Vulgan, Fortina's Palace and Money Boat also carrying a fair amount of public money.

A late rush of money in the last few days before the race reduced to 14/1 the price of nine-year-old gelding Well To Do, a chestnut gelding providing a direct link to a National winner 35 years ago. By the French stallion Phebus out of Princess Puzzlement, he was bred by Mrs H. Lloyd Thomas, whose late husband Hugh had owned and often ridden Royal Mail, winner of the 1937 Grand National. Bought for Mrs Heather Sumner by her trainer, Captain Tim Forster, when an unbroken three-year-old, Well To Do took time to mature and it was not until late April 1968 that he made his first appearance on a racecourse. His first success came some 17 months later in a handicap hurdle race at Devon and Exeter and before the end of that season he achieved his first victory over fences by winning the Wisborough Green Novices 'Chase over three and a quarter miles at Fontwell on 3 March 1970. From six outings during the 1970–71 campaign Well To Do visited the winner's enclosure four times, finishing second and third in his other two ventures and by now was looked upon as a safe and reliable steeplechaser of some promise. Tragically, his owner Mrs Sumner died from cancer in June 1971 and under the terms of her will Well To Do became the property of his trainer, Captain Forster. Although entered for the 1972 Grand National, Tim Forster was somewhat reluctant to run the horse at Aintree and it was with barely 15 minutes to spare that he despatched a telegram to Weatherby's confirming Well To Do as a runner. His five races before the National, of which he won one, were designed to bring the gelding to peak fitness for the big day and ridden by his regular jockey, Graham Thorner, the early odds of 25/1 before the race were quickly snapped up. Twenty-three-year-old Graham Thorner came from a Somerset farming family and upon leaving school joined Captain Forster at Letcombe Bassett in Berkshire, turning professional during the 1967-68 season. In 1971 he became champion jockey, having ridden a total of 74 winners, and that same year had his first taste of the Grand National when riding Bowgeeno into fourth place, a little over four lengths behind the winner.

The big field raced away led by Fair Vulgan. Over Becher's Fair Vulgan was still in command, with Miss Hunter, General Symons, Astbury, Specify and Bright Willow hard on his heels but the Brook proved too much for Lisnaree, Swan Shot and Beau Parc. The leader, Fair Vulgan, was badly hampered by the riderless Gay Buccaneer at the water jump, though with a superhuman effort his jockey, Macer Gifford, kept him upright and they continued in front back into the country. Black Secret led over Becher's from Specify, General Symons, Gay Trip and the improving Well To Do. Jumping the fourth from home, the race lay between just four horses, rank outsider General Symons, Black Secret, Gay Trip and Well To Do, with the remaining survivors well strung out in the far distance. Coming to the last fence almost in perfect line, the four took it together, with Well To Do on the inside rails landing marginally in front and producing a good turn of foot he raced on towards victory. At the winning post it was Well To Do the winner by two lengths from Gay Trip. Three lengths further back Black Secret and General Symons were declared to have dead-heated for third place, the first occasion when a dead-heat for any of the placings had entered the National's records.

Yet again it had been a rousing finish to a thrilling race, the crowds revelling in every second of the drama, and although there was a hint of sadness in the eyes of owner-trainer Captain Tim Forster, he received the deluge of congratulations with calm dignity.

Of the 38 runners for the 1973 Grand National, the handicap top spot was shared between L'Escargot and the brilliant Australian-bred Crisp, with each set to carry 12st, just 1lb more than Mr Edward Courage's Spanish Steps. Black Secret and General Symons were competing again but the majority of the contestants were newcomers to the National and although Glenkiln was one of this number, he was the most recent winner over the big fences.

It was another from Donald McCain's yard though which had captured the public's imagination sufficiently to share favouritism with the Fred Winter-trained class performer Crisp and this was the eight-year-old Red Rum. Bred by Martin McEnery in County Kilkenny, he was by the grey stallion Quorum out of a mare called Mared. Bought originally by former jockey Tim Molony, who was now training at Melton Mowbray in Leicestershire, Red Rum won three times on the flat for owner Maurice Kingsley. His first-ever appearance on a racecourse was coincidentally at Aintree, on the day before the 1967 Grand National in the Thursby Selling Plate over five furlongs, in which he dead-heated for first place with Curlicue. In due course Red Rum became the property of Mrs Lurline Brotherton and entered the yard of veteran trainer Bobby Renton and proceeded to win over hurdles and fences. For a brief period after Mr Renton's retirement, the gelding was trained by a man who partnered him in many races, the Irish jockey Tommy Stack, and then by Anthony Gillam, but Red Rum went through a period of indifferent form and shortly after running a great race to finish fifth in the Scottish Grand National he was sent to Doncaster sales. It was here that Donald McCain entered the life of Red Rum and it was an encounter which was to change the lives of both horse and trainer, together with those of many others. Bidding on behalf of his most important patron, the elderly Liverpool-born Mr Noel le Mare, McCain secured Red Rum for 6,000 guineas and was brought back across the Pennines to the trainer's yard behind a used-car showroom in Birkdale. Within days came the shattering discovery that Red Rum was afflicted with the dreaded pedalostitis, a crippling disease of the foot. Had the horse gone to any other trainer, his racing days would most certainly have been at an end, but the only gallops available to 'Ginger' McCain were the sands of Southport beach and miraculously a half-hour walking in the sea cured Red Rum's lameness. It was a new horse which went to Carlisle on 30 September 1972 to represent his new owner and trainer and his victory in the Windermere Handicap 'Chase was followed in quick succession by four others. Rested then for two months, his Grand National preparation was brought along steadily from the end of January 1973, with just three races in which he finished second once and third in the other two. His jockey for the National was Brian Fletcher, who since winning the Grand National five years before with Red Alligator, had suffered horrendous head injuries in a fall at Stockton which all but put an end to his career. At the off Red Rum and Crisp were joint favourites at 9/1.

After a delay of only three minutes, the starter sent them on their way and on fast firm going the pace was hot right from the start. Jumping like a stag, Crisp drew ahead of his rivals. Back on the racecourse, Crisp was 12 lengths ahead of the rest jumping the Chair, and the second circuit began with Crisp still a long way in front. Landing over the 19th, Brian Fletcher decided the leader was getting too far ahead and took Red Rum in pursuit, but jumping Becher's for the last time Crisp was at least 20 lengths clear and still jumping beautifully. Over Valentine's and running back towards the racecourse Richard Pitman and Crisp looked uncatchable. Crisp was beginning to show signs of tiredness as he jumped the last fence, but once on the flat strode out towards the winning post still 15 lengths ahead and with Red Rum putting in a good jump over the final obstacle he was certainly running on well. As Crisp neared the elbow he was visibly distressed, his stride shortening and for several moments staggering through exhaustion but he regained his equilibrium, running now solely on instinct. Still six lengths clear inside the final 100 yards, only a horse and rider as gutsy and determined as Red Rum and Brian Fletcher could have made up the ground and in the very last strides of the contest Red Rum got up to win by three-quarters of a length. Twenty-five lengths behind came L'Escargot in third place, with Spanish Steps fourth.

The crowds went wild with delight, a locally trained horse, which most had backed, winning in the final moment of a memorable race and a brave and heroic front runner finishing second. Donald McCain was the man of the moment and understandably relished every second of the happiest moments of his life.

Somewhat unkindly, it was repeatedly pointed out that Red Rum in winning the race had done so only because he was receiving 23lb from the gallant runner-up.

Aintree racecourse was finally sold to the Liverpool property developer Mr Bill Davies on 19 November 1973 and the reign of Mrs Mirabel Dorothy Topham came to an end.

The principal newcomers in 1974 were the management and owners of the racecourse, with the players well versed in the requirements of the test ahead of them.

Most-fancied of the 42 starters was the eight-year-old Scout and at 7/1 favourite was recognised as an out-and-out stayer. Second spot in the betting was held by last year's third-placed L'Escargot on 17/2, unquestionably the class horse in the field.

Facing the stiffest test yet imposed on him with top weight of 12st was Red Rum, the champion of Merseyside, but this time third in the betting at 11/1. His final race before the National was in Haydock Park's Greenall Whitley Handicap 'Chase in which, uncharacteristically, he unseated jockey Brian Fletcher at the first fence after being hampered. Possibly his most brilliant performance since winning the National came in the Hennessy Cognac Gold Cup at Newbury. Jumping splendidly throughout, Red Rum battled like a lion in the closing stages in a ding-dong tussle with Red Candle, only to be beaten a short-head by a horse receiving a stone from him.

Apart from Scout and L'Escargot, his most-fancied opponents included Spanish Steps, Rough House, Straight Vulgan, Francophile, Royal Relief and Sunny Lad.

The start was delayed due to the unladylike behaviour of Princess Camilla, who brought cheers from the crowd with an exhibition of rearing and bucking, but when at last the starter released the barrier, the whole field proceeded in an orderly if fast manner. Landing over the first in front were Sunny Lad, Charles Dickens, Rough Silk and Pearl of Montreal, with the only faller here being Royal Relief. With little change in the order over Becher's, there were surprisingly few fallers but at the Canal Turn Argent, Karacola, Huperade and Dublin's Green all came down. Back on the racecourse it was Pearl of Montreal leading from a tightly packed bunch, the most prominent of which were Rough Silk, Straight Vulgan, Charles Dickens, Sunny Lad and L'Escargot and maintaining the strong pace set from the start, they began the final circuit. At Becher's, Red Rum struck the front. With Charles Dickens, Scout, L'Escargot and Spanish Steps well in contention, Red Rum was in front somewhat earlier than his connections would have wished for but Brian Fletcher set out to give them all a race they'd never forget. Jumping fast and fluently, 'Rummy' galloped with the determination which had become his hallmark. Jumping the final two fences as cleanly as all those before, Red Rum ran out the easiest of winners by seven lengths. L'Escargot was second, just a short-head in front of the third horse, the outsider Charles Dickens. Spanish Steps again put up a splendid performance to finish fourth.

In becoming the first horse since Reynoldstown in the mid-1930s to win the race in successive years, Red Rum not only won his race under top weight like a truly great racehorse, but made many critics of the previous year's victory eat their words. The congratulations bestowed on Donald McCain were well earned, for he had produced Red Rum again in beautiful condition and the proud owner, Noel le Mare, had achieved his lifelong ambition to win the Grand National, twice over.

It is extremely rare for Liverpudlians to allow criticism of a fellow 'scouser', yet in 1975 even they expressed their anger at Aintree's owner, Bill Davies, for again increasing admission charges for 'their race'.

Not surprisingly, top weight for the race was again Red Rum with 12st, conceding weight to all his 30 opponents, but he started as a red-hot favourite at the unrealistic odds of 7/2. Red Rum's reputation had, of course, been tremendously enhanced by his brilliant victory in the Scottish Grand National at Ayr, just three weeks after that emphatic second Aintree National success.

L'Escargot was the second choice of backers at 13/2, while the other best-supported horses included Rough House, Land Lark, Money Market, Junior Partner and Rag Trade.

L'Escargot was bred by Mrs Barbara O'Neill in Mullingar, County Westmeath, and was by the French-bred stallion Escart III. His dam, What a Daisy, was a half-sister to Mr What, the 1958 Grand National winner. As a foal L'Escargot was bought for 950 guineas by the former jump jockey Jimmy Brogan, who sadly died within days of the transaction and his widow looked after the youngster until sending him to Ballsbridge sales in 1966. Bought by trainer Dan Moore for 3,000 guineas on behalf of his patron, Mr Raymond Guest, the American Ambassador to Ireland, L'Escargot was put into training. After six races on the flat, which brought two wins and an unplaced journey in the Irish Cesarewitch, L'Escargot graduated to jumping, winning his début event in the Osberstown Hurdle at Naas on 2 March 1968. Seventeen days later at the Cheltenham Festival, L'Escargot made every inch of the running to easily win Division 2 of the Gloucestershire Hurdler. A natural jumper, the gelding proved to be even better over the major obstacles. L'Escargot won the Cheltenham Gold Cup in both 1970 and 1971, then with advancing age the edge went from his speed and although still a force to be reckoned with, this was to be his fourth Grand National and he had been beaten decisively by Red Rum in the last two. Tommy Carberry had partnered L'Escargot in almost all his races and again took the mount at Aintree, having so far that season ridden the winners of the Topham Trophy 'Chase, the Irish Grand National and the Cheltenham Gold Cup.

Once on their way the pace was good with Zimulator leading over the first fence. As Glanford Brigg and Beau Bob took them towards Becher's, Zimulator found the fourth fence too much for him. Rough House fell at the fifth, while Castleruddery refused and the leading positions over Becher's were held by Glanford Brigg, Beau Bob, Feel Free and Southern Quest. At the next fence L'Escargot hit the top very hard, shooting Tommy Carberry forward and for several moments the jockey was clinging on to his mount's head. Only a horseman of his stature could have made the recovery he did and before reaching the Canal Turn L'Escargot was on the heels of the leaders. At the Chair Land Lark came to grief. Back in the country again Glanford Brigg still led, from Southern Quest, Beau Bob, High Ken and after a gap came L'Escargot,

Red Rum, The Dikler, Manicou Bay and Money Market. At the Brook Beau Bob came down, leaving Southern Quest and Red Rum at the head of affairs. A magnificent jump by L'Escargot at the Canal Turn brought him right into contention and Red Rum had the crowds cheering as he went to the front. Joined almost at once by L'Escargot, the two came back to the racecourse stride for stride and rose at each of the final two fences side by side. Touching down fractionally ahead of his rival over the last, Red Rum stuck to his task in his usual brave manner but once Tommy Carberry got L'Escargot into his stride, the Irish chestnut surged ahead. At the winning post it was L'Escargot the winner by 15 lengths from Red Rum, with Spanish Steps eight lengths away in third place and Money Market fourth.

Owner Raymond Guest proudly led in L'Escargot, the horse who had given him a National victory after 20 years of trying. L'Escargot was immediately retired from racing and given to the trainer's wife, assured of a comfortable and loving future.

Fourteen

1976-1985

Mr Bill Davies fell into a dispute with the Jockey Club which once more threatened the future of the Grand National. Mr Davies was given a deadline by which to reach an agreement, after which they declared their intention of transferring the big race to Doncaster, albeit in name only.

It at once became apparent that this was no idle threat and with just days to spare, in late December 1975, a solution was reached when Ladbrokes the Bookmakers entered into an agreement with Bill Davies to manage the racecourse until his problems could be resolved.

Of the 32 runners making up the National field, Barona emerged as 7/1 favourite, with Red Rum at 10/1 and Jolly's Clump, Money Market and Tregarron all on 12s. Others to attract attention in the betting included Spanish Steps, The Dikler and the horse which finished tenth and last in 1975, Rag Trade.

By Menelek out of The Rage, Rag Trade was bred in Ireland by Mr Ian Williams, whose father Evan had ridden Royal Mail to victory in the 1937 National. Trained by George Fairbairn at Hallington in Northumberland for his breeder, the gelding won a couple of races before being offered for sale at Doncaster shortly before the 1975 National. Rag Trade was knocked down for an amazing 18,000 guineas to the representative of Mr P.B. Raymond, whose finest moment in racing had come in 1963 when Ayala won Aintree's big race, and his final preparation for the National was conducted by Arthur Pitt at Epsom. After at least getting round in the 1975 National, Rag Trade repaid a portion of his purchase price three weeks later with a convincing victory in the Midlands Grand National at Uttoxeter. Transferred in the close season to trainer Fred Rimell's Kinnersley yard, Rag Trade ran five times before making a second attempt at the National, his final effort being a winning one in Chepstow's Welsh Grand National. At 14/1 he was ridden by 23-year-old Irishman John Burke, stable jockey to Fred Rimell.

As a result of a disagreement early in the season, Red Rum found himself with a new partner, the man once briefly responsible for training him, Tommy Stack, while Brian Fletcher took the mount on the mare Eyecatcher.

Away to a good start, Spittin Image, Money Market, Tregarron and Nereo led over the first and, with Money Market and Spittin Image disputing the lead over Becher's, Tregarron, Glanford Brigg and Tudor View failed to survive the Brook. Rounding the Canal Turn, Spitting Image led from Nereo, Money Market, The Dikler, Golden Rapper, Highway View and Rag Trade and in this order they came back to the racecourse. Landing over the Chair, Spanish Steps and Spittin Image touched down together, with Red Rum at this point lying about 12th. Back out in the country Golden Rapper's rush to the front came to an abrupt end when crashing head first at Becher's. Approaching Valentine's Spittin Image and Churchtown Boy held the narrowest of leads over The Dikler, Red Rum and Eyecatcher, with Rag Trade, Ceol-na-Mara and Barona in close touch. At the second-last fence five horses were in line, all seemingly with a chance, Red Rum, Eyecatcher, Rag Trade, Ceol-na-Mara and The Dikler but by the time the final obstacle was reached the last two had dropped behind. Touching down slightly ahead of Eyecatcher, Red Rum looked certain to notch a third incredible National victory, when suddenly and with a tremendous burst of finishing speed, Rag Trade flashed to the front. Battling back in the courageous way of his Red Rum rallied in the last 200 yards to reduce the deficit. At the post Rag Trade won by two lengths from Red Rum, with Eyecatcher eight lengths back in third place, followed by Barona.

It was a first National win for jockey John Burke, the second for owner Mr Raymond and a record four victories in the race for trainer Fred Rimell.

Always the optimist, Don McCain made the same prediction as the previous year, that they would be back at Aintree come the spring.

The year 1977 was a turning point in the history of Aintree racecourse, even before the Grand National meeting began, for through the enterprise of Ladbrokes the racecourse abandoned flat racing completely and devoted its activities to jumping.

With over £41,000 on offer to the winner of the Grand National, the race attracted 42 runners, which consisted of some of the finest 'chasers on either side of the Irish Sea.

Heading the handicap for the fourth time in as many years was Red Rum with 11st 8lb. With but a single win, and that in a three-horse race, from seven outings that term, 'Rummy' was at 12 years of age considered by most pundits to be way past his best.

Form horse and favourite at 15/2 was Andy Pandy, winner of four good races that season and with the same trainer-jockey combination of the previous year's winner, Fred Rimell and John Burke. Quickly back into action two days after a 15-length win in the Topham Trophy 'Chase on the opening day of the meeting was Churchtown Boy, backed down to 20/1 as a result of his handling of the big fences. Miss Charlotte Brew rode her own horse, Barony Fort, marking another milestone in the history of the great race.

The sun shone, the going was good and the assembled thousands waited in good humour and with a sense of expectancy for the National to begin, unaware that they were about to see history being made.

After a delay of nine minutes, the race began and the very first fence brought the downfall of Pengrail, War Bonnet, High Ken, Duffle Coat, Spitting Image, Willy What and Huperade. Amid all this chaos, Sebastian V had continued unscathed in the lead and he approached Becher's with a three-length lead over Boom Docker. Jumping well, it was the drop on the landing side of the Brook which caught Sebastian V out, his fall leaving Boom Docker in command. Boom Docker raced back onto the racecourse 15 lengths clear of Sage Merlin, Hidden Value, Rag Trade, Andy Pandy and the improving Red Rum and Boom Docker cleared the water jump over 20 lengths ahead, to start the second circuit a very long way in advance of the rest. Without the slightest warning Boom Docker ran straight at the inner wing of the 17th fence, refusing to go any further. In an instant the whole pattern of the race changed, the favourite, Andy Pandy, being left in front and jumping brilliantly at each fence down to Becher's, he increased his advantage with every leap. Fully 12 lengths ahead rising at Becher's Brook, Andy Pandy met the obstacle well, only to crumple to the ground as he landed and all at once Red Rum was in the driving seat. Left in front much earlier than Tommy Stack wanted, he wisely decided to let 'Rummy' bowl along and force his pursuers to match his pace. Rounding the Canal Turn in super style Red Rum was well clear of What a Buck, Churchtown Boy, Happy Ranger, Sir Garnet and The Pilgaric and from there on he proceeded to keep up the pressure. With faultless precision Red Rum jumped fence after fence down the canal side on his way back to the racecourse. Crossing the Melling Road for the final time, the cheering began in earnest as Red Rum appeared about to stamp his greatness as no other horse had ever done. On that long run to the second-last fence, Churchtown Boy began making ground, threatening with every stride to extinguish the hope now rampant in everybody watching. Red Rum cleared that obstacle as purposely as he had ever jumped an Aintree fence but Churchtown Boy, now just two lengths behind, smacked into it, costing him several lengths. Majestically and still powerfully Red Rum jumped the last, his 150th Grand National fence, to actually sprint up the run-in the winner by 25 lengths from Churchtown Boy. Eyecatcher was a further six lengths away in third place, followed by The Pilgaric.

Aintree was alive with excitement and joy, the realisation that the horse of humble origin, from just down the road near Southport, had totally rewritten the record books, giving the many thousands present a feeling of gratefulness for merely being at Aintree on an historic and unforgettable occasion.

Donald McCain had achieved the impossible with Red Rum, in bringing the horse in five successive years fit to conquer the toughest racecourse in the world. In winning the Grand National an unprecedented three times, his and Red Rum's name would forever be a very valuable part of racing folklore.

When the 68 entries for the national were published in January 1978, it was clear that trainer Donald McCain intended keeping to his word, for the now 13-year-old Red Rum was among them but 24 hours before the race the dreadful news broke that Red Rum was a doubtful runner as a result of an injury incurred on the gallops. Withdrawn from the race at the very last moment, the wise decision was taken to retire Red Rum there and then and as a mark of esteem for the old warrior Aintree's management insisted that he lead the parade before the big race.

The men with satchels hastily formed a new market with former winner Rag Trade the 8/1 favourite from the Irish challenger Tied Cottage and locally owned Master H. A late rush for the nine-year-old Lucius made the gelding a 14/1 chance at the off.

Bred by Dr Margaret Lloyd from a pairing of the stallion Perhapsburg and the mare Matches, Lucius was still an unbroken three-year-old when bought by Gordon W. Richards for 1,800 guineas. While in the process of preparing him for racing, Gordon Richards sold Lucius to one of his owners, Mrs Fiona Whittaker. His first appearance on a racecourse was two days after Christmas in 1972, when running unplaced in Wetherby's Christmas Juvenile Novices Hurdle, but the gelding improved sufficiently to win twice over timber before the end of his first season's work. From nine races in the run-up to the National, Lucius was only once out of the first two, winning three times. Trainer Gordon Richards hailed from the west country and after becoming too heavy for flat racing, switched to riding 'over the sticks'. His career was cut short after suffering back injuries in an event at Perth and upon recovery bought a livery stable at Bamburgh in Northumberland. While the movie *Becket* was being filmed at nearby Bamburgh Castle, Richards supplied the horses used in the production but, unable to resist the excitement of steeplechasing, he took out a licence to train in 1964. Moving to the former establishment of Tommy Robson, at Greystoke Castle in the Lake District he was soon recognised as one of the most effective trainers in the north. The stable jockey, David Goulding, was injured just before the National and the last-minute replacement to partner Lucius was Bertram Robert Davies. Brother-in-law of Terry Biddlecombe, Bob

Davies holds a BSc in Agriculture, began riding at an early age and rode his first point-to-point winner when only 14.

With hardly any delay at the start, the field dashed away led by the headstrong Tied Cottage, who landed in front over the first fence. Tied Cottage was several lengths clear of the rest, but jumping to the right at the Brook, Tied Cottage fell, as also did Gleaming Rain and Henry Hall. Side-stepping the fallen horses in front of him, Double Bridle took the lead, with Shifting Gold, Lucius and Sebastian V in close attendance. With Lucius in the lead, the survivors came back onto the racecourse. Double Bridle crashed out at the 13th and Churchtown Boy fell at the Chair and the first circuit was completed with Sebastian V leading over the water jump. As Sebastian V continued making the running back to Becher's, Lucius moved to within a length of the leader. The two leaders jumped splendidly all the way back towards the stands. At the final obstacle Sebastian V landed first, a length and a half ahead of Collishall, and in a thrilling finish which involved no less than eight horses, Lucius produced a terrific burst of speed to win by half a length from Sebastian V. The fast-finishing Drumroan got up to snatch third place, only a head behind Sebastian V, with Coolishall fourth.

Lucius was a most popular winner, especially for the manner in which he found that extra turn of foot in the closing stages of the race and the only person suffering any real disappointment was the unfortunate David Goulding, denied the opportunity of a dream ride into the record books through the perils of his trade.

The general election victory of Mrs Margaret Thatcher in 1979 gave Britain its first woman Prime Minister and the return of a Conservative Government, just weeks after a car bomb planted by terrorists killed Mr Airey Neave, a senior aide to Mrs Thatcher, as he drove out of an underground car park at the House of Commons. Later in the year Lord Mountbatten, a cousin of the Queen, was also the victim of terrorism when blown up on his estate in Ireland. In the United States, the Oscar-winning Hollywood star John Wayne lost his long fight against cancer at the age of 72, and in the Middle East the Shah of Iran was deposed and driven into exile by supporters of Ayatollah Khomeini.

Of the 34 runners in the Grand National, the 1976 Cheltenham Gold Cup winner Royal Frolic headed the handicap with 11st 10lb, while the most recent Gold Cup winner, Alverton, was the 13/2 favourite.

Among eight competitors on offer at 25/1 was the ten-year-old Scottish-trained Rubstic, bred by Mrs Robert Digby. By the stallion I Say, who finished third in the 1965 Epsom Derby, his dam was the unraced brood-mare Leuze, and upon being sold as a yearling for 500 guineas, Rubstic entered the yard of trainer C.H. Bell at Hawick in Roxburghshire. The gelding's first effort on a racecourse came at three years of age in the Cross Fell Novice Hurdle at Carlisle, in which he finished a well-beaten third of four. His owner, the former British Lions rugby international John Douglas, switched him to the stable of Gordon W. Richards at Penrith at the start of the next term, from where he was sent to win two long-distance 'chases at Haydock Park and Cheltenham. Returning to Scotland, Rubstic was placed with his third trainer, John Leadbetter, at Denholm, Roxburghshire. Regularly displaying an abundance of stamina, Rubstic won the Durham National 'Chase over three and a half miles at Sedgefield in two successive years and was twice second in the Scottish National before making his bid at Aintree. His jockey, 28-year-old Maurice Barnes, was the son of Tommy Barnes who finished second in the National on Wyndburgh in 1962 and for Maurice it was his first ride in the big race.

From a good start, Bob Champion was the first to show in front on Purdo and he raced safely away from the first fence. Purdo was still at the head of affairs jumping Becher's, only to crumple on landing, leaving Zongalero, Alverton and Rubstic disputing the lead. With two loose horses slightly ahead of them, the leaders approached the Chair with Zongalero, Rubstic and Wagner in line abreast just in front of the favourite Alverton. In the blinking of an eye the riderless horses brought chaos at the biggest obstacle on the course when they veered right across those following them. In the ensuing mêlée nine horses were put out of the race. Unaffected by the turmoil behind them, the four leaders cleared the water and went off on the final circuit, with Wagner holding a narrow lead over Rubstic and Zongalero. At this stage it appeared as if Alverton had only to stand up to win, for he was simply cantering. Changing his stride though coming to the Brook, Alverton completely misjudged the fence, hit it very hard and fell on the landing side fatally injured. With the pace quickening Rubstic was left some lengths after jumping the Canal Turn. Rubstic came under pressure from Maurice Barnes on the long run to the penultimate fence, in an effort to rejoin the leaders and responding well the gelding was right on the heels of Rough and Tumble, Zongalero and The Pilgaric jumping the fence. As The Pilgaric and Wagner began to fade, the three leaders jumped the last in perfect line, Rough and Tumble on the inside rail having the slightest edge over the other two. Rubstic ran on gamely, passing the post a length and a half in front of Zongalero, with Rough and Tumble five lengths back in third place. The Pilgaric was fourth.

As the first Scottish-trained horse to win the Grand National, Rubstic was given a rousing reception as he was led in and all concerned with the winner were naturally in high spirits.

A field of 32 runners for the 1980 Grand National was reduced by two on the morning of the race when the trainers of top weight Man Alive and Wagner saw the state of the course.

Rubstic was 8/1 favourite, his nearest rivals so far as the bookies were concerned being Jer, Zongalero, Rough and Tumble, Another Dolly and Prince Roc.

The 12-year-old Ben Nevis had been strongly fancied in the race the previous year, but was now on the 40/1 mark and again ridden by American merchant banker Mr Charlie Fenwick, whose father-in-law, Mr Redmond C. Stewart, owned the gelding, was considered to have missed his chance of success. Bred in England by A.S. Pattenden Limited, by Casmiri out of Ben Trumiss, Ben Nevis was originally bought by Mrs Jane Porter, a Yorkshire point-to-point rider as well as a civil servant. After a couple of disappointing displays, the son of Casmiri won a point-to-point at the third attempt, after which he was sold to Mr Stewart after a dinner party in Yorkshire while the American gentleman was visiting this country. Taken back to the United States, the small and rather excitable Ben Nevis was prepared for racing over timber. Thriving on his new surroundings, Ben Nevis went from strength to strength, winning 12 consecutive races in America, including the Maryland Hunt Cup in 1977 and 1978. Mr Stewart's son-in-law, Charlie Fenwick, proved to be the ideal partner for Ben Nevis. Charlie's grandfather, Mr Howard Bruce, had been the owner of Billy Barton, second in the disastrous National of 1928, and some of the magic associated with Aintree's great race had obviously passed down the generations to the grandson. Setting out to find an English trainer to prepare Ben Nevis for Liverpool, the final choice was Captain Tim Forster of Wantage in Oxfordshire, and the chestnut gelding duly returned across the Atlantic to the country of his birth. Sadly it all came to nought when they were brought down in the pile-up at the Chair. This time round Charlie Fenwick just came over to ride the horse when it raced, returning to America immediately afterwards. From the 12 races he had competed in since returning to Britain, his mount was still without a victory, the heavy ground was the worst possible conditions for the horse and shortly before leaving the paddock Ben Nevis had begun to sweat up.

The jockeys set off at a sensible pace towards the first fence, which Delmoss jumped in front and it was Delmoss, Zongalero and Rubstic who proceeded to cut out the running. With the leaders jumping well over Becher's, So and So and Another Dolly both came down here and the last horse to jump the Brook first time round was Ben Nevis. The field was well strung out as Delmoss made his way back to the racecourse in the lead. Over the water Delmoss was ten lengths clear of the rest and starting the second circuit he was followed by Kininvie, Prince Roc, Zongalero, Rough and Tumble and the improving Ben Nevis. At the 19th seven of the 21 survivors came to grief and Ben Nevis was almost level with the leader Delmoss. Zongalero refused at the 20th and Becher's saw the departure of the leader Delmoss, Three to One and Jimmy

Miff, leaving Ben Nevis in command. Over Valentine's the nearest danger was John Francome on Rough and Tumble. Approaching the final fence, Ben Nevis was still six lengths clear of Rough and Tumble and jumping it resolutely, Ben Nevis romped in a very easy and praiseworthy winner by 20 lengths from Rough and Tumble, with The Pilgaric ten lengths further back in third place. The only other to survive was Philip Blacker on Royal Stuart.

Captain Tim Forster had saddled his second national winner, the numerous American visitors were delighted with the victory and awed by the spectacle, and Charlie Fenwick had served both his father-in-law and the memory of his grandfather well. Ben Nevis returned to America justifiably an equine hero, who would never have to prove himself to anyone again.

Just two months after the 1980 Grand National, Mrs Mirabel Dorothy Topham passed away at the age of 88. Often controversial, too often unfairly maligned, but always with the best interests of Aintree and the Grand National uppermost in her heart, Mrs Topham served racing better than most and her sad loss was truly the end of an unforgettable era.

Only in the Grand National can the deeds of man and horse weave a magical tale to uplift the spirit, dispel anger and malice and inspire the soul to a greater sense of well-being and purpose, and never was this more graphically demonstrated than in that emotion-packed epic race of 1981.

Nobody who was at Aintree on 4 April of that year will ever forget the fairytale brought to reality before their eyes, nor would they for one moment wish to. Such was the magnitude of the performance that day, and for many painful months before, that it would serve little purpose to be scant in the telling. In truth it would be an injustice.

Of the 39 runners Spartan Missile was a worthy favourite at 8/1, as twice winner of the Liverpool Foxhunters 'Chase over one circuit of the National course. Bred, owned, trained and ridden by 54-year-old John Thorne, Spartan Missile had been and still was the leading hunter 'chaser in the country and no more popular or likeable person could one wish to meet than John Thorne.

Largely more on sentiment than good judgement, Aldaniti held second spot in the betting on 10s. Aldaniti was bred by Tommy Barron at his Harrogate stud in Darlington and was by Derek H out of Renardeau. Sent to Ascot bloodstock sales in 1974, he was bought for 3,200 guineas by jockey turned trainer Josh Gifford, and carrying the trainer's wife's colours won his first race over hurdles at Ascot, ridden by Bob Champion. One of Gifford's owners, Nick Embericos, was so impressed with the horse that he soon became the new owner but Aldaniti never won again over hurdles and, worse still, he suffered a serious strain of a tendon in his off foreleg. The gelding was off the racecourse for 13 months but, after returning to training, Aldaniti won his first steeplechase at Ascot on April Fools' Day in 1977. Developing into one of the most promising young 'chasers in training, Bob Champion was convinced that one day he would win the Grand National, and after running a good third in the Hennessy Cognac Gold Cup at Newbury, the prophecy appeared well founded. Unfortunately, Aldaniti had chipped two pieces of bone from the pastern of his off hind leg and was again consigned to a long period of rest. Once more in the loving care of Liverpool-born Beryl Millem, head girl at the Barkford Manor Stud where Aldaniti was confined, he was gradually restored to fitness. Jockey Bob Champion was also about to encounter his own problems, which quickly became a veritable death sentence. Champion was diagnosed as having cancer and a long, painful and anxiety-fraught period of chemotherapy treatment began. Through the darkest moments of his suffering, and there were many, his determination to survive and conquer was emboldened by the desire to one day ride Aldaniti in the Grand National. In the interim period, however, the horse had broken down for the third time and even the most optimistic observer had to admit that Aldaniti's racing days were numbered. Responding to his agonising treatment, Bob Champion made progress, Aldaniti was 'patched up' and reunited, the pair won the Whitebread Trial 'Chase at Ascot on 11 February 1981 and their next appointment was at Aintree on 4 April.

From a level break Kininvie took an early lead and in company was Carrow Boy, Zongalero and Pacify cleared the first. Over Becher's the leading positions were Kininvie, Chroal Festival, Zongalero, Carrow Boy, Pacify and Tenecoon. In mid-division at this point was Spartan Missile, while well to the rear raced Aldaniti. Aldaniti quietly moved through the field to land first over the 11th, at which Tenecoon became a casualty. Back on the racecourse, Aldaniti jumped the Chair closely accompanied by Sebastian V, Royal Stuart and Zongalero, and once back in the country Aldaniti opened up a six-length lead. He continued in front on the way to Becher's for the second time, followed by Royal Mail, Rubstic and Royal Stuart, with Spartan Missile making rapid headway from the rear. Making no mistake at the Brook, Aldaniti jumped it beautifully, soaring through the air in a majestic leap which defied the many injuries he had suffered. Aldaniti raced across the Melling Road with the cheers of many thousands willing him on. Landing safely over the final fence, Aldaniti was fully 15 lengths ahead. Suddenly, approaching the elbow, Spartan Missile answered the call of his rider, John Thorne, and the favourite surged forward to narrow the gap between himself and the leader. Gaining ground with every yard, the challenger drew closer but the wonderfully brave Aldaniti pulled out that little bit extra to hold on for the victory the whole world most wished for. Aldaniti won by four lengths from Spartan Missile, with Royal Mail two lengths back in third place and Three to One fourth. The first person to congratulate Bob Champion after passing the post was John Thorne, in a marvellous example of genuine sportsmanship.

Not for many years had such a scene of happiness been witnessed on a racecourse as that which Aldaniti and Bob Champion engendered on that joyous afternoon at Aintree, when everybody had a smile on their face and a lump in their throat.

Barely six weeks before the next National, John Thorne was tragically killed while riding in a point-to-point, his unrealised dream of winning the Grand National sadly dying with him.

The invasion of the Falkland Islands by Argentine forces, the day before the 1982 Grand National, put Britain on a war footing with the immediate formation of a task force implemented to recapture the British Crown Colony in the South Atlantic.

These unexpected developments naturally overshadowed the resurgent uncertainty concerning the future of Aintree racecourse, for the 1982 Grand National was to be the end of Ladbrokes' management of the event. With owner Bill Davies setting a price of £7 million on Aintree, the future of the venue looked bleak indeed.

Notwithstanding these problems, the 1982 race was the richest National yet competed for, with a value to the winning owner of £52,507, and the 39 runners bidding for the prize were an appropriate assortment of jumping talent for such rich pickings. Top weight with 11st 10lb was the Stan Mellor-trained Royal Mail, just 1lb ahead of the previous year's tear-jerking winner Aldaniti. Others well supported in the market included Again the Same, Mullacurry, Rough and Tumble and Rambling Jack.

Clear favourite on the day was nine-year-old Grittar, the country's leading hunter 'chaser, who the previous season had carried off both the Cheltenham and Liverpool Foxhunters events. Bred, owned and trained by Mr Frank Gilman of Uppingham in Leicestershire, Grittar was by the former useful flat racehorse Grisaille, from the mare Tarama, a winner over hurdles. Grittar's first appearance on a racecourse came at Nottingham when still a raw two-year-old, in a five-furlong maiden plate and finishing unplaced, it was not until his jumping career began that his real talent became obvious. Developing into a strong, compact gelding and a superb jumper with boundless stamina, Grittar finished sixth behind Silver Buck in the Cheltenham Gold Cup. Charged with the responsibility of partnering the big race favourite was a 48-year-old Northamptonshire farmer, Dick Saunders, who until that fateful day had never seen a Grand National live. A close friend of the late John Thorne, Dick Saunders had regularly ridden Grittar in his races with much success.

Delmoss was again the tearaway front runner as soon as the race began and the first fence brought the highest number of fallers for many years when Aldaniti, Three to One and Rambling Jack were among the ten whose race ended almost as soon as it began. Delmoss continued in front to lead over Becher's by three lengths. Next in line came Carrow Boy, Grittar and Saint Fillans. Racing back in front of the stands, Delmoss was still dictating affairs ahead of Carrow Boy, Saint Fillans and Good Prospect, with Grittar, Loving Words, Tiepolino, Tragus and Hard Outlook a little distance further back. Back in the country Delmoss started to feel the effects of his pacemaking and was overtaken by Carrow Boy, Saint Fillans and Tragus, with Grittar hugging the inside rail and beginning to make ground on the leaders. At Becher's Saint Fillans pecked badly and Grittar galloped past into the lead, quickly opening up a decisive advantage. Unhindered and still full of running, the favourite never looked like being headed as he made his way back to the racecourse. The grey Loving Words, although jumping the obstacle well, was hampered by two fallen horses in front of him and dislodged his rider, Richard Hoare, who performed well to get back in the saddle and continue. Well clear coming to the last fence, Grittar made his only mistake here, brushing through the top of the fence, but once on the flat there was no stopping him. Grittar raced past the winning post, a 15-length winner from Hard Outlook, with a long way back the remounted Loving Words in third place and the long-time leader Delmoss fourth. Cheers and Mrs Geraldine Rees came in eighth and last, the lady from Tarleton, near Preston, becoming the first of her sex to complete the National course.

As the first favourite to win the race since Merryman II in 1960, Grittar was a very popular winner and his rider, Dick Saunders, the fourth amateur since the Second World War to succeed, immediately announced his retirement from race-riding. A member of the Jockey Club, Mr Saunders is now a steward of the Grand National meeting, a role to which he applies the same thoroughness and judgement as when winning the race.

Bob Champion and Aldaniti also departed from the sport they had graced and brought glory to, their dual energies becoming responsible for raising many much-needed thousands of pounds for cancer research through the Bob Champion Cancer Trust.

That the Grand National Appeal had run into difficulties soon became obvious early in 1983 when a breathing space was granted to allow fund-raising to continue until 1 May 1983.

Of the 41 competitors in that year's National, the most recent winner, Grittar, was top of the handicap with 11st 12lb, and now partnered by the accomplished professional Paul Barton, went off favourite at 6/1.

Among others finding most favour with the betting public were Peaty Sandy, the popular Irish raider Greasepaint, Mid Day Gun, Keengaddy and an eight-year-old chestnut named Corbiere.

By Harwell out of Ballycashin, Corbiere was bred by M. Parkhill and joining Mrs Jenny Pitman's Weathercock House establishment at Upper Lambourn in Berkshire at three years of age, began his racing at National Hunt events, winning his first over two miles at Nottingham. Presented as a 21st birthday gift to Brian Burrough, of the Henley brewing family, Corbiere was named after the lighthouse close to their Channel Islands home and always a very game and consistent performer, rapidly demonstrated his ability over both hurdles and fences. Of his eight races on the run-up to the 1983 National, Corbiere won two, the first being an outstandingly brave performance in the Welsh National at Chepstow. Ridden by 23-year-old Ben de Haan, his regular pilot, Corbiere was one of three runners in the race trained by Mrs Pitman, the others being Monty Python and Artistic Prince.

From a good start, Delmoss once more attempted to make the running, this time accompanied by Corbiere, and together they led over the first, at which Tower Moss, Midday Welcome and Mid Day Gun came down. With Delmoss still in the lead over Valentine's, Corbiere was just a length behind and continuing to make the running they came back onto the racecourse, closely followed by the improving Hallo Dandy. Quick thinking by jockey Bill Smith on Delmoss prevented a nasty moment when a loose horse hampered them at the 13th and they were still in front landing over the Chair. Moving up on the outside approaching the 17th, Hallo Dandy struck the front, with Corbiere, Colonel Christy and the rapidly improving Greasepaint well in attendance. In this order they took Becher's for the final time in fine style. Over Valentine's Hallo Dandy and Corbiere raced neck and neck, while behind them Colonel Christy, Yer Man, Grittar and Political Pop struggled to keep pace and Greasepaint appeared to be biding his time. Unsuited by the going, Hallo Dandy began to fade between the last two fences, leaving Corbiere to go on and clear the last a good four lengths up on his nearest rival, Greasepaint. Producing a splendid run from his mount after passing the elbow, amateur rider Mr Magnier brought Greasepaint with such a determined effort that only a stout-hearted horse could have withstood. Holding on in the bravest manner, Corbiere won by three-quarters of a length from Greasepaint, with another Irish horse, Yer Man, 20 lengths further back in third place. Hallo Dandy was fourth.

With tears of joy in her eyes, the first woman to train a Grand National winner, Jenny Pitman welcomed her hero 'Corky' back into the winner's enclosure. Only she could have known the agonies of those last 200 yards to the winning post, no doubt rekindling unhappy memories of a Grand National ten years earlier, when her then husband, Richard Pitman, on Crisp was caught on the line by Red Rum. Since the heartbreak of a divorce, the struggle to bring up two young boys and the fight to establish herself in a predominantly male preserve, Mrs Pitman had risen above every adversity.

At last the long-drawn-out battle concerning the future of the Grand National was forever resolved at the eleventh hour in 1984. Not as the result of the Jockey Club's appeal but through an article written by a racing journalist, whose eloquent description of the National's allure and value caught the attention of the chief executive of an international company.

The journalist could only have been Lord Oaksey who, as Mr John Lawrence, came so close to winning the 1963 Grand National on Carrickbeg, and the chief executive was Major Ivan Straker, of Canadian Distillers Seagram. So inspired by what he read, Major Straker wasted no time in contacting his boss and what had eluded the British racing authorities for almost 20 years was resolved in a matter of hours. Seagram entered into an agreement to sponsor the National for the foreseeable future and enabled the Jockey Club to purchase the racecourse from Mr Davies through its holding company, Racecourse Holdings Trust.

In an attempt to improve safety in the race, the Aintree executive dramatically altered the conditions of entry for the race and stipulated that the maximum number of runners for the race would be limited to 40.

Favourite at 9/1 was Greasepaint who had changed ownership and among others prominent in the betting were Lucky Vane, Broomy Bank, Grittar, Corbiere and Eliogarty.

Also strongly fancied was the previous year's fourth-placed Hallo Dandy at 13/1. By Menelek out of Dandy Hall, he was bred by Mr J.P. Frost and costing 10,000 guineas as an unbroken three-year-old, found his way in due course into the stable of Donald McCain. Of limited ability over hurdles, Hallo Dandy came on by leaps and bounds when put to 'chasing and before too long Gordon Richards, the Penrith trainer, was given responsibility for the gelding. Shortly before the 1983 National Hallo Dandy was purchased for £20,000 by London insurance broker Mr Richard Shaw. Again ridden by Welshman Neale Doughty, whose third ride in the race it was to be, they now had the type of ground which Hallo Dandy performed best on.

Away to a perfect start, Peter Scudamore on Burnt Oak went immediately to the front on the wide outside of the course, with Golden Trix his closest rival. Jumping Becher's with a 12-length lead, Burnt Oak was followed by Earthstopper, Two Swallows, Spartan Missile, Mid Day Gun, Imperial Black and Ashley House. Well to the rear at this stage was Hallo Dandy, with just a handful of horses behind him. Showing distinct signs of tiredness once back on the racecourse, Burnt Oak was just six lengths ahead of the rest as they came to the Chair, at which Ashley House and Carl's Wager both unseated their riders and Hallo Dandy, though jumping brilliantly, was not in the first 20. Eliogarty held a slight lead landing over Becher's, from Greasepaint, Earthstopper and Two Swallows, but with a sensational leap, Hallo Dandy overtook a number of horses in mid-air to land in sixth place. Rounding the Canal Turn, with the race really on in earnest now, Greasepaint struck the front, followed by Earthstopper, Grittar, Eliogarty, Two Swallows and Hallo Dandy and it was clear to all that the winner was sure to come from this half dozen. Five from home the result lay between just two, Greasepaint and Hallo Dandy. Greasepaint still had the edge until Hallo Dandy outjumped him at the second last and for the first time was in the lead. Another fine jump at the final fence gave Hallo Dandy a two-length lead but as in the previous year's race, Greasepaint rallied as Hallo Dandy hung sharply over to the stands rails. At the elbow Greasepaint was within half a length of the leader and racing flat out, and it was then that Neale Doughty showed his mastery by riding out Hallo Dandy in copybook style to draw away and win by four lengths from Greasepaint. Corbiere, coming late on the scene but full of running, was a length and a half back in third place, with Lucky Vane fourth.

It was a great triumph for all concerned with Hallo Dandy, the one-horse owner Richard Shaw, genial Cumbrian trainer Gordon Richards and the highly talented Neale Doughty, who had taught himself to ride as a boy on the pit ponies in the valleys of south Wales.

As an introduction to the Grand National, sponsors Seagram could not have wished for a better contest than this their first involvement in the race.

After finishing twice runner-up in successive years, Greasepaint was again all the rage with punters for the 1985 race and shared favouritism with the newcomer West Tip at 13/2.

One competitor for whom his odds of 50/1 could be considered rather flattering was the 11-year-old Last Suspect, thought, and not without justification, to be something of a wilful character who would be totally unsuited to Aintree. Bred by the Countess of Mount Charles, the gelding was by the former highly successful flat racehorse Above Suspicion. The dam, Last Link, was also a meritorious performer on the turf, having won many 'chases in Ireland, including the Irish Grand National. Trained by Jim Dreaper at Kilsallaghan in County Dublin, Last Suspect began his racing career as a five-year-old, competing in National Hunt flat races and after winning his second event at Fairyhouse was bought by Anne, Duchess of Westminster, whose mighty Arkle had taken the jumping world by storm during the mid-1960s. When transferred to Captain Tim Forster's Wantage yard in 1982, Last Suspect took time to settle in and although beating Corbiere at Chepstow early in 1984, was often troublesome during his races and on occasion simply pulled himself up.

Demonstrating this wayward streak again in his final race before the National at Warwick, both owner and trainer decided to withdraw him from the Aintree race. Only at the very last moment was jockey Hywel Davies able to use his persuasive powers on the Duchess of Westminster and convince her that Last Suspect was worthy of one last chance to prove himself. Twenty-eight-year-old Welshman Hywel Davies rode his first winner under rules at Fontwell in 1977 on Mr Know All and after a spell as an amateur attached to Josh Gifford's yard, turned professional and in turn became first jockey to Captain Forster.

Once again there was no trouble at the start, the field getting away evenly and the outsider Dudie landed in front over the first fence. Landing over Becher's in order of running was Dudie, Roman Bistro, Glenfox, Corbiere, Musso and Greasepaint, and at this point Last Suspect was some way off the pace, lying about 11th. Jumping the Chair in a group, Greasepaint and Scot Lane were lucky to survive after making mistakes but they recovered well, thanks to the skill of their jockeys, and as Dudie showed signs of tiring on the way back to the 17th, his pursuers closed on him. Approaching Becher's for the second time, nothing was going better than Richard Dunwoody's mount, West Tip, but as he landed a close second to Corbiere, the drop caught him out and as he tried to recover, a loose horse ran into him from behind and floored him. Peter Scudamore was enjoying a dream ride on top weight Corbiere, who hadn't put a foot wrong the whole way and after jumping the Canal Turn led towards Valentine's from Rupertino and Last Suspect, with Greasepaint and Mr Snugfit the only others close enough to cause any danger. Crossing the Melling Road with just two fences left, Corbiere was four lengths clear and looked certain to record a second victory. Having treated the final ditch with some flippancy, Last Suspect was a good way back and Hywel Davies was patiently allowing him time to recover. Joining Corbiere at the second last, and with the weight beginning to tell, Mr Snugfit landed first over the final fence with Corbiere battling on in his usual game manner. At least eight lengths behind here, Last Suspect suddenly found an extra gear and racing up the centre of the run-in brought the crowds to their feet as he passed the brave Corbiere and with his tail swishing in alarming fashion, closed on the leader. In the last 100 yards Last Suspect drew level, then ahead, to win by a length and a half from Mr Snugfit, with Corbiere three lengths away in third place. Greasepaint was fourth.

Winning jockey Hywel Davies had put up 3lb overweight to ride Last Suspect, but his faith in the horse was well rewarded, providing the Duchess of Westminster with her first victory in the race she would never allow her champion, Arkle, to endure. For Captain Tim Forster it was a third visit to the National winner's enclosure and his surprise at Last Suspect's performance was shared by many other experts.

Chapter Fifteen

1986-1996

Adding an international flavour to the 1986 Grand National was the sporting involvement of the top weight, Essex, from Czechoslovakia, an eight-year-old entire who, not having raced three times in this country, was automatically allocated the maximum burden.

Since running so well to finish second in the previous year's National, Mr Snugfit had been bought by Mr Terry Ramsden and again ridden by Phil Tuck was the 13/2 favourite. The three previous winners competing again, Last Suspect, Hallo Dandy and Corbiere, each featured prominently in the betting.

Still fresh in people's memory was the fine performance last time of West Tip. Second favourite at 15/2, he had been specially prepared this season with the Grand National in mind and again ridden by the up-and-coming Richard Dunwoody, was a name on most shortlists. Bred by Mr Thomas J. Hayes in Ireland, West Tip was by the stallion Gala Performance, from an unraced mare named Astryl, and was sold as a foal at Ballsbridge for 850 guineas. Returning to Ballsbridge when a yearling, West Tip was knocked down this time for 5,400 guineas and three years later, still without ever having appeared on a racecourse, was sold again for 3,000 guineas at Goff's August sale. His fourth owner was Mr Peter Luff and this man at least intended racing the gelding, for he at once installed him with trainer Michael Oliver at Droitwich in Worcestershire. A few days after Christmas 1982, West Tip made his first racecourse appearance a winning one, in a two-mile novices hurdle at Warwick. From his remaining seven races that term, he was only once out of the first four and apart from scoring a second victory, by far his most promising performance was in finishing a very good third in the Sun Alliance Novices Hurdle at the Cheltenham Festival. Just as consistent the following season when competing in novice 'chases, West Tip won at Wolverhampton and Haydock and was placed five times. Success followed success in the run-up to his first National attempt in 1985, West Tip winning four times on the trot in very good company and having teamed up with a jockey of rare ability in Richard Dunwoody, he had very sound claims in the 1986 National. Twenty-two-year-old Richard Dunwoody was without doubt the jockey find of the decade, for since riding his first winner less than three years before on Game Trust at Cheltenham, he had become one of the most exciting and talented jockeys seen in years.

Early morning snow had eased the going somewhat and from a good start they raced to the first fence, where Port Askaig and the well-fancied Door Latch fell. Uncharacteristically, Corbiere came down at the fourth when up with the leaders. Jumping well and fast, Tacroy, Doubleuagain and Essex led over the Brook, followed by a well-bunched group and the only one to drop out here was the remounted Dudie, who unseated his rider for the second and final time. With Tacroy and Doubleuagain clear of the rest coming back onto the racecourse, Vaclav Chaloupka ran into trouble when part of his tack broke and sadly he was forced to pull Essex up before reaching the Chair. Following Tacroy and Doubleuagain over the water, Kilkilowen, Classified and The Tsarevich headed the rest. Still going well, the two leaders rose to take the 17th fence when a riderless horse ran right across them, knocking Doubleuagain to the ground and so badly hampering Tacroy that he dislodged his jockey two fences later. Landing in front over Becher's, Classified and Kilkilowen were closely attended by The Tsarevich, Young Driver, Northern Bay, West Tip and the improving Monanore. In the same order they jumped Valentine's, making their way back to the racecourse well clear of the remainder, but approaching the second last the Scottish-trained Young Driver had gained a useful advantage over Classified and West Tip and these three had drawn away from the others. Touching down in front over the last fence, Young Driver, a 66/1 shot and ridden by Chris Grant, strode away as if to become another shock winner, but Richard Dunwoody waited patiently with West Tip until nearing the elbow. Striking at just the right moment, Dunwoody and West Tip raced smoothly into the lead, and although Young Driver stayed on bravely, he had to be content with second place, two lengths behind West Tip. Twenty lengths further back Classified finished third, with the fast-finishing favourite Mr Snugfit securing fourth place.

West Tip and his jockey received a tremendous ovation upon returning to the unsaddling ring and together with owner Peter Luff and trainer Michael Oliver, Richard Dunwoody became the first winners to be presented with the new Seagram Grand National trophy. A magnificent bronze depicting three horses jumping Becher's Brook, it had appropriately been sculpted by former National jockey Philip Blacker.

In 1987 the prize money for the Grand National reached a new high, with £80,000 being added to the sweepstake, making the value to the winning owner a most attractive £64,710.

Favourite at 5/1 was West Tip, with the Gordon Richards-trained grey Dark Ivy just behind on 11/2.

One man who had been trying to win the National longer than he cared to remember was 92-year-old Mr H.J. Joel. His runner this time was the 11-year-old Maori Venture, easy to back at 28/1 and considered by the knowledgeable ones to be too chancy a jumper to survive even one circuit of Aintree.

Bred in Wales by Mr Dai Morgan, the chestnut was named after a period in the breeder's life when he played rugby in New Zealand. By the stallion St Columbus out of the mare Moon Venture, Maori Venture didn't appear on a racecourse until he was five years of age, when trained by Mrs A. Finch the gelding won a National Hunt flat race at Taunton at 50/1. Passing into the ownership of Major Jack Rubin, Maori Venture came under the care of trainer Jim Old in Bristol, who introduced the gelding to 'chasing and achieved some success with him. Upon the death of Major Rubin, Maori Venture was despatched to the Ascot sales where he was bought by Andrew Turnell on behalf of Mr Jim Joel. Now a trainer at East Hendred in Oxfordshire, Andy Turnell was the son of that great jockey and trainer, Bob Turnell, and after his own very successful career in the saddle came to an end, Andy succeeded his father. In Mr Joel's famous black jacket and scarlet cap, Maori Venture became something of a Lingfield specialist, but he remained prone to losing concentration during a race and still had a frustrating habit of making silly mistakes at his fences. On his run up to the 1987 National, Maori Venture won one race at Newbury, finished a respectable third in the Hennessy Cognac Gold Cup, and in his final event before Aintree ran a splendid race to finish second in the Grand Military Gold Cup at Sandown. His partner in the National was stable jockey, 32-year-old Steve Knight, who had served his apprenticeship with flat-race trainer Richard Hannon until increasing weight forced him to try his luck 'over the sticks'.

Straight from the off, the Stan Mellor-trained Lean ar Aghaidh set about making every post a winning one, leading over the first in runaway fashion. Rank outsider Big Brown Bear moved up to dispute the lead with Lean ar Aghaidh as they showed the way over Becher's and Maori Venture was very fortunate to survive the Brook when coming down right on his nose before recovering. Back on the racecourse Lean ar Aghaidh was still in command, closely followed by Big Brown Bear, Northern Bay and You're Welcome, and these four led in that order over the Chair. With little change in the order of running, Maori Venture began making ground from the rear as they raced towards the second Becher's and jumping the Brook well on the outside of the course, he moved to within six lengths of the leading group. With Lean ar Aghaidh still in front over Valentine's, he was going so strongly that it just seemed possible he could actually win the race after making all the running. But crossing the Melling Road a whole bunch of challengers were at his heels. Touching down in front over the final obstacle, Lean ar Aghaidh held a length advantage but was immediately challenged by Maori Venture on his outside and The Tsarevich coming up on the inner. It was Maori Venture who outstayed them all, gaining the upper hand at the elbow and coming away to win by five lengths from The Tsarevich, with the gallant Lean ar Aghaidh four lengths away in third place. West Tip was fourth.

It was a fabulous triumph for all concerned, particularly Andy Turnell, who in only his second season as a trainer had saddled the unconsidered Maori Venture to win the National and also prepared Tracy's Special who finished an honourable sixth.

Owner Mr Jim Joel was not at Aintree to see the victory he had dreamt of for so many years; he was many thousands of feet above the ground flying back from South Africa. Given the news of Maori Venture's triumph aboard the plane, he made the decision there and then that the horse had run his last race. Present the following day at the stable's celebrations, Mr H.J. Joel announced Maori Venture's retirement and his intention to leave the horse in his will to the man who had partnered him to glory, jockey Steve Knight.

Long associated with quality themselves and respecting the finest aspects of tradition, Grand National sponsors Seagram paid the highest tribute in 1988 to probably the greatest horse ever to grace Aintree's hallowed turf, the incomparable Red Rum. Having commissioned jockey turned sculptor Philip Blacker some two years before to create a bronze statue of the nation's favourite racehorse, the completed work was unveiled two hours before the 1988 National by HRH the Princess Royal.

It was the newcomer Sacred Path, trained by Oliver Sherwood and with just 10st, who started the 17/2 favourite from joint second market choice Lean ar Aghaidh and Rhyme 'N' Reason on 10s. The Aintree stalwart West Tip was again heavily supported at 11/1, with Hard Case, Repington, Bucko, Border Burg and The Tsarevich also receiving the support their ability demanded.

Although the current star of steeplechasing, that attractive and highly talented grey wonder, Desert Orchid, was not targeted at the National, choosing instead to run away with the Chivas Regal Cup on Aintree's opening day, his stablemate, Rhyme 'N' Reason, was a more than worthy substitute. Bred by Mrs J.F.C. Maxwell at the Ballee House Stud in Downpatrick, County Down, Rhyme 'N' Reason was by the highly successful French-bred stallion Kemal. The dam was the unraced mare Smooth Lady, a half-sister on her dam's side to Grand National winner Hallo Dandy. After winning two Irish bumper events on the flat when trained by his breeder's husband, Rhyme 'N' Reason was bought by Michael Dickinson, the Harewood, West Yorkshire trainer, and proceeded to reward the former jockey's confidence by winning his first three novice hurdles over three miles for him in the colours of owner Miss Juliet E. Reed. Upon Dickinson turning his talents to preparing horses for the flat, the gelding was transferred to the Upper Lambourn yard of David Murray-Smith. Completely unfazed by his change of abode, Rhyme 'N' Reason completed his first season in Murray-Smith's care as a steeplechaser of outstanding ability by winning the Irish Grand National at Fairyhouse when still only six years of age and very much a novice. Flattering to deceive was the obvious assumption, when from four races during the next season the best he could achieve was to run second at Cheltenham on his final outing in January 1986. After another disappointing period in the 1986-87 season, when his jumping frequently let him down, Rhyme 'N' Reason was transferred to the Whitsbury stables of David Elsworth at Fordingbridge in Hampshire. In an amazing return to form, the gelding won four of his eight races in the run-up to the 1988 Grand National. The man in the saddle was 27-year-old Irish-born Brendan Powell, who began his riding as an amateur and enjoyed his first victory aboard Button Boy at Windsor early in 1982.

As they came under starter's orders, a number of runners rushed the tape causing it to snap and by the time it was repaired they were sent on their journey six minutes late. To a groan of despair, the favourite Sacred Path fell at the first fence. Jumping Becher's well, Big Brown Bear, Lean ar Aghaidh, Insure, Kumbi and Eaton Rouge were first over, but Marcolo fell and brought down Lucisis, while Rhyme 'N' Reason was involved in an incident which will be remembered as long as people speak of the National. Having jumped Becher's perfectly in mid-division Rhyme 'N' Reason lost his footing on landing and, with his forelegs splayed out, slithered on his belly and was brought to a halt. Through a brilliant example of horsemanship, Brendan Powell not only kept his seat but brought his mount upright and from a walk, set off in seemingly hopeless pursuit, the last of 33 still in the race. Still in front rounding the Canal Turn, Big Brown Bear and Lean ar Aghaidh showed the way back towards the racecourse. Lean ar Aghaidh had taken over from the rapidly improving Gee-A. The latter, ridden by leading lady jockey Gee Armytage, had jumped brilliantly from the start and after clearing the Chair within a length of the leader, took up the running early on the second circuit. Amazingly, Rhyme 'N' Reason had somehow by this time battled on to be among the leading 12 horses. Champion jockey Peter Scudamore rushed Strands of Gold into the lead after jumping the 19th from Gee-A, Little Polveir, Course Hunter and the still improving Rhyme 'N' Reason. Travelling smoothly and with a good lead, Strands of Gold rose at Becher's in fine style, only to be caught out by the drop on landing and fell, leaving Little Polveir in front of Rhyme 'N' Reason, Gee-A and the northern-trained Durham Edition moving into contention. Striding out well Little Polveir maintained his advantage over Valentine's, only to take one chance too many at the next, falling dramatically as Rhyme 'N' Reason became the new leader, followed by Monanore, West Tip, Lastofthebrownies, Durham Edition and Attitude Adjuster. Durham Edition landed running and proceeded to clear the final fence three lengths to the good. For jockey Chris Grant it was the second year he had landed first over the last in the National and as with Young Driver, he found himself run out of it in the final 300 yards. Hard at work on Rhyme 'N' Reason, Brendan Powell conjured up a spirited run from his mount to win by four lengths from Durham Edition, with Monanore 15 lengths further back in third place. West Tip was fourth.

Before being able to celebrate his outstanding victory, Brendan Powell was called before the stewards to explain what they considered excessive use of the whip in the closing stages of the race. It would have taken much more than this slight hiccup to dampen the winning jockey's spirits though, after such a remarkable recovery when down but not quite out at the first Becher's.

Rhyme 'N' Reason never ran in the Grand National again.

In 1989 the Grand National celebrated its 150th birthday, the great race having thrilled and intrigued successive generations each year, apart from interruptions by two world wars.

Adding that always valuable element of class to this year's field was the 11st 10lb top weight The Thinker, winner two years before of the Cheltenham Gold Cup and the pride of Arthur Stephenson's Bishop Auckland yard. His stablemate, Durham Edition, was preferred by the punters, going off the 15/2 second favourite behind the 7/1 principal market choice and winner of the recent Ritz Handicap 'Chase at Cheltenham, Dixton House.

Making his fourth appearance in the National and at 12 years of age thought by many to be way past his best was Little Polveir, a 28/1 shot who in his three previous attempts had completed the course just once when ninth in 1986. Bred by Mr F.G. Harris in County Antrim, the gelding was by Triumph Hurdle winner Cantab from the mare Blue Speedwell and was bought without ever having appeared on a racecourse by trainer John Edwards for his client Michael Stone. Settling well into the trainer's routine at his Ross-on-Wye establishment, Little Polveir developed into a very useful handicapper, enjoying his best year in 1987, when consistency through that season was rewarded by a ten-length victory in the Scottish Grand National at Ayr. After winning a 'chase easily at Fontwell in October 1988, the gelding ran well in his seven other races up to the 1989 National without recording a victory and some six weeks before his main appointment at Aintree, changed ownership. Bought for £15,000 by Mr

Edward Harvey, Little Polveir was purchased solely for the purpose of providing Mr Harvey's son, Captain David Harvey, with a mount in the Grand Military Gold Cup at Sandown Park. It was his final race before tackling the Grand National again and he ran well enough to finish fourth without troubling the winner. With a new owner, the gelding also acquired a new trainer in the form of Toby Balding. Entrusted with steering Little Polveir round was 30-year-old Jimmy Frost, son of a Devon farmer and stable jockey to Mr Balding, and unlike his mount, it was to be the jockey's first encounter with the National.

On their way at last, Stearsby was prominent over the first, at which Cerimau was the only faller, but at the next the Irish challenger Cranlome also came down. With Stearsby landing first over Becher's from West Tip, Newnham and Team Challenge, the favourite Dixton House fell, together with Sergeant Sprite, Hettinger, Brown Trix and Seeandem. Stearsby and West Tip continued to dispute the lead over the Canal Turn, closely chased by Team Challenge, Newnham and Mithras, and continuing over Valentine's Little Polveir was not too far behind the leading group. Taking the Chair in line abreast, West Tip, Mithras and Little Polveir thrilled the crowds with a perfect display of jumping and although the race was still wide open at this the halfway point, the three leaders appeared still full of running. Over Becher's again Little Polveir held a four-length advantage over Bonanza Boy, Gala's Image, West Tip and Lastofthebrownies, with Durham Edition and Team Challenge still well in the hunt. Crossing the Melling Road for the final time, it was still Little Polveir, strongly pressed by Lastofthebrownies, Durham Edition, Team Challenge, West Tip and Bonanza Boy. The Thinker moved into third place at the last fence, a little over two lengths behind Little Polveir and Durham Edition, and it was the latter who looked most dangerous at this stage. Once on the flat though, Durham Edition faded quickly, leaving the rallying The Thinker and West Tip to pursue Little Polveir on the run to the winning post. The riderless Smart Tar was a blessing in disguise for the leader in the closing quarter mile of the race, for matching strides side by side Little Polveir continued his gallop all the way to the line to win by seven lengths from the gallant West Tip, with the top weight The Thinker just half a length back in third place. Lastofthebrownies was fourth, Durham Edition fifth and Monanore sixth.

Winning trainer Toby Balding graciously gave all the credit for Little Polveir's fitness to the winner's former trainer, John Edwards, although his own ability was clearly endorsed by his saddling of Beech Road and Morley Street, both winners at Aintree that afternoon.

As would be expected, the media were most critical of the incident at Becher's Brook, which caused the death of two brave horses and such was the outcry from various sources, the Jockey Club immediately ordered an investigation. After many months of intensive scrutiny from every available source, the landing side of Becher's was drastically altered long before the next National, with that notorious sloping bank levelled to what was considered a more reasonable form.

Amid the height of the Becher's controversy the worst disaster in British sport befell 96 football supporters when they lost their lives at Hillsborough in Sheffield during the FA Cup semi-final between Liverpool and Nottingham Forest. The loss, pain and senselessness of that horrifying tragedy is still greatly felt on Merseyside and regrettably far from satisfactorily resolved.

Possibly more than any previous Grand National, the 1990 event attracted more attention simply because of the major alterations made to its most famous obstacle. Opinion was divided as to whether the changes were necessary, but bowing to overwhelming criticism from certain animal welfare bodies and a well-intentioned, if sometimes ill-informed, media, the very future of the race was yet again in danger.

In complete contrast to the previous year, the going at Aintree for the 1990 race was firm, guaranteeing a fast-run contest but even this type of ground was unsuitable for some, resulting in two late withdrawals, leaving 38 runners.

Heading the handicap with 11st 9lb was the dual Welsh National winner Bonanza Boy, the mount of champion jockey Peter Scudamore.

Favourite at 7/1 was the recent Cheltenham winner Brown Windsor, from Bigsun, Durham Edition, Rinus, Call Collect and Ghofar. Appearing in the race for the sixth and final time was the 1986 winner West Tip.

Others of proven ability who caught the eye of the gambling public included Polyfemus, Lastofthebrownies, Mr Frisk and the Maryland Hunt Cup winner Uncle Merlin, and these last two, both American-owned, were at the same odds of 16/1.

By Bivouac out of the mare Jenny Frisk, Mr Frisk was bred on the North Yorkshire moors by Mr Ralph Dalton and made a name for himself in the point-to-point world by winning four times. When put up for sale at Doncaster in May 1986, the gelding fetched 15,500 guineas when knocked down to an American lady, Mrs Harry Duffey, whose father had bred Battleship, winner of the National in 1938. What may have seemed a considerable amount of money for a mere point-to-pointer was soon made to look like a bargain price when Mr Frisk won seven of the nine races he competed in during his first season. Trained by Kim Bailey at Upper Lambourn, the credit for the gelding's success lies solely with the trainer, for in his early days Mr Frisk was such an awkward individual that much of his preparation was conducted with the horse riderless and led by Bailey's wife on her hunter. His second season was as encouraging as the first, Mr Frisk winning twice, at Warwick and Doncaster. His original objective for 1989, the Grand National, was ruled out at the eleventh hour due to the heavy going but there could be little doubt that Mr Frisk was ready to give a good account of himself at Aintree, despite his nervousness before a race. During the 1988–89 campaign, Mr Frisk won three of his eight races, in the last of which, Sandown's Anthony Mildmay, Peter Cazalet Memorial Trophy, he demonstrated his unflinching courage in a prolonged struggle with Run and Skip and Castle Warden to win by half a length. Having won the second of his six outings prior to the 1990 National, Mr Frisk seemed to many set fair for a fine performance on the type of ground he relished and ridden by 25-year-old leading amateur Marcus Armytage was a most popular fancy on the day.

From the moment the barrier rose the pace was fast and furious, with Star's Delight at the head of the cavalry-like charge to the first fence. Gala's Image was the only faller here and before reaching the next Uncle Merlin took the lead from Brown Windsor, Gee-A and Mr Frisk. Maintaining a red-hot pace, Uncle Merlin held a two-length lead over Becher's from Star's Delight, Mr Frisk and Polyfemus. Rejoining the racecourse, Uncle Merlin and Mr Frisk were several lengths clear of the rest and jumping perfectly, still kept up the scorching gallop. Uncle Merlin landed over the Chair just half a length ahead of Mr Frisk, followed by Polyfemus who was very lucky to recover from a terrible mistake at this big ditch. With the two American-owned horses still in the ascendancy, they returned to Becher's with Uncle Merlin again clearing the obstacle well in front, but landing awkwardly, he unseated his jockey, Hywel Davies, and Mr Frisk was left six lengths clear of his rivals. In what must have been a difficult situation for Marcus Armytage, left in front so far from home, he demonstrated commendable judgement by taking advantage of his mount's exuberance and bold jumping by continuing to ride him into his fences while keeping something in reserve for the final run to the post. Over the final fence Mr Frisk was two lengths ahead of Durham Edition and with the latter running on strongly, they were almost level at the elbow. It was here that Marcus Armytage, having ridden an exemplary race throughout, rode a finish which any jockey could be justly proud of. He rode out the chestnut with hands and heels to win by three-quarters of a length from Durham Edition, with Rinus 20 lengths back in third place. Brown Windsor was fourth. Departing from Aintree as honourably as he had always appeared, West Tip finished tenth.

It was a very happy scene in the winner's enclosure as usual, the more so when the announcement was made that Red Rum's record time for the race, which had stood since 1973, had been broken by an amazing 14.1 seconds. The new record now stood at eight minutes 47.8 seconds and is very likely to stay at that for some considerable time.

For winning rider Marcus Armytage his work was still not over, for as a leading racing journalist he had to prepare an article for the *Racing Post* describing the 1990 Grand National. It is hard to imagine anyone better qualified to perform such a task.

Aintree racecourse welcomed Her Majesty Queen Elizabeth the Queen Mother back to its historic setting on 4 April 1991 to open the new stand named in honour of steeplechasing's most respected and valuable patron.

Also returning to Aintree that year was East European Master of Sport Vaclav Chaloupka, who five years before had ridden Essex in the National and was hoping to do better this time with the mare Fraze.

Far and away the most exciting prospect of what, as always, promised to be a thrilling contest was the very real possibility that the recent Cheltenham Gold Cup winner, Garrison Savannah, could equal the unique record of Golden Miller by winning the Grand National in the same year as the Cheltenham classic. Trained by Jenny Pitman and ridden by her eldest son Mark, Garrison Savannah was a lightly raced eight-year-old who, with just 11st 1lb to carry in the National, attracted sufficient support to make him joint second favourite with Rinus at 7/1. Overall market leader was Bonanza Boy on 13/2, representing the powerful Martin Pipe stable.

Of the 40 horses assembled for that year's race, none had travelled further to be at Aintree than the 11-year-old chestnut gelding Seagram, a highly appropriate name for a contestant in the Seagram Grand National. Bred by Mrs J.A. Broome in New Zealand, the gelding was by the English-bred stallion Balak from the unraced mare Llanah. Devon trainer David Barons had for some time been visiting New Zealand to purchase young horses which he found made good steeplechasers and it was his wife, Jenifer, who bought the then three-year-old Seagram on one of their earliest trips to the southern hemisphere. Costing 80,000 New Zealand dollars, which is about £3,600, the youngster settled well at David Barons' Hendham Farm at Kingsbridge, and in the colours of his Liverpool owners, Maincrest Limited, won a novice hurdle at Ludlow before finishing a good second in the Liverpool Hurdle in his first season. The following year Seagram continued to improve, winning the White Satin Handicap Hurdle at Aintree, and during the 1986-87 campaign won over both hurdles and fences before breaking down after a victory at Hereford. It was about this time that Maincrest gave up its involvement in racing and ownership of the now invalid New Zealand horse reverted to David Barons. Off the racecourse for over a year, Seagram had carbon-fibre tendon implants in both forelegs as part of the treatment to restore him to full fitness but at one point it was feared he would never race again. Making a promising comeback by winning two 'chases, a half share in Seagram was bought by Sir Eric Parker and it was in this owner's colours that he was successful in another two handicaps before the season's end. By now established as a game and very useful steeplechaser, Seagram was twice offered to Seagram UK Limited but on each occasion the company chairman, Major Ivan Straker, declined. As a ten-year-old, Seagram had his busiest season yet, taking part in 11 races, of which he won three and, thriving on competition, it was a similar programme in 1991 when his main objective was the National. Winning twice from seven outings before Aintree, Seagram displayed his well-being when taking the Ritz Club National Hunt Handicap 'Chase at Cheltenham in fine style, some three weeks before the National. Ridden by 25-year-old Nigel Hawke, who like his mount was making his first Grand National appearance, Seagram was a strongly fancied fifth in the betting at 12/1.

A rowdy demonstration delayed the start for eight minutes, after which the field got away to a first-rate break and the usual dash to the first fence culminated in Docklands Express being the only faller there. Oklaoma II and Golden Freeze soon opened up a slight gap between the rest with fast jumping on the run to Becher's, which they took cleanly from Over the Road, Garrison Savannah, Mr Frisk, Rinus and General Chandos and there was little change in the leading position on the run back to the racecourse. Golden Freeze and his stable companion Team Challenge led over the Chair and to the delight of trainer Jenny Pitman, Garrison Savannah lying third at this stage meant that the three leaders were all from her stable. Back in the country Golden Freeze was still in front, jumping the 17th just ahead of Rinus, New Halen and Over the Road. Two fences before Becher's Rinus fell, leaving Garrison Savannah and Golden Freeze at the head of affairs, with New Halen, Over the Road, Auntie Dot and the improving Seagram in close pursuit. In this order they jumped Becher's safely. Coming back onto the racecourse Golden Freeze faded, his place being taken by Durham Edition, but Garrison Savannah by now was looking certain to repeat Golden Miller's long-standing record. Touching down clear after the last fence he strode on to be eight lengths in front of Seagram as they approached the elbow. With Nigel Hawke hard at work on the latter and Mark Pitman not yet having moved, Garrison Savannah on the far rails looked the certain winner, until suddenly Seagram began to gain ground up the centre of the course, and with the Gold Cup winner unable to find anything extra, Seagram raced past to win by five lengths from a very game Garrison Savannah. Eight lengths back in third place came Auntie Dot, with Over the Road fourth in front of Bonanza Boy and Durham Edition.

For the whole Pitman family it must have seemed like re-enactment of the closing stages of the 1973 National when Mark's father, Richard Pitman, suffered the same fate aboard the exhausted Crisp, but as always Mrs Jenny Pitman was gracious in defeat, her major concern being that all her horses and riders had returned safely.

Amid the congratulations for the winning connections, Major Ivan Straker assisted in the presentation ceremony, bravely disguising his disappointment in refusing to buy Seagram when he had the chance.

Seagram Limited handed over sponsorship of the National to their subsidiary company, Martell, in 1992, having not only saved the race from extinction but restored it to its former status and with the French firm's generous increase in added money that year's Grand National became the richest yet.

Heading the handicap with 11st 7lb was the Gordon Richards-trained Twin Oaks, a powerful, sound jumper who had become a Haydock Park specialist, winning six times over the nearby course.

Favourite at 15/2 was Docklands Express, a first-fence faller the previous year but with an impressive record of consistency that term. Others in demand on the day included Laura's Beau, Twin Oaks, Auntie Dot and the biggest horse in training, Party Politics.

A highly popular tip as a result of the British general election being less than a week away, the Nick Gaselee-trained gelding stood over 18 hands high and started at 14/1. Bred by David Stoddart, a Buckinghamshire farmer, he was by the American-bred stallion Politico out of Spin Again. Subsequently placed with trainer Nick Gaselee in Upper Lambourn, Party Politics won two of his five steeplechases in his first season, both at Warwick. Even at this early stage in his career, the gelding became the subject of high praise from many pundits, and continuing on the right lines he chalked up another three good victories for his owner-breeder in his second term under rules. It speaks volumes for the horse that while still only eight years of age and in just his third season of racing, he was earmarked for the 1992 Grand National and although without a win from four outings before Aintree, there could be no doubt that he possessed abundant stamina and was a force to be reckoned with. Just days before the big race he was bought for a reputed £80,000 by Mr David Thompson, who presented him to his wife, Patricia, as a gift. With his regular jockey Andy Adams injured, the very capable 26-year-old Welshman Carl Llewellyn took the mount.

After just a two-minute delay the race began, with a fast early gallop being set by Golden Minstrel, who led over the first from Forest Ranger and Willsford. Racing on to Becher's, with little incident on the way, Golden Minstrel maintained his lead. A mid-air collision between Forest Ranger and Brown Windsor led to the latter falling heavily and Carl Llewellyn worked wonders in steering Party Politics clear of the prostrate Brown Windsor. Willsford overtook Golden Minstrel at the Canal Turn and proceeded to show the way back to the racecourse with an enormous number of runners still in the race. Willsford and Golden Minstrel led over the Chair, with Ghofar, Hotplate, Party Politics and Forest Ranger well up and 34 runners went back out for the final circuit. Hotplate led over Becher's followed by Ghofar, Golden Minstrel, Romany King and Party Politics. At the Canal Turn Romany King took up the running from Hotplate and Willsford but at the fourth from home Party Politics cruised smoothly past these three to lead them back across the Melling Road. Four lengths in front jumping the second last, Party Politics stayed on well to maintain a decisive advantage over the final fence, and although Romany King rallied bravely to narrow the gap passing the elbow, Party Politics was ridden out for a two-and-a-half-length victory from the very game Romany King. Fifteen lengths further back the Irish-trained Laura's Beau came in third, with Docklands Express fourth.

Winning owner Mrs Thompson was a very delighted lady when presented with the winner's trophy as well as £99,943, and also enjoyed the satisfaction of seeing her other runner, Roc du Prince, finish the course in 17th place.

For jockey Carl Lewellyn it was a case of third time lucky, as on both his other rides in the race he failed to get round, and in a sporting gesture typical of this rare breed of horseman, he paid tribute to the injured Andy Adams who had watched the race on crutches from the weighing room.

With so many shocks, surprises and sensational happenings having been regular components of Aintree's colourful history for so long, what occurred on Grand National day 1993 could well have been considered just another chapter in the so often incredible story of the race.

Unfortunately, that sad day reduced the greatest steeplechase in the world to an object of ridicule and farce, leaving British horseracing reeling from the shambles which its greatest showpiece had been subjected to.

With so much already written about the National that never was, suffice it to say that after two false starts, a race of sorts did take place, amid confusion, ineptitude and chaos, which was 'won' by the Jenny Pitman-trained outsider Esha Ness, but of course it didn't count and the race was declared void. The subsequent official investigation was thought by many to be lacking in something, though few knew what, and the only certainty to emerge from it was that the names of starter Captain Keith Brown and flag-man Mr Ken Evans would be the most remembered characters of the 1993 Grand National.

The only good thing that can be said of that unfortunate incident is that valuable lessons were learned and the importance of constant vigilance and attention to detail became watchwords for all future administrations, not just at Aintree but at all sporting venues.

A new starting procedure, tried and tested by the Jockey Club, was implemented at Aintree for the 1994 Grand National, together with additional flag-men positioned at clearly visible points in an energetic and purposeful effort to avoid anything remotely similar to 1993's débâcle.

What nobody could plan for was of course the weather and with heavy snow falling continuously through Friday afternoon and evening, the stewards called for an early morning inspection of the course on Grand National day. Amazingly, shortly before the time for the race, the sun appeared, the skies cleared to a perfect blue and, apart from the going, it was an ideal day for the National.

Of those at the top of the handicap the most interesting was the French-bred gelding The Fellow. Recent winner of the Cheltenham Gold Cup, he was a frequent visitor to these shores and the winner of a number of our richest races. It was a bold decision by his trainer, François Doumen, to tackle the National so soon after the Gold Cup but racegoers appreciated it and The Fellow was joint third favourite with Master Oats at 9/1.

Moorcroft Boy was the 5/1 favourite, with the leading hunter 'chaser Double Silk a popular choice at 6s, then on 16/1 came Young Hustler, Zeta's Lad, Mr Boston and the choice of local punters, the 11-year-old Miinnehoma.

Owned by Liverpool-born comedian Freddie Starr, the gelding was bred by Mr Patrick Day in Ballycogley in County Wexford and was by the stallion Kambalda out of Mrs Cairns. Bought for 35,000 guineas at Doncaster spring sales in 1988, he was first trained by Owen Brennan at Newark, winning his first of three outings, a National Hunt flat race at Uttoxeter. In his second season, when now with Martin Pipe at Wellington in Somerset, he raced for the first time over hurdles, setting up a sequence of four victories from five races and showed every likelihood of developing into a promising 'chaser. Sidelined for a season, Miinnehoma came back with a vengeance for the 1991–92 campaign, to run unbeaten in his three races at Newton Abbot, Chepstow and Cheltenham, and the final one the valuable Sun Alliance Steeplechase at the National Hunt festival. After such sparkling performances, his four outings without a win the following year was disappointing to say the least and the gelding's usual faultless jumping was absent from each of these attempts. Another lengthy spell off the racecourse came to an end when Miinnehoma returned to the winner's enclosure after winning a 'chase at Newbury in March 1994 and after running unplaced behind The Fellow in the Gold Cup, he came to Aintree comparatively lightly raced for an 11-year-old. Ridden by the incomparable Richard Dunwoody, the pair had a huge following of local support simply because of Freddie Starr was the owner.

The oldest competitors in the race were the 13-year-old gelding Fiddler's Pike and his 51-year-old rider, Mrs Rosemary Henderson, who also owned and trained him and had received special permission from the Jockey Club to partner her horse in the race.

To the relief of everyone, particularly the racecourse officials, the starting gate worked perfectly, and to the cheers of the crowds the field charged out towards the first fence. Prominent from the off were Miinnehoma, Garrison Savannah, Riverside Boy and Young Hustler. Double Silk and Riverside Boy were dictating the pace, followed by Young Hustler, Garrison Savannah, The Fellow and Master Oats, and in this order they led over Becher's, with Miinnehoma well in touch and benefiting from the experienced guidance of Richard Dunwoody. Double Silk, jumping superbly, led round the Canal Turn, with Garrison Savannah in close attendance on the inside rail and Riverside Boy also well to the fore. On the long run back to the racecourse, Riverside Boy took up the running just ahead of the rail-hugging Garrison Savannah and Double Silk, but at the 13th Double Silk, possibly distracted by the loose horse ahead of him, fell. Almost in the same instant Master Oats and Mr Boston also came down and Mighty Falcon was brought down in the mêlée. Leaping the water Garrison Savannah led from Riverside Boy, Miinnehoma, The Fellow, Ebony Jane and Moorcroft Boy. Jumping Becher's The Fellow on the inside pecked badly as he landed at the deepest side, while Miinnehoma also pitched so heavily that his nose scraped the ground, but both recovered well and Dunwoody's handling of his predicament displayed horsemanship at its finest. Slightly in front over the Canal Turn, Miinnehoma turned towards Valentine's with Just So just to his rear, and as The Fellow fell here, Mister Ed ran right into the French horse and unseated his rider. Taking Valentine's superbly, Just So went on from Miinnehoma, Ebony Jane, Moorcroft Boy and Into the Red, and from here on these five had the race to themselves. Landing first over the final fence, Moorcroft Boy strode away towards the winning post with Miinnehoma being patiently held in check by his jockey and with the riderless Young Hustler preceding them they came to the elbow. With the coolness of an ice cube, Richard Dunwoody moved Miinnehoma confidently and smoothly into the lead and with Moorcroft Boy unable to resist, Freddie Starr's horse looked set to record an easy victory. Coming from some way back, after being eight lengths adrift at the last fence, Simon Burrough produced Just So with a terrific spurt, gaining ground with each stride until reaching the girth of the leader, but digging deep into his reserves of energy, Miinnehoma found that vital bit more with which only the greatest races are won. Miinnehoma passed the post a length and a quarter in front of Just So, with Moorcroft Boy 20 lengths back in third place. Ebony Jane was fourth, in front of the only other two to finish, Fiddler's Pike and Roc du Prince.

Winning owner Freddie Starr was unable to be at Aintree due to showbusiness commitments, but on the telephone he congratulated trainer Martin Pipe and Richard Dunwoody while they were interviewed by Desmond Lynam on TV.

Creating her own important piece of racing history, Mrs Rosemary Henderson tried unsuccessfully to hide her delight and pride at finishing closest to a National winner than any other member of her sex on a horse who, like his rider, had obviously thoroughly enjoyed a run around Aintree.

Once more, in 1995, the Grand National fell short of its complete number of runners, this time with 35, falling five short of the maximum permitted. To many critics it constituted a problem which would soon need to be addressed.

Top weight with 11st 10lb was Master Oats, probably the most improved 'chaser in training and unbeaten in his four races this season, which included his most recent victory in the Cheltenham Gold Cup.

It was apparent from the betting that gamblers were using the Gold Cup result as an indicator for Aintree, with the runner-up behind Master Oats at Cheltenham, the mare Dubacilla, holding the second spot in the market on 9s. Also receiving good support were Young Hustler, Country Member, Miinnehoma, Crystal Spirit, Lusty Light and Garrison Savannah.

The last two mentioned formed part of a six-pronged assault on the race by trainer Mrs Jenny Pitman, whose other runners included Superior Finish, Do Be Brief, Esha Ness and Royal Athlete.

By the French-bred stallion Roselier out of Darjoy, Royal Athlete was bred by Mr John Brophy in Ireland and was bought at Ballsbridge sales by Jenny Pitman for 10,000 Irish guineas, on the same day she also purchased Garrison Savannah and Esha Ness. The gelding developed into a good staying 'chaser under Mrs Pitman's care, but his career was beset with a series of injuries. After surprising everybody, except his trainer, by running a sheer blinder to finish third in the 1993 Cheltenham Gold Cup behind Jodami, Royal Athlete started the new season by contesting the Hennessy Gold Cup at Newbury. In an horrendous injury, the gelding needed almost 40 stitches in his leg and during the 13 months he was out of racing it seemed doubtful if he would ever race again. Other problems affecting the chestnut included soft feet, which are very easily bruised. Behind all those physical drawbacks, however, Royal Athlete possessed that so rare blend of courage, tenacity and unflinching determination, without which no Grand National can ever be won. Without a win from his four races up to Aintree, the gelding was ridden by 24-year-old Irish-born Jason Titley, who himself had encountered problems since arriving in England after a brilliant succession of victories in his native land. Royal Athlete started at 40/1.

With hardly any delay the starter got them away well and in the usual dash across the Melling Road Master Oats, Camelot Knight and Into the Red were prominent. At the head of affairs Master Oats cleared Becher's on the wide outside of the course. Rounding the Canal Turn, with the pattern of the race beginning to take shape, Superior Finish led from Into the Red, Garrison

Savannah, Do Be Brief and Riverside Boy, with Royal Athlete handily placed on the inside just behind the leaders. Back on the racecourse they approached the Chair with Do Be Brief holding a slight advantage over Crystal Spirit, Camelot Knight, Ebony Jane and Master Oats and in this order they began the final circuit. Over the 17th Royal Athlete had taken command, followed by Topsham Bay, Do Be Brief, Master Oats, Into the Red and Over the Deel and it could be clearly seen that Jason Titley was giving Royal Athlete a tremendous ride. After clearing the Canal Turn it developed into a duel for a number of fences between Master Oats and Royal Athlete as these two began to open up a gap, but by the last fence in the country Royal Athlete had taken the measure of Master Oats and proceeded to make his way back towards the stands. Jumping the last fence with a clear lead, Royal Athlete raced for home chased by the fast-finishing Party Politics and a bunch of others, but sprinting away from the opposition, Royal Athlete won by seven lengths from Party Politics, with Over the Deel six lengths away third. Staying on really well, Dubacilla was a close-up fourth, in front of dead-heaters Into the Red and Romany King.

A jubilant Jenny Pitman again took her place in the winners' enclosure, together with owners, the brothers Garry and Libby Johnson, who were generous in their praise for their trainer's brilliance.

But the biggest smile came from Jason Titley who, in his first-ever Grand National, performed with an excellence rarely seen in one so young.

In the first week in May 1995, Aintree's best-loved winner, Red Rum, celebrated his 30th birthday and the racecourse management marked the occasion in the most appropriate manner by holding an evening meeting over the Mildmay course in his honour.

The majority of the many thousands who attended Aintree that evening were people without any interest in horseracing, yet they flocked to the racecourse to pay their respects to a horse who had captured the hearts of everyone who admires bravery and the will to rise above adversity. No one could have known it would be the last time they would see this four-legged legend who completely re-wrote the record books and whose fame had reached the furthest corners of the world.

On Wednesday, 18 October 1995, Red Rum was put to sleep after suffering a heart attack and the horse who changed the lives of so many was thoughtfully and with dignity laid to rest alongside the winning post at Aintree racecourse.

The many thousands of visitors for the 1996 Grand National at the end of March gazed in reverence at Red Rum's grave, remembering all he achieved on this course and what an inspiration he had been to so many.

The 1996 race saw the greatest fall in the number of runners for 36 years, with only 27 taking their place at the start. Young Hustler was at the top of the handicap with 11st 7lb, with two brilliant Irish challengers, Life of a Lord and

Son of War, just behind him in the weights, together with Deep Bramble. Rather appropriately 'Ginger' McCain ran the rank outsider Sure Metal who provided Donald McCain junior with his first ride in the race.

Most heavily backed horse on the day was the recent runner-up in the Cheltenham Gold Cup, the ten-year-old Rough Quest. Bred by Mr Michael Healy in Ireland, he is by Crash Course out of the mare Our Quest, and after twice finishing fourth in National Hunt flat races in Ireland, came to England as the property of Mr Andrew Wates and entered the yard of trainer Tim Etherington. Showing little ability over hurdles, Rough Quest came into his own when put over fences, developing quickly into one of the leading novice 'chasers. It was at this juncture that Irishman Terry Casey entered the picture. Having trained in England for a number of years, with some success, Mr Casey was on the verge of packing in training and returning to Ireland when he answered an advertisement placed by Andrew Wates for a trainer. A fine amateur rider himself, Mr Wates rode the winner of the 1970 Liverpool Foxhunters Steeplechase, Lismateige, as well as getting as far as the water jump in the 1968 National. Now 55 years of age, the owner and trainer struck up an ideal working partnership, persevering through a number of problems with Rough Quest and was rewarded in 1995 when the son of Crash Course won a splendid race at the Cheltenham Festival. With just one victory and three second places from his six outings in the current season, his finest performance to date was undoubtedly running the Irish star Imperial Call to four lengths in the Gold Cup at Cheltenham. Not fully fit that day, Rough Quest had suffered a muscle enzyme affliction which resulted in his fading at the end of his races and the worry of that still existed on the big day at Aintree. Ridden by 25-year-old Mick Fitzgerald, who was born in Cork City and raised in County Wexford, it was the jockey's second ride in the National.

Stepping in as the starter this year was Mr Gerry Scott, making his own piece of Aintree history by becoming the first Grand National winning jockey to be responsible for starting the race and it was a strange coincidence that when he won on Merryman II in 1960, the field then consisted of just 26 runners.

From a splendid start that famous charge to the first fence proceeded. Already showing prominently, Young Hustler raced with Sure Metal and Three Brownies, setting a good gallop, and with Sir Peter Lely, Superior Finish and Over the Deel also well up, they raced on to Becher's. Jumping beautifully Sure Metal led over Becher's Brook from Three Brownies, Over the Deel, Sir Peter Lely and Young Hustler. With little change in the order they took the Canal Turn, the leaders closely tracked by a tightly packed group. Still in front approaching the Chair, Three Brownies showed just ahead of Young Hustler, Sure Metal, Greenhill Raffles, Over the Deel, Superior Finish and Sir Peter Lely, and once over the water they turned back into the country. Rough Quest had been brought quietly up on the outside on the approach to Becher's, lying just off the pace in about ninth position, and another who made up an enormous amount of ground to be right in contention was Encore un Peu, who took Becher's in fourth place behind Young Hustler, Sir Peter Lely and Three Brownies. With Rough Quest and Life of a Lord hot on their heels, a terrific finish looked likely, and going to the front on reaching the racecourse, Encore un Peu was running on strongly. Tracked by Three Brownies, Young Hustler and Rough Quest over the second last, Encore un Peu went to the last fence a good five lengths ahead of the challenging Rough Quest and, landing safely on the flat, ran on well towards the finish. Having timed his challenge to perfection, Mick Fitzgerald brought Rough Quest on with a tremendous run, drawing level at the elbow where, hanging left for the briefest of seconds, he came close to his rival but raced past in a matter of strides. Staying on brilliantly, Rough Quest resisted the renewed challenge of David Bridgwater on Encore un Peu to win by a length and a quarter, with Richard Dunwoody getting up on the line for third place with Superior Finish, 16 lengths behind the second horse. Sir Peter Lely was fourth, Young Hustler fifth and Three Brownies sixth. Eleven others completed the course, the last of which was Donald McCain junior on the long-time front runner Sure Metal.

Even before the winner reached the unsaddling enclosure the announcement was made over the Tannoy that there was to be a stewards' enquiry, obviously concerning that so brief moment when the two principals came close together.

For the connections of Rough Quest the next 15 minutes were as anxiety filled as any time during the race itself, but to everyone's relief the decision finally came through that the result was to stand and the placings remain unaltered.

The congratulations continued in the winner's enclosure longer than anyone knew or cared and another Grand National had reached its conclusion and produced its rewards.

Sixteen

1997

There have been countless dramatic moments in the long history of the world's greatest steeplechase, yet never before and, hopefully, never again has anything happened to compare with the shock or the feeling of helplessness which occurred at Aintree on 5 April 1997. On that day, which was set to record the one hundred and fiftieth running of the Grand National, many thousands of people lived through what will be remembered as Liverpool's long weekend.

After two days of splendid racing and with fine weather forecast for the big occasion, the crowds flocked to Aintree in anticipation of a race as thrilling as any witnessed in the past and with the annual hope that they would beat the bookies in the difficult task of finding the winner. There had been a sort of forewarning of what was to come on the opening day of the meeting when much disruption was caused to most of the motorway network leading to Liverpool. Warnings received concerning bombs planted on these highways by IRA activists were of course treated with great urgency by the authorities, and the emergency measures taken resulted in many racegoers arriving late at the racecourse. The most distinguished among these was champion trainer Martin Pipe, who arrived barely in time to saddle his runners for the first race.

But all of that was two days beforehand, no bombs had been found and when the sun shines bright on National day, all thoughts turn to less troublesome matters.

Despite the previous year's winner, Rough Quest, being an absentee through injury, there was still sufficient talent among the big race field to tempt, excite and intrigue. Among the leading fancies, the striking and highly talented grey Suny Bay appealed to many as a lively choice, while the consistent Go Ballistic, partnered by 1996's successful jockey Mick Fitzgerald, had flattered when finishing fourth in the recent Cheltenham Gold Cup. Jenny Pitman's Smith's Band and Nahthen Lad held sound credentials and Irish challengers, stablemates Wylde Hide and Feathered Gale, were both considered good enough to provide a long overdue victory for the Emerald Isle.

A comparative newcomer to England, however, had attracted enough admirers in recent months to place him among the favourites, and on the minimum mark in the handicap Lord Gyllene stood out as good value at around 10/1 on the morning of the race. Bred in New Zealand by Mrs N.M. Taylor, the bay gelding had won a couple of 'chases in his native land before being purchased in a somewhat unusual manner by Mr Stanley W. Clarke and brought to England at the start of the 1996 season. Having only seen the horse in a video recording sent to him, Mr Clarke, the chairman of both Uttoxeter and Newcastle racecourses, felt there was something about Lord Gyllene which reminded him of the great Red Rum. Placed in the care of Shrewsbury trainer Steve Brookshaw, the gelding scored a hat-trick of victories at Uttoxeter in 1997 and with five seconds to his credit had failed only once from ten outings to make the frame. More importantly, Lord Gyllene had proved beyond any doubt that he could stay extreme distances over fences.

The name Brookshaw was one which was well known to older racegoers, principally through the outstanding reputation of his uncle Tim who, as a highly talented jockey in the 1950s and 1960s became a household name. Champion National Hunt jockey with 83 winners in 1959, he also, that year, performed one of the greatest feats of horsemanship ever witnessed in the Grand National. Partnering the Scottish trained Wyndburgh, Tim Brookshaw lost an iron when challenging for the lead at Becher's Brook second time round and, from that point on, rode without stirrups for the remainder of the race. Despite this additional handicap, Tim brought his mount safely home within a length and a half of the winner, OXO. It was a tremendous loss to racing when this most gallant of horsemen became paralysed from the waist down after a fall from Lucky Dora in a hurdle race at Aintree in December 1963.

Following in the formidable family tradition, Steve Brookshaw had already distinguished himself as a most talented amateur rider before taking out a full trainer's licence just two years ago and even in that short period of time had tasted the joys of Aintree victory. Sending out the veteran jumper Rolling Ball to win the 1996 Martell Foxhunters' Steeplechase in the colours of Stan Clarke's wife, Hilda, augured well for his first attempt at the Grand National with Lord Gyllene.

As usual there was plenty of pre-race entertainment at Aintree as the stands and enclosures rapidly filled up, with the band of The Royal Ghurka Rifles playing somewhat more sedate melodies than the vibrant sounds of reels emanating from the ever popular Irish Bar. There was an abundance of famous faces to be seen, from that great Hollywood actor Gregory Peck to the prominent member of the then Labour Shadow Cabinet John Prescott and, of course, surrounded by a posse of security men, the unmistakable figure of HRH the Princess Royal. Her Royal Highness, a regular visitor to the National over the years, was attending on this occasion to perform a very special function, the unveiling of a bronze bust of that best known and most respected sports commentator Peter O'Sullevan CBE.

Internationally known and admired as 'The Voice of Racing', Peter O'Sullevan was about to give his fiftieth and final commentary on the Grand National, for he was to retire from broadcasting at the end of the year. There could be no doubt that he had set the standard for all others to strive for, nor that his easily understood and so accurate descriptions of any race he covered would be sadly missed, and the imaginative gesture by the Aintree executive in marking the contribution he had made to horseracing was appreciated as a suitable send-off by everyone. With the unveiling ceremony completed, everyone's attention then turned to finding the winner of the first race, no mean feat with a large field of hurdlers. As things turned out the outsider Shankar got the afternoon's proceedings well under way, providing trainer David Nicholson with his sixth winner at the meeting so far and bringing attention to the trainer's representative, Turning Trix, in the National.

At approximately 2.50 p.m., with less than an hour before the start of the big race, the first of two coded telephone calls was received by Merseyside police, warning that certain devices had been placed on the racecourse. Under the circumstances there could be no alternative but to evacuate the stands and enclosures and within minutes the racecourse management's 'Operation Aintree' plan went into action. With television monitors and the public address system urging everyone to vacate the stands, complex and adjacent enclosures, and to move towards the centre of the racecourse, the evacuation was carried out surprisingly well. The majority felt that this interruption of the day's activities was nothing more than a minor hiccup which would quickly be resolved. However, when closer inspection revealed that the running rails had been flattened to enable the crowds to stream into the central enclosure and beyond, it became obvious that the situation was far more serious. It could also be clearly seen that a number of the fences had been damaged during the mass evacuation. Mounted and foot police good naturedly, yet firmly, urged the throngs further and further away from the stands, while two police helicopters hovered low, repeating the instructions of their colleagues.

In far greater detail, the affairs of that fateful day and the following 48 hours are described in the superb book, *Everyone Must Leave*, by Nigel Payne and Dominic Hart, published by Mainstream in 1998. All that this writer can convey are his own personal experiences throughout that unique weekend, for example, being shepherded across the racecourse by armed response officers, in company with jockeys Graham Bradley, Norman Williamson and Richard Dunwoody, when the main concern of Brad was that he had left his fags behind. The interminable waiting in the horsebox yard off Melling Road to see whether we'd be allowed back to the jockeys' room to retrieve our belongings and the frustration when informed most emphatically that, 'There's no chance lads, the bomb squad haven't cleared there yet.' With the dipping of the sun, Aintree became a very cold place, as it can even in the middle of summer, thanks to that wind from Liverpool Bay. It was only then that the real plight of our jockey companions in distress really came home to those of us who were more conventionally dressed. With just their silks, breeches and lightweight boots to protect them from that chilling wind, this toughest breed of sportsmen merely cracked jokes, suggested most unlikely answers to their predicament and, without a penny between them and with no recourse to credit cards of any description, behaved impeccably. When, some time after 7.30 that night, the majority of the horses were allowed to leave, the expressions of relief on the faces of those jockeys would have served well as an object lesson for certain animal rights activists. Those oh-so-gallant young men were so very obviously more concerned with the welfare of the horses than their own discomfort. Although some did cadge lifts in the horseboxes in the hope of perhaps finding digs somewhere down the M57 or M58, others made pals of some local lads and were promised a good night out in, 'de 'Pool, an' a kip in are 'ouse'. All over that vast area of north Liverpool that evening, many thousands of stranded and bewildered people discovered generosity and kindness way beyond their wildest imaginings as Liverpudlians everywhere opened their hearts and homes to all in need.

By this point, everyone knew that it was impossible to retrieve their vehicles until Sunday lunchtime at the earliest and from then on even the simplest request from a stranger at any door to be allowed to use the toilet finished up with total strangers from all walks of life being not only granted that most basic of all favours but food, a bath and somewhere, somehow a bed for as long as it was needed. For those old enough to remember, it was like stepping back in time 57 years, to the dark and deadly days of the Blitz, and the friendships cemented that night would unquestionably last forever. It was a rare opportunity for scousers, myself included, to feel proud to be able to say we came from Liverpool and some representatives of certain newspapers must have felt a pang of conscience for the way they had portrayed this area of the country in the past.

The whole city of Liverpool responded magnificently to the unexpected emergency, with the city council organising accommodation in sports centres, school and church halls and laying on free transport, food and telephone communications for the stranded masses.

At Aintree racecourse itself, the area still threatened by the unknown, there were others rising above the trauma and possible danger thrust upon them. The racecourse management and staff, under the supreme example set by managing director and clerk of the course, Charles Barnett – the police and security people still delving into the unknown in their efforts to declare the area safe – and two stable 'boys' whose determination, despite the threat of arrest, to feed, water and generally secure the welfare of the horses still remaining in the racecourse stables most surely extended way 'above and beyond the call of duty'. Phil Sharpe and Simon Malloy resisted the appeals and threats of the police and security people in order to stay with those horses still left at Aintree and although as employees of trainer Charlie Brooks their main concern was for their own Suny Bay, they catered for the needs of every animal as if their lives depended on it. Yet another lesson for animal rights belligerents.

If Saturday had been a long and trying day, Sunday was little different, except for the fact that we could rejoice, as we kept an anxious vigil at the Melling Road course entrance from early morning, that the National was to be run at 5 p.m. on the Monday evening. This decision was ambitious indeed on the part of the racecourse executive, for the whole track would need to be gone over with a fine-tooth comb, many of the fences repaired and whole sections of running rail re-erected. It was, however, a comforting thought to sustain us through that quiet Sunday morning: the realisation that the authorities had not bowed to intimidation and that the spirit of the National had prevailed. If racing was show business, then the dictate would surely have been that, 'the show must go on', and so it was to be in what, to many, is the greatest show on earth.

As if in celebration of this news, the trainer of the recently deceased and without doubt the greatest fairytale National winner ever, Aldaniti, Josh Gifford invited a whole party of us low-spirited and emotionally drained souls to share a drink with him in the nearby Railway Working Men's Club on Melling Road. Despite his round possibly being the largest he has ever had to order, Josh nonetheless was the life and soul of probably the most pleasant interlude of that entire weekend of despair and uncertainty.

At long last, at 3.40 p.m. that afternoon, we were finally allowed back into the weighing room to collect our belongings, albeit under an armed escort. The experience of walking past those deserted hospitality suites, with half-eaten meals still on the tables, mink coats and personal belongings randomly strewn over chairs and tables, left an eerie feeling akin to what the first aboard the floundering *Marie Celeste* must have gone through. There could be no question that my companions felt the same as me, for those usually ebullient, ever jocular jockeys were on this occasion as sombre, subdued and preoccupied as me.

With just the one race set for Monday, 7 April 1997, came thoughts of America's Maryland Hunt Cup, which is also just a one-race-a-day affair, but there exists a world of difference between Virginia and Aintree and despite the no vehicle rule applying to this particular Grand National and the fact that everyone, known or unknown, was to be subjected to a body search, the crowd exceeded the estimated attendance by almost three to one.

The Princess Royal was back as guest of honour as was, of course, Peter O'Sullevan, still determined to record his 50th commentary on the race, whatever the circumstances.

With the number of runners now reduced to just 36, there was a rapid change in the betting, with Go Ballistic coming in as the 7/1 favourite, ahead of Suny Bay at 8/1, Wylde Hide on 11s and Avro Anson together with Smith's Band at 12/1. Lumped together on the 14/1 mark were Nahthen Lad, Antonin, Lo Stregone and, surprisingly, Lord Gyllene.

At precisely one minute past five o'clock, starter Simon Morant sent them off to as near a perfect start as one can reasonably expect and with the somewhat depleted crowds in the stands cheering them on, they raced across the Melling Road towards the first fence. Smith's Band, Dextra Dove and Lord Gyllene led a steady gallop into this fence, after which it could be clearly seen that Lord Gyllene had touched down in front. Full of Oats was the only faller at this obstacle but his exiting caused no problems for any other competitor and the run down to the first Becher's was unusually trouble-free. Displaying a wisdom way beyond his years, jockey Tony Dobbin allowed Lord Gyllene to make his own pace, which was such that it kept him at the head of affairs and, although closely pressed by Suny Bay and Smith's Band, Lord Gyllene maintained his advantage over Becher's Brook. At the next obstacle, Back Bar fell and Glemot unseated his rider and by this time everyone had noticed the difference between this National and those they were accustomed to. With no spectators allowed out in the country for security purposes, it appeared very odd indeed that the only people close to the fences were security personnel, whose attention seemed to be anywhere but on the historic event taking place. The vast bank between the first and fourth obstacles, usually packed full of excited people, was bare except for armed police spaced out at intervals along its peak and only a few of the normal squads of press photographers had been allowed at selected fences to record the action.

With fallers mercifully few and far between, all the attention was centred on the bold jumping front-runner Lord Gyllene travelling so smoothly on the inside of the course, but closely tracked by Suny Bay, Smith's Band, Northern Hide, Nahthen Lad and Wylde Hide. The positions remained the same rounding the Canal Turn and galloping back towards the racecourse, the pace was still strong, and many at the rear of the field were already finding it difficult to keep in touch. At the big open ditch after Valentine's, Nuaffe came down when racing in mid-division and as Lord Gyllene led them back across Melling Road at the Anchor Bridge, only four of the original thirty-six were missing from the contest. With the leading positions unaltered they jumped the thirteenth fence cleanly, but at the rear of the field Don't Light Up fell and Straight Talk came down at the next. Running to the Chair, Smith's Band moved up on the outside, almost drawing level with Lord Gyllene and with Suny Bay in third place on the inner, these leaders jumped the mighty ditch in fine style. In mid-division behind them, Celtic Abbey paid the penalty for a clumsy jump with an ugly looking fall, but within seconds the horse was back on his feet and continued in the hunt although riderless. It was another loose horse, however, which almost brought disaster to the long time leader. As the final obstacle on the first circuit, the Water Jump, loomed up before Lord Gyllene and Smith's Band, the riderless Glemot suddenly raced forward, forced his way between the two front-runners and having headed them, immediately cut to the left, straight across the path of Lord Gyllene. It could not possibly have happened at a more dangerous moment, for they were just yards from the take-off point, yet as cool as a cucumber, Tony Dobbin slightly checked his mount to allow the intruder to pass in front of him and allowing Lord Gyllene to stretch out over the wide expanse of water, swung left-handed back out towards the country. And all this without once surrendering their position at the head of the field.

Now on the final circuit, Lord Gyllene was still in command, hugging the inside rail, with Suny Bay right behind him, Smith's Band lying third in the centre of the course and Northern Hide, Dextra Dove, Valiant Warrior and Avro Anson also in close attendance. At this point the favourite, Go Ballistic, was well to the rear, as was the struggling Wylde Hide, who'd done extremely well to survive a dreadful mistake at the thirteenth.

Totally misjudging the twentieth and despite the superb jockeyship of his partner, Richard Dunwoody, Smith's Band crashed straight into the fence and tragically was fatally injured. From that point on, Lord Gyllene continued to dictate the race completely and although those awesome fences can never be treated lightly, the New Zealand gelding never looked like making the semblance of a mistake. With Suny Bay and Master Oats appearing the only two likely to pose a threat on the run for home, Lord Gyllene remained foot perfect at each obstacle and at the final open ditch, the twenty-seventh, Suny

Bay ruined any chance he might have had by barging his way through the obstacle.

With ears still pricked, Lord Gyllene romped home the easiest of winners by 25 lengths from Suny Bay; the fast finishing 100/1 outsider Camelot Knight was third, Buckboard Bounce fourth, Master Oats fifth and Avro Anson sixth of the 17 to complete the course.

With cheers as loud as any ever heard after a Grand National, the winner was led in to a rapturous welcome, though in all probability the cheers were not for the brave Lord Gyllene and his connections alone. It could well be that the reduced crowd at this long-waited-for event were also applauding everyone who had lived through and survived with such stoicism and dignity that long weekend at Aintree. All were heroes in their own private way, for they had proved beyond any question that ordinary decent people can always overcome threats and intimidation.

Seventeen

1998

Within weeks of Lord Gyllene becoming the second New Zealand-bred horse to win the National since Seagram in 1991, Aintree racecourse had come to look very much like a huge building site.

As had been well planned in advance, the latest in the on-going programme of modernisation and improvement to the venue had swung into place with first, the demolition of the north end of the large Victorian County Stand, which was to be followed by the construction of a brand new stand in its place.

Not only was it a race against time to complete the project before the 1998 Grand National meeting but, to anybody regularly passing the site through those early summer months, it appeared that it was a race which was certainly going to be lost. The evening meeting over the Mildmay course in mid-May took place amid what seemed to be a confusion of mounds of rubble, contractors' vehicles and demolition equipment all apparently frantically going nowhere. Even at Aintree's November Becher fixture, although the new structure was by then in place, it seemed long odds against it being ready in time for the many thousands intended to occupy it in just under five months time.

As the 1998 Grand National approached, however, and with work continuing around the clock, Aintree's new skyline had well and truly emerged and it could be seen to all that any disruption over the past months had been well worth while.

For the second year running the most recent winner of the race was to miss the event, Lord Gyllene having met with an injury, as had Rough Quest after his victory and, although the latter was back attempting to repeat his triumph of 1996, it was disappointing that the New Zealand horse was unable to compete.

Suny Bay, such a courageous runner-up in 1997, was back again and after a dramatic and convincing win in Newbury's Hennessy Gold Cup the previous

November, had convinced many of his improving ability to such an extent that the grey was always among the favourites in the ante-post betting on the race. Even when the handicapper burdened Suny Bay with top weight of 12 stone for the 1998 National, the Charlie Brooks-trained gelding retained his appeal.

Also among the principal contenders this time were the consistent Him of Praise, Martin Pipe's Challenger du Luc, the Aintree Becher 'Chase winner Samlee, Nahthen Lad, Banjo and the Irish mare Dun Belle. There was also something of an international flavour added to the contest through the inclusion of the French challenger Ciel de Brion, the mount of eighteen-year-old Thierry Doumen whose father François trained the horse.

One of the most interesting and inspiring stories to emerge from this contest surfaced through ten-year-old Earth Summit at last appearing at Aintree. Bred by Mr R.P. Fry and trainer Jim Old, the gelding was by Celtic Cone out of Win Green Hill and by all accounts was a most difficult character to handle when a youngster, proving very hard to break. Purchased as a two-year-old on behalf of Peter Scudamore Bloodstock Ltd, the son of Celtic Cone was allowed to mature before being consigned two years later to the Doncaster May Sales of 1992. Here, he was knocked down for merely 5,800 guineas to Peter Scudamore's partner, the Gloucestershire trainer Nigel Twiston-Davies. So it was, that for this sum Earth Summit, named after the Earth Summit conference in Brazil, became the property of a syndicate consisting of six owners. The most notable of this sextet, in terms of horseracing experience at least, was none other than Nigel Payne, a man associated with Aintree racecourse for many years and undoubtedly the instigator of the ownership enterprise. Originally the marketing director of the betting shop division of Ladbrokes, Nigel's first professional involvement with the Grand National came about when Ladbrokes took over management of Aintree racecourse in 1976. His roles now include that of marketing consultant and press officer and one would be hard put to find a busier official at any Aintree fixture.

In Earth Summit's first season the gelding won one three-mile hurdle race at Chepstow from eight outings and from that initial campaign it became apparent to everyone concerned with the preparation of the horse that the youngster favoured softish ground and that a test of stamina was his forte. By the end of his second season, while still only a six-year-old, Earth Summit rounded off a superb term with a runaway victory in the Scottish Grand National, whereupon Nigel Payne backed his horse at odds of 33/1 to win Aintree's supreme prize before the end of the century.

Two years later, at Haydock Park, the sky fell in for the syndicate of owners officially registered as The Summit Partnership, when Earth Summit suffered a serious injury to the suspensory tendon and they were informed by the racecourse vet that the horse would never race again. With infinite patience and dedicated care, Earth Summit was slowly nursed back to fitness by trainer Nigel Twiston-Davies and his assistant, former champion jockey Peter Scudamore, but it was a long and frustrating process. Despite being entered a couple of times for the Grand National, the horse was withdrawn on each occasion because of doubts concerning his fitness. After two somewhat disappointing runs in the early part of the current season, Earth Summit stormed back into the headlines with a performance which put him slap bang in line for that long awaited tilt, the National. On heavy going, in Chepstow's Welsh National shortly before the end of 1997, Earth Summit gave a superb display of jumping and stayed on extremely well to win from that very impressive grey Dom Samourai. It was a rewarding and promising turning point for everyone associated with the horse and in spite of finishing down the course on his final two appearances before the big race, hopes were high that the demands of Aintree would bring out the best in Earth Summit.

As was only to be expected, after the scares of the previous year, security was very intense over the entire meeting, yet none of the precautions deterred the crowds from flocking to Aintree, especially on National day. The new grandstand was named after the person who officially opened it, HRH the Princess Royal, and in terms of design and splendour is a tribute to all involved in its construction, affording as it does the finest vantage point of the whole vast Aintree acreage.

Constant rain over the preceding couple of days had turned the ground heavy by the time the 37 runners made their way out on to the racecourse for the parade and, with these conditions making the race an even more severe test of stamina than usual, there was a late reshuffling of betting odds in the ring. Earth Summit came in for most attention in this respect and by the time the starter mounted his rostrum, he had been installed the 7/1 favourite from Samlee and Him of Praise, both at 8s.

After a delay of just three minutes the starting gate rose and apart from Fabricator who dwelt, the remainder got away evenly to the usual roar from the crowds. First to show as they crossed the Melling Road was Scotton Banks and Greenhill Tare Away, and as these led away from the first fence they had already left five fallers behind them, Banjo, Challenger du Luc, Pashto, What a Hand and one of the two greys, Diwali Dancer. The reluctant starter, Fabricator, fell by the wayside at the third, while the next two obstacles accounted for the exits of Do Rightly, Griffin's Bar and Celtic Abbey. At this stage of the proceedings Earth Summit was on the wide outside of the course and well to the rear of the field. Greenhill Tare Away held a slight lead over Decyborg and Ciel de Brion going over Becher's

Brook, where Choisty and Court Melody came down, and by now Earth Summit had moved into mid-division, although it was noticeable that jockey Carl Llewellyn was still taking him the longest way round. With little change in the order over and round the Canal Turn, the Irish challenger Dun Belle lost her rider at Valentine's Brook and at the open ditch two fences later Damas refused, Nahthen Lad unseated his rider and General Crack was pulled up. It was still Greenhill Tare Away in front coming back on to the racecourse, with Decyborg breathing down his neck and Ciel de Brion, Go Universal, Scotton Banks and Rough Quest also well to the fore, and despite the attentions of two loose horses at the fourteenth the leaders raced on to the Chair. Ciel de Brion landed first over the huge ditch from Greenhill Tare Away, Decyborg, St Mellion Fairway, Scotton Banks, Go Universal, and the improving Earth Summit, still on the wide outside. After they had all cleared the water safely, the second circuit began with Suny Bay and Rough Quest starting to make ground on the leaders, but by now Maple Dancer, Joe White and Pond House had all called it a day by pulling up. With the strain now beginning to tell, four more were wisely pulled up at the seventeeth, Go Universal, Into the Red, Hillwalk and Radical Choice and with Ciel de Brion still dictating the pace the race was rapidly taking its final form. Ciel de Brion made a couple of mistakes on the run down to Becher's which allowed Greenhill Tare Away to lead him over the Brook, but Earth Summit now looked comfortable, jumping brilliantly in third place on the far side, with Suny Bay, Brave Highlander, St Mellion Fairway and Rough Quest the nearest of the few still left in the contest. At the Canal Turn, Suny Bay moved smoothly into third place tight on the inside rail and just to his rear Brave Highlander unshipped his jockey, enabling Rough Quest to secure fifth place just behind Earth Summit. As Ciel de Brion fell at the plain fence after Valentine's when lying a close second, both Suny Bay and Earth Summit easily overtook Greenhill Tare Away and when the long-time leader came down at the next, Suny Bay and Earth Summit were left with the race between them. Drawing ever further away from the handful still in the race, a duel developed between Graham Bradley on Suny Bay and Carl Llewellyn on the blinkered Earth Summit. Stride by strength-sapping stride the two brave horses battled on, still foot perfect at the remaining three fences but over the final fence it was obvious that it was an unequal struggle, for the gallant grey Suny Bay was conceding a cruel 23lbs to his rival. Drawing clear after passing the elbow, Earth Summit galloped on relentlessly to the line to win by 11 lengths from Suny Bay, with a distance back, in third place, Richard Dunwoody on Samlee, who ran on from seemingly nowhere in the closing stages. St Mellion Fairway was just a length and a quarter away from

Samlee in fourth, and almost out of sight, Gimme Five came home fifth and Killeshin, after unseating his rider and being remounted, finished sixth and last. The very brave Rough Quest, who found the going completely against him and was going well in third place approaching Melling Road for the final time, became very tired from that point on and his jockey, Mick Fitzgerald, sympathetically pulled him up at the second-last fence.

Although in modern day terms it had been a slowly run race, what must be taken into consideration is the desperate state of the ground they raced over and that because of those conditions the race was a far more demanding and exhausting event than normal. Equally importantly, it must be remembered that, although fifteen horses fell on the first circuit, when competitors began showing signs of distress second time round they were immediately pulled up by their riders. Only one horse actually fell on the second lap of the race.

Joy and intense emotion were displayed in great profusion by all connected with the winner when Earth Summit entered the winner's enclosure and, taking a few minutes off from his numerous duties, Nigel Payne was the first of the owners to be interviewed by Desmond Lynam. With tears of joy and relief still in his eyes, the Aintree press officer actually apologised for displaying such intensity of feeling in those vital closing moments of the race. Of the other syndicate members Ricky George, who 26 years earlier had caused a major sporting shock when scoring the goal for Hereford which knocked Newcastle United out of the FA Cup, admitted that being part-owner of a Grand National winner gave him greater satisfaction. The other co-owners were Mike Bailey, a local government officer from the Wirral, chartered accountant Peter Earl of Lewes and two Londoners, media agency owner Bob Simms and the only retired member of the victorious team, Gordon Perry. The celebrations were set to continue long into the night and probably far into the following morning and once she had tucked up this year's National hero for the night, Earth Summit's devoted stable girl, Marcella Bayliss, would no doubt be joining them. Throughout the whole of that most thrilling race her main concern was for the welfare of the horse who meant so much to her.

Another year, another victory and as so often in over a century and a half, another glorious and sublime fairytale. If anyone still doubts that the Grand National is the place where dreams really can come true, then just ask any member of The Summit Partnership.